Townhouse Design

Layered Urban Living

Chris van Uffelen

Townhouse Design

Layered Urban Living

BRAUN

CONTENTS

Subtle

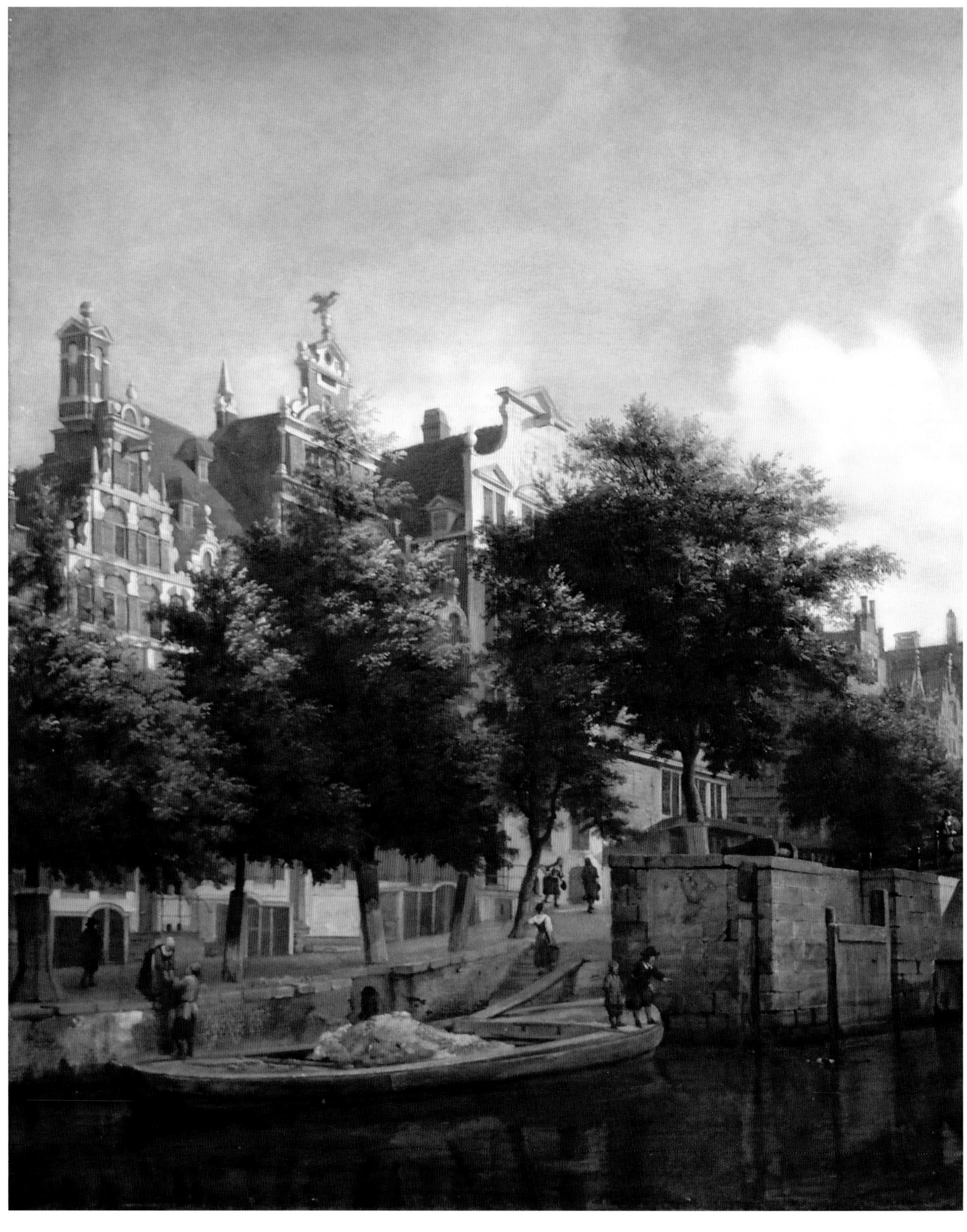

"Through Difficulties to Greatness"

(Victor Hugo)

by Chris van Uffelen

Townhouses are a special kind of dwelling, and their form is derived from the specific requirements of the building itself within the context of a city or town. When settlements were fortified, the space within the walls became more important – and more valuable. City walls can't be moved easily, so buildings began to increase in height to cope with increasing housing demands. The height first rose to two stories, and then eventually to five. The distance between the buildings became smaller and over time disappeared completely in many areas; this had the disadvantage that light and air were only able to enter the building through the façade openings on the street and garden sides. In addition, building taxes increased proportionately with the width of the façade on the street side, which resulted in the construction of small, deep houses to save money. The precious façade area was reserved for important rooms, rather than secondary spaces, which led to the stairwell being located towards the center of the building volume, illuminated through the roof above.

In many places, local interpretations of the townhouse typology began to arise, for example in Amsterdam, where the city was extended by the construction of the Amsterdam Canal District and the confiscation of land, which was later drained and sold in smaller plots at a much higher price. Most of the buildings in this area have the same width, except for those belonging to particularly wealthy citizens, who bought more than one plot of land and were then able to build a house wider than the typical three window axes. Because of the risk of flooding, the houses were given raised basements, above which the ground floor rose as a principle level, or Bel Etage. A short staircase led upwards, and the entrance to the basement was located beneath this. The construction and illumination of the sidewalk directly in front of the house was also the owner's responsibility; this was often designed at the same time as the house and the entire ensemble created not just a work of architecture, but also often a work of art. Townhouses are designed to accommodate a specific function and this can alter their appearance. While merchants along the Amsterdam canals initially used the upper stories for storage, which required beams and pulleys to raise the goods to the necessary height, craftsmen and bakers opened their shops on the ground floor. The façades didn't serve any structural purpose because the ceilings were spanned between the two sidewalls, so they could be redesigned at will and adapted to suit any new requirements. The ground floor façades facing the street were often built of wood, while the upper floors were usually built of brick or stone. As the façade served no load-bearing purpose, it was also possible to add large window openings.

Initially, townhouses were mostly timber-framed buildings. Each story usually protrudes very slightly further out than the one below. This gives the floor plates a counterweight, which meant they could support more weight in the rooms and also stopped them curving downwards under the pressure. Doing this also gained more living space, which meant that the upper floors began to protrude more into the street space; sometimes an oriel was also used to gain

← | **Jan van der Heyden: Houses on the Herengracht and the old Haarlemmersluis, Amsterdam,** circa 1670, detail

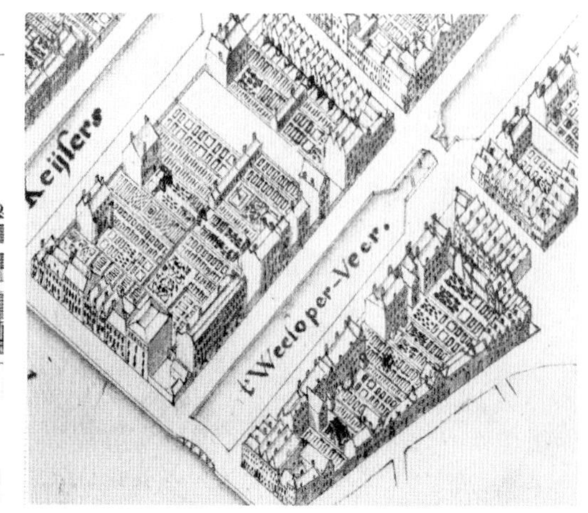

space. This new development was soon strictly regulated to stop the buildings jutting too far outwards. In some places, the protrusion of the upper floors was even used after timber-framed construction became less popular because it stopped the floor plates curving under the weight.

However, this practice largely disappeared in order to keep pace with more modern stylistic developments. Not just timber-frame buildings, but also the brick gothic with its corbie gable were designed with the gable facing the street. At the beginning of the Modern era, the triangular gables were considered unattractive. For practical reasons saddle roofs were also built oriented towards the street, but these were ornamented with modern architecture: balustrades and cornices, or sculptures that hid the roof behind. In Italy, the Renaissance led to the development of a new type of townhouse for the upper classes; this was inspired by the city palace typology. In contrast to the townhouse, this type of building is wider and encloses an inner courtyard. Townhouses had gardens to the rear of the house; if one was able to afford two plots one behind the other the site then reached backwards to join the next street and created enough space to build a coach house. Splendid private gardens were often built, and in the cities where these have been preserved, or where the townhouse tradition still survives today there is often a green area that is usually open for communal use.

In the 19th century, old townhouses were often divided to serve as rented properties, and the "new" rental houses were often narrower but similar in form. In many places, it is possible to see the difference in height of the spreading city, where windowless walls tower above lower residential buildings. However, as the perimeter block development began to gain a bad reputation because of its negative effects on the health of the residents, rows of houses began to take precedence over the typical block developments. Since the 1980s the townhouse has once more seen a rise in popularity. Urban living is becoming more desirable than living in the countryside, although owning your own four walls is still just as desirable. Single townhouses fill holes in the urban fabrics left by the larger developments and the historical existing buildings also often undergo modernization work. This volume shows the entire scope of this type of residential construction, which often consciously represents the different traditions that preside in the local area, sometimes even succeeding in giving these a new interpretation.

↖↖ | **Various façades along Keizersgracht,** Amsterdam
↑ | **Block development at Keizersgracht,** Amsterdam
↗ | **Reconstruction of townhouses on the Römerberg,** Frankfurt/Main
↗↗ | **Gothic Wulflamhaus,** Stralsund
→| **Herengracht, Amsterdam,** the Huis Bartolotti was built across two plots in the middle of the row, built by Hendrick de Keyser (1617) and Philips Vingboons first "neck-front"-house to the right (1638)

APOTHEKE
1998

SELF-CONFIDENT

Elding Oscarson

↑ | **Front view,** white façade
→ | **Townhouse within context**

Townhouse

Landskrona

This narrow site is sandwiched between old buildings in Landskrona, Sweden. The site is barely five meters wide with a tiny area of just 75 square meters. The clients wanted a house that would also serve as a public gallery. The architects built a single space softly partitioned by thin exposed steel slabs. These span the entire width of the house and divide its program – kitchen, dining, living, library, bed, bath, and a roof terrace. The simple system creates an array of different spatial experiences. The interior opens up to the street, to the middle of the block, and to the sky above. This openness in all directions generates a building volume that is both monolithic and transparent. Energy consumption is 57 percent lower than regulations demand.

PROJECT FACTS

Address: Landskrona, Sweden. **Client:** confidential. **Completion:** 2009. **Gross floor area:** 125 m². **Number of rooms:** 1. **Main materials:** masonry, metal. **Situation:** part of existing development in city center.

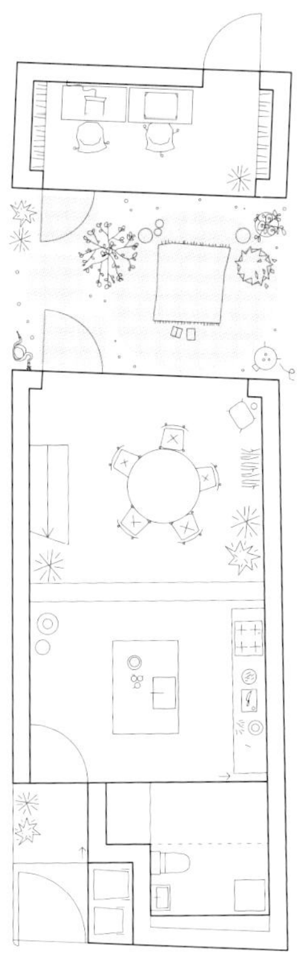

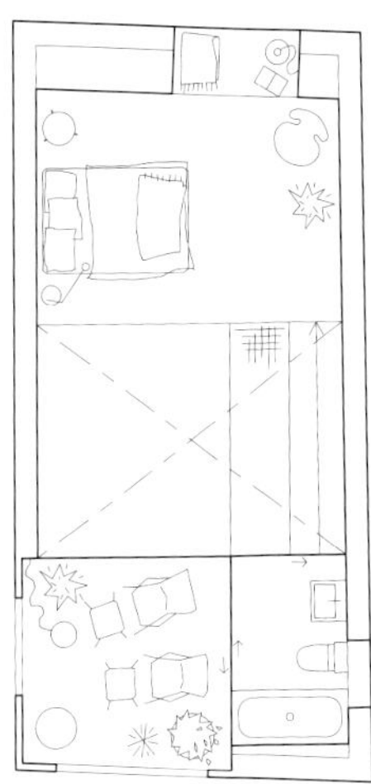

← | **Street view**
↖ | **Ground, first and second floor plans**
↓ | **Interior,** view of garden

Craig Steely Architecture

↑ | **View through garden,** looking west
↓ | **Garage door opening sequence**

→ | **East elevation**

Peter's House

San Francisco

Located above San Francisco's Dolores Park on a steep site bordering a public garden, this decidedly small house uses the site as efficiently as possible. Peter's House comprises a cast-in-place concrete garage at the lowest level and builds a three-story glass tower above it, altering the land and native hillside drainage very little. The top living floor then spans from a flat plateau at the top of the lot to the tower like a bridge. Beyond the structural challenges, the biggest issue in designing Peter's House was opening the building to the expansive view while maintaining a level of privacy from the sidewalk and garden that pass alongside. 90 solid wood louvers made from Monterey cypress wood regulate openness and privacy.

PROJECT FACTS

Address: 1 Dolores Park, Mission District, San Francisco, CA 94114, USA. **Client:** Peter Russell-Clarke. **Completion:** 2013. **Gross floor area:** 170 m². **Number of rooms:** 4. **Main materials:** glass, concrete, cypress wood. **Situation:** semi-detached building in urban context.

↑ | **Kitchen,** terrace in background

← | **First floor plan**

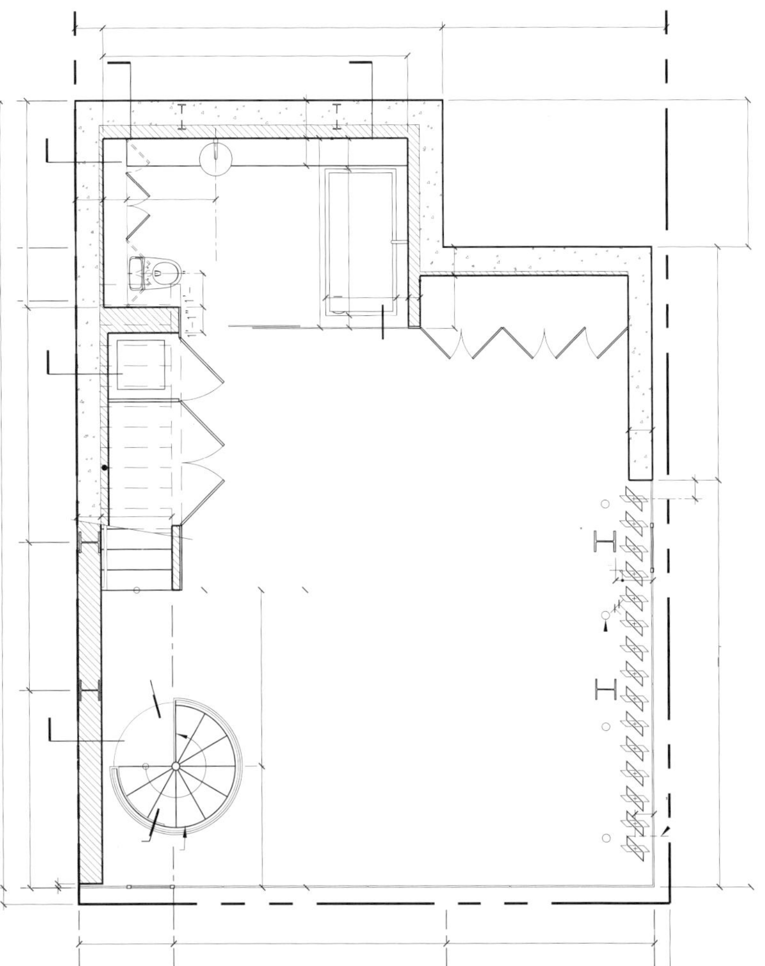

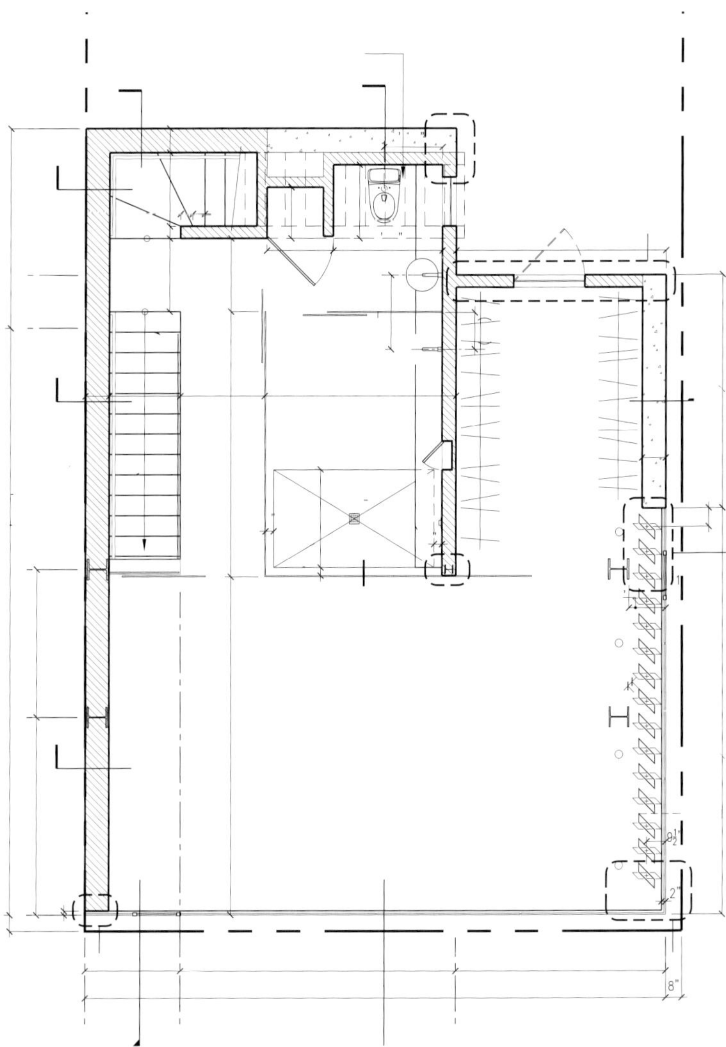

← | Second floor plan

↓ | Master bedroom

dIONISO Lab

↑ | **Façade,** worm's-eye view
→ | **Front side,** evening light

House 77

Póvoa de Varzim

Póvoa de Varzim is a city profoundly related to the sea and fishing. Its cultural richness influenced this project. The house is simple; the social areas are on the lower floors, with private areas above. The interior was structured into half floors in order to achieve an interesting spatial arrangement and dynamic interconnections between spaces. The west façade is covered by aluminum venetian blinds that help to insulate the house. The east façade is covered with stainless steel panels, perforated with the "siglas poveiras". These symbols are a writing system once used as a way of communication and to mark personal belongings. In this way the house responds to the city, revitalizing a legacy that has been progressively forgotten and abandoned.

PROJECT FACTS

Address: Rua Antonio Graca, n77, 4490 Póvoa de Varzim, Portugal. **Client:** confidential. **Completion:** 2010. **Gross floor area:** 232 m². **Number of rooms:** 5. **Additional use:** atelier. **Main materials:** concrete structure, birch wood floors, stainless steel panels, aluminum shutters. **Situation:** part of existing development in city center.

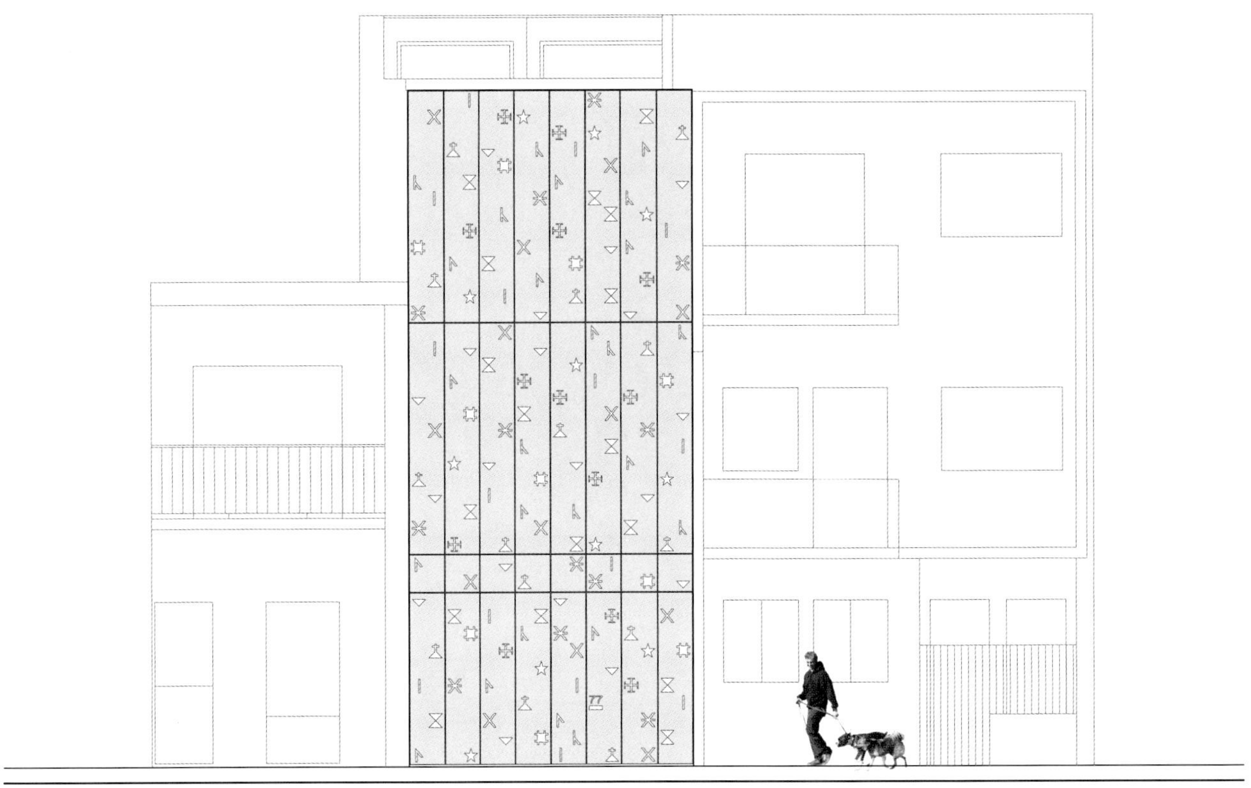

↑ | Elevation
← | Façade detail

← | Rear of building at dusk
↓ | General view

AAW Architektenbüro Arno Weirich

↑ | **Building in context**
↗ | **Living area,** second floor
→ | **Rear side terrace above garage**

Closing the Gap

Bonn

For more than 66 years, there has been a hole in this densely built area in the center of Bonn, directly opposite the Remigiuskirche. Because of access rights, the ground floor of this townhouse serves as both an access route and parking space. Structurally, the three upper floors have been conceived to allow the complete depth of the building to be designed in an open-plan way. The large glazed surfaces draw natural light deep into the interior. The façade facing the street is clad with limestone and fitted with colored panels. Energy is supplied by a geothermal heat pump and a 95-meter-deep geothermal well. In addition, the entire building is equipped with a ventilation system with heat recovery.

PROJECT FACTS

Address: Brüdergasse 21, 53111 Bonn, Germany. **Client:** Arno Weirich. **Completion:** 2011. **Gross floor area:** 393 m². **Number of rooms:** 7. **Main materials:** reinforced concrete, glass. **Situation:** part of existing development in city center.

← | **Façade,** large windows give house an open and transparent appearance

↑ | **Section and first floor plan**
↙ | **Oriel,** view of church
↓ | **Staircase**

↑ | **Aerial overview**

Urban Hybrid

Emmen

Investment corporation Senn BPM AG, together with MVRDV, won the Feldbreite competition to design a housing block with 95 homes. Instead of the housing block asked for by the brief, MVRDV created a mixed urban block with small apartment buildings at the corners, townhouses along the streets and garden and patio houses inside the block. Each house or apartment will have its own façade color, emphasizing its individual ownership. The interior of the block is divided into both private and public spaces, with dividing walls used to hang tables or benches and parts of the walls which can be rotated and used for table tennis. The garden and patio houses in the center of the courtyard have their own entrance doors at the outer perimeter of the block.

PROJECT FACTS

Address: Mooshüslistrasse, 6032 Emmen, Switzerland. **Client:** Senn BPM AG, St. Gallen. **Completion:** ongoing. **Gross floor area:** 13,959 m². **Number of apartments:** 97. **Number of rooms per building:** various. **Additional use:** services, underground parking. **Situation:** new development in urban context.

↑ | **Townhouses around Emmen Square**

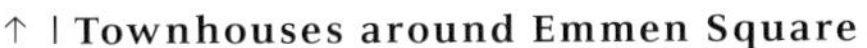

↓ | **Ground floor plan,** property boundaries indicated

↑ | **Sample floor plans,** three-story family house and two-story garden house

↓ | **View from roof terrace**

brandt + simon architekten

↑ | **General view,** south-east
→ | **Façade detail**

Schuppen

Berlin

The unusual tiled façade gives this building a striking character, making it stand out from the rest of the row. The large number of tiles and the chosen colors create a changing interplay between traditional building materials and the almost digital, pixelated appearance of the façade as a whole. The sequence of colors is planned as a repeated pattern and reflects both the former use of the site as a garden center, and the desire for a summerhouse. The façade of roof tiles is a solid and durable solution, because they offer not only comprehensive design possibilities but also an optimal cladding for the insulated timber construction behind. The energy needed to heat the water and support the heating is provided by the sun and also complements the 'green thinking' behind the design.

PROJECT FACTS

Address: Maximilianstraße 10, 13187 Berlin, Germany. **Client:** confidential. **Completion:** 2009. **Gross floor area:** 215 m². **Number of rooms:** 5–7. **Main materials:** wood, tiles, cellulose. **Situation:** part of existing development in urban context.

← | **Entire building,** view from backyard
↓ | **Ground floor plan**

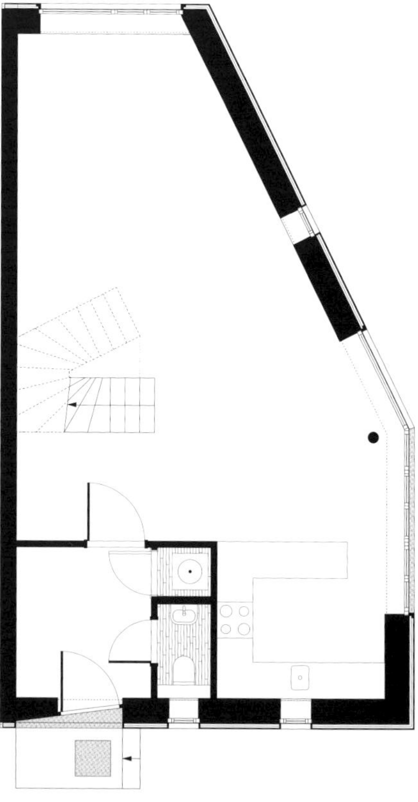

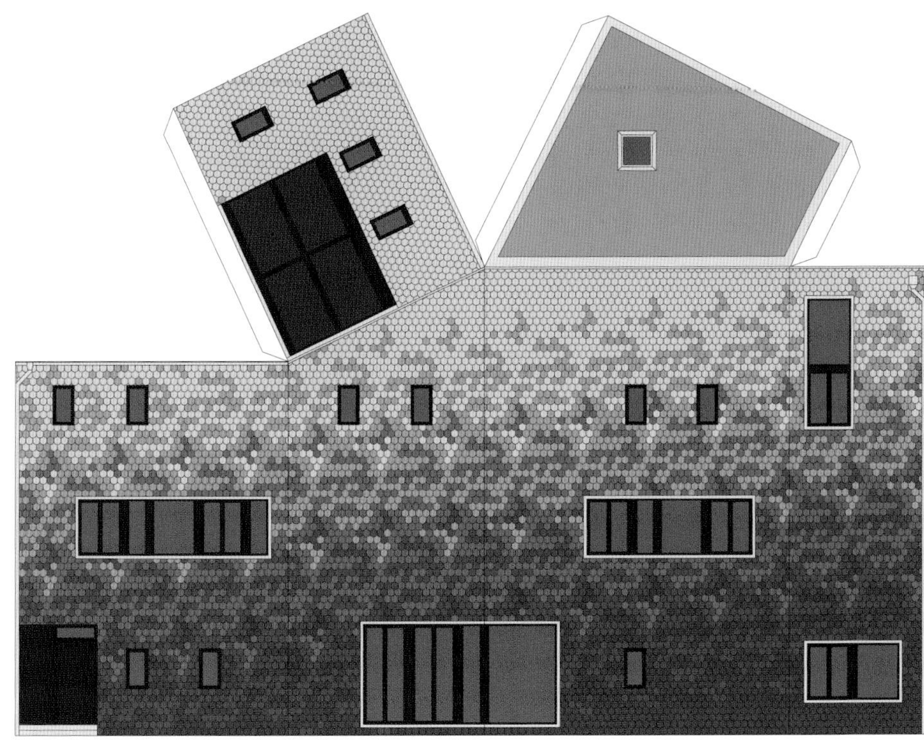

↖ | Façade diagram
↓ | Library interior

MDS

↑ | **Living room and terrace at dawn**
→ | **Façade,** south elevation

Shirokane House

Tokyo

The site for this residence is surrounded on four sides by other buildings. The architects maximized the amount of natural light brought into the building from above and designed the interior so that light reaches all the way to the lower levels. The living room is located on the top floor, with a terrace connected to it and a second roof terrace facing onto the void above it. Light and fresh air from the terraces and void pour into the first-floor dining room and kitchen. The southern side of the house, which faces onto the road and has no windows aside from those in the entryway, gives the impression of a closed-off, somber structure. Inside, however, the mood is entirely different, with light and shadow fluctuating throughout the day to create a diversity of scenes.

PROJECT FACTS

Address: Minato-ku, Tokyo, Japan. **Client:** confidential. **Completion:** 2013. **Gross floor area:** 102 m^2. **Number of rooms:** 5. **Main materials:** reinforced concrete. **Situation:** detached building in urban context.

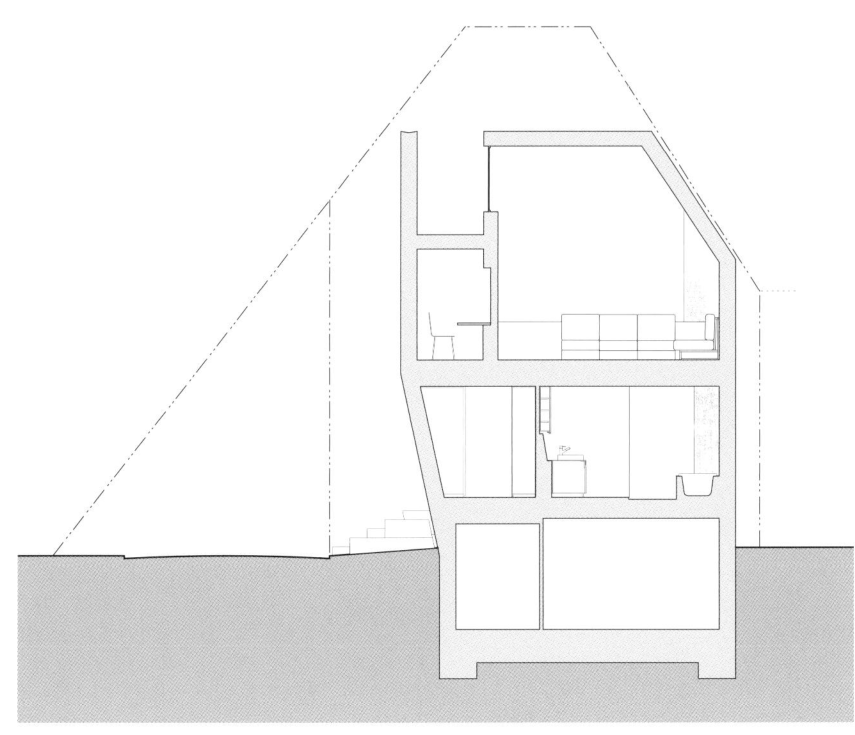

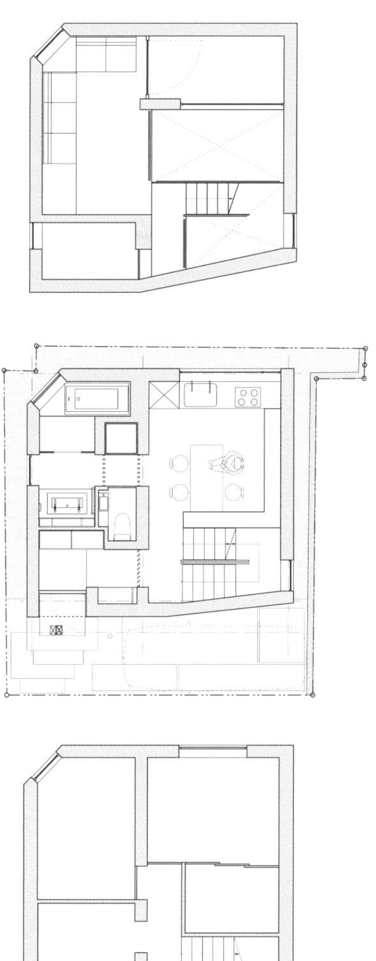

←←| **Living room,** top floor
↑ | **Section and basement, ground and first floor plans**
← | **Void,** upper floor

Fujiwara-Muro architects

↑ | **Front view,** façade
→ | **Entrance area at night**

House in Hakusan

Hakusan

This design develops from the client's concerns about limiting excessive heat from sunlight at the front of the house, and about how to optimize the flow of air. A wide staircase has been built at the center of the house, thus allowing a gentle breeze to flow downwards. An inbuilt table is positioned at the top of the staircase, providing a cool, bright and airy space for the inhabitants to sit. The rooms on the second floor are arranged around the staircase. The architects restricted the size of the windows in order to provide some respite from the sun, opening these windows allows sunlight to reflect off the lower portion of the staircase, providing illumination from the bottom up.

PROJECT FACTS

Address: Hakusan-shi, Japan. **Client:** Ogiso family. **Completion:** 2011. **Gross floor area:** 95 m². **Number of rooms:** 4. **Main materials:** wood. **Situation:** detached building in suburban context.

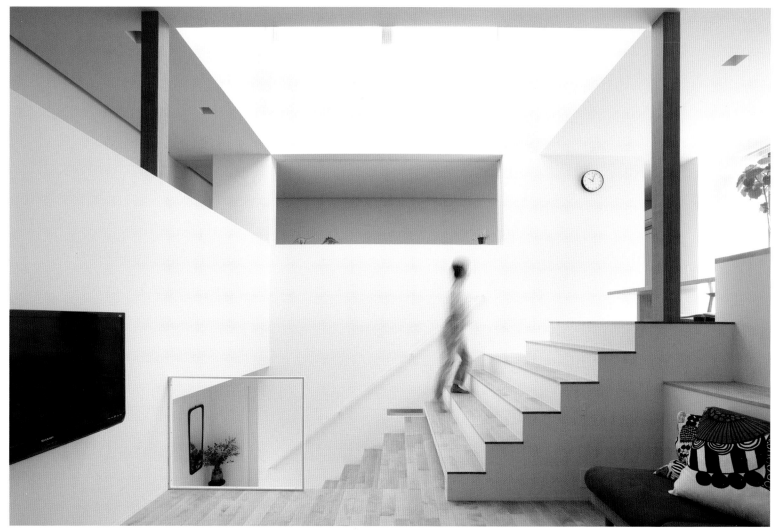

↑ | **Interior,** open ceiling
← | **Stairs and living area,** seen from above

← | Stairs and open ceiling

↓ | Ground and first floor plans, section

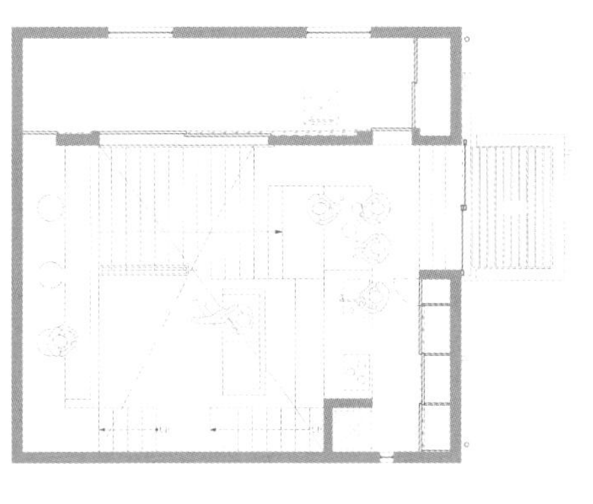

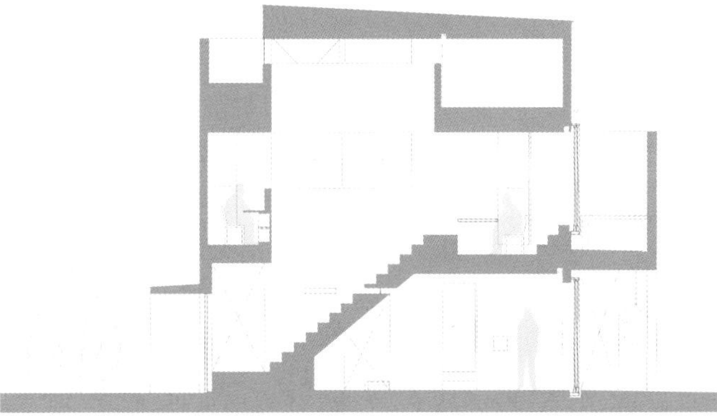

Buddenberg Architekten

↑ | Building in context
→ | Entrance

Extension of Hinterhofhaus

Düsseldorf

This project involved the extension of Hinterhofhaus, German for backyard house, to create more space for the owners, a young family with two children. Changes to building regulations allowed the construction of a staggered upper level. Two cubes were 'docked' onto the plain gray 'shoe box'. The cubes on the roof house the two children's bedrooms and a bathroom. A smaller cube on the ground floor serves as the entrance and also contains a rubbish separation system. The garden design picks up on the arrangement of the house, comprising low cubes that serve as seating elements and flower beds. The glazed orange larch wood and anthracite gray used for the existing building have been reversed on the new extension, which is clad with wood and has anthracite window frames.

PROJECT FACTS

Address: Tannenstraße 9, 40476 Düsseldorf, Germany. **Client:** Oliver Buddenberg, Inge Tauchmann. **Completion:** 2010. **Gross floor area:** 45 m². **Number of rooms:** 2. **Main materials:** larch wood. **Situation:** detached building in city center.

↑ | View of terrace
↓ | Extension and ground floor plans

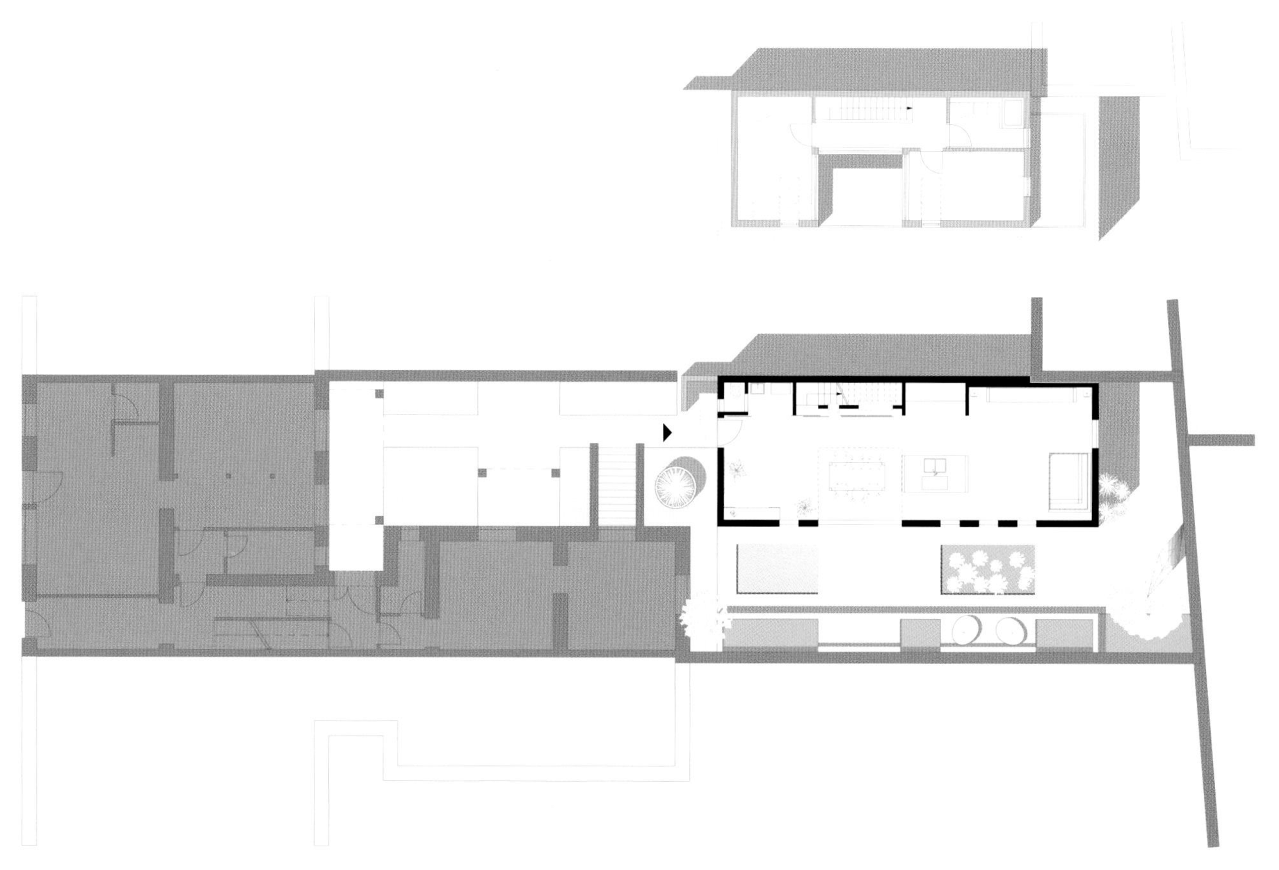

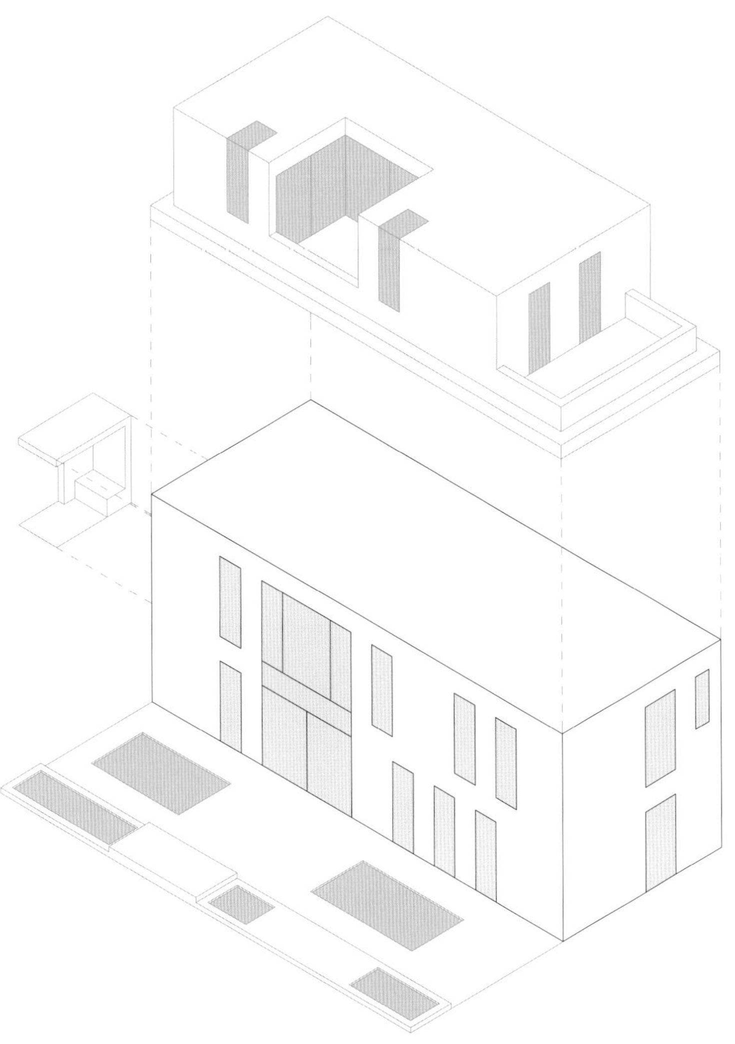

← | Axonometry
↓ | Garden

apool

↑ | **Street façade,** sky reflection
→ | **Entrance,** sliding door

Townhouse Oberwall

Berlin

This project involved the transformation of a half-finished townhouse into a flagship store for a fashion label and a second home for the designers. The building structures were dismantled and redesigned. The new design makes the most of the typical vertical orientation of a townhouse. The façade concept is radically minimalist in style. The façade gives the house its unique character, creating an unmistakable face for the company. A fully glazed sliding door forms the entrance to the store; this is six-and-a-half meters tall and just as tall as the building is wide. The seven-story building houses two duplexes. Working and living environments are united under one roof. The reduced color pallet focuses on white, natural white, and concrete gray, thus emphasizing the effect of natural light.

PROJECT FACTS

Address: Oberwallstraße 16, 10117 Berlin, Germany. **Client:** Studio Rundholz GmbH. **Completion:** 2012. **Gross floor area:** 540 m². **Number of rooms:** 7. **Additional use:** flagship store. **Main materials:** aluminum, glass, concrete. **Situation:** part of new development in city center.

← | Rear façade at night

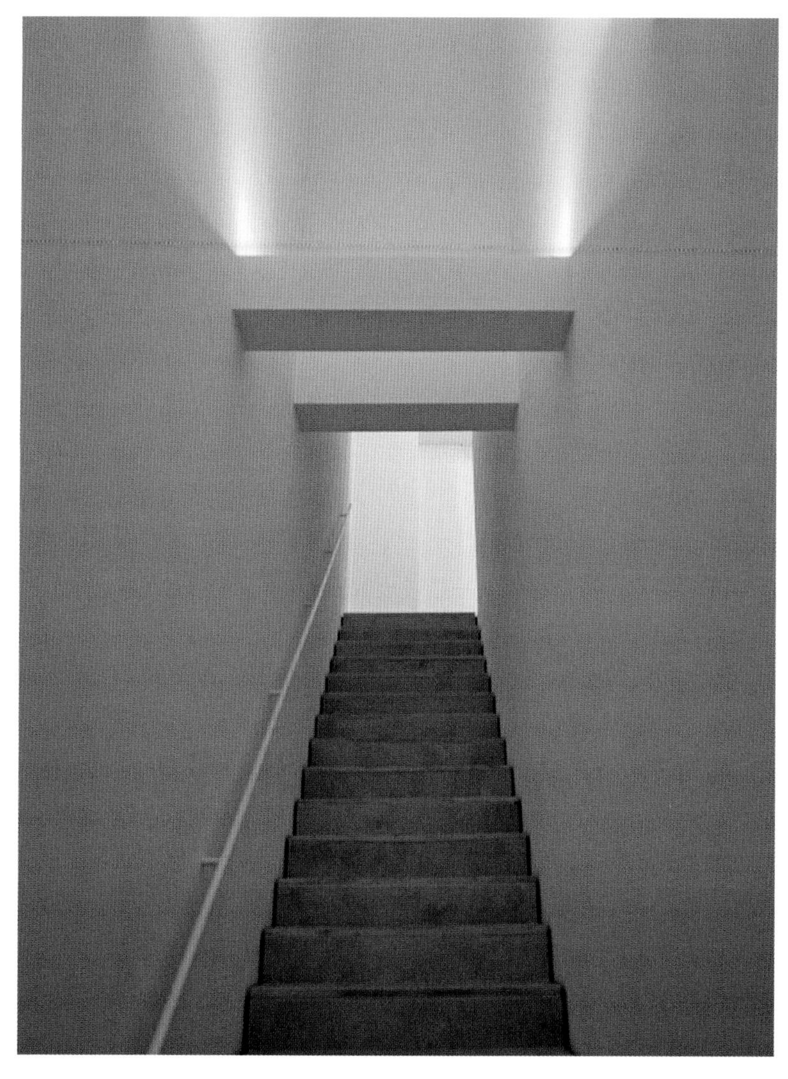

← | Staircase
↙ | Section

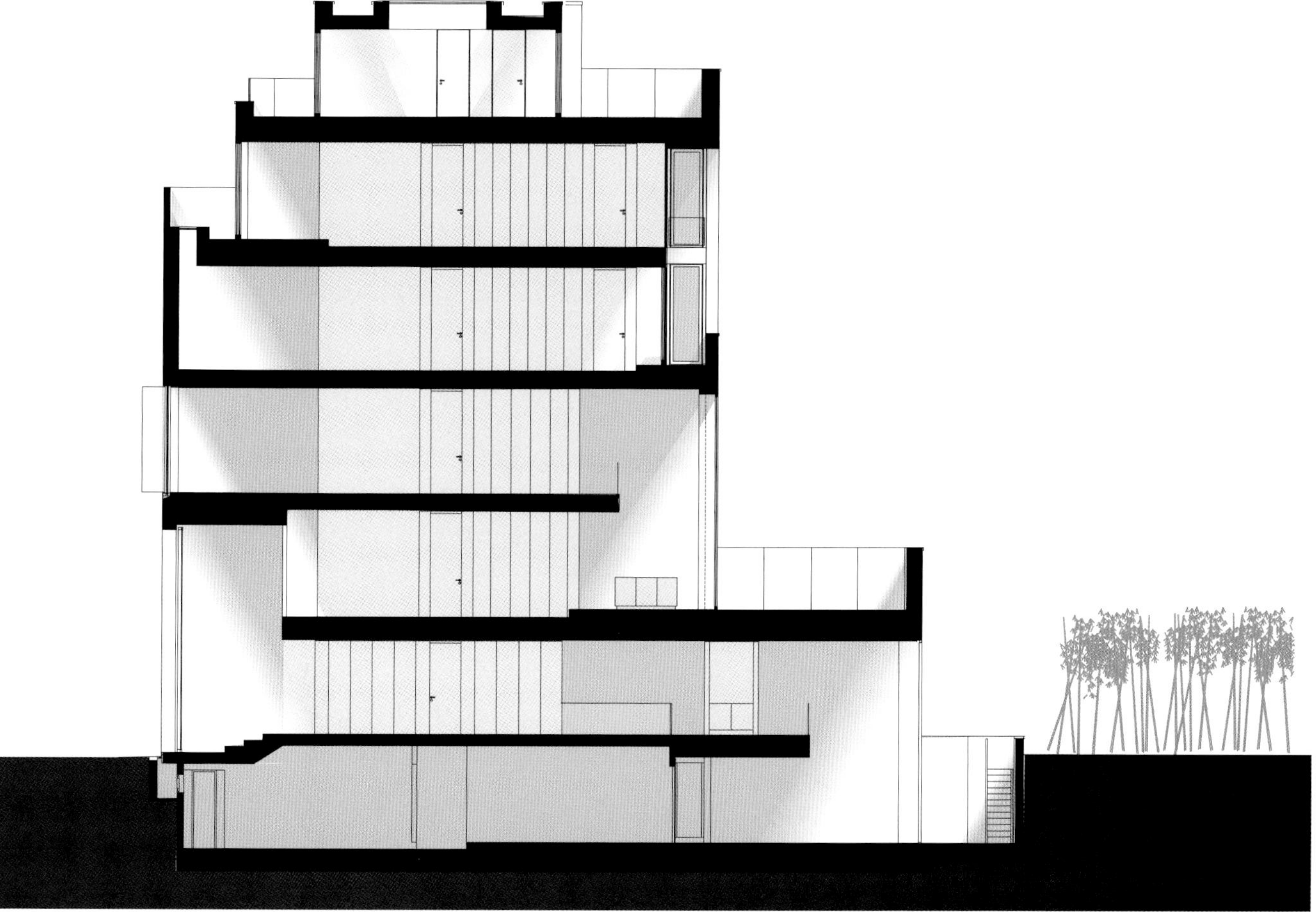

Katsuhiro Miyamoto & Associates

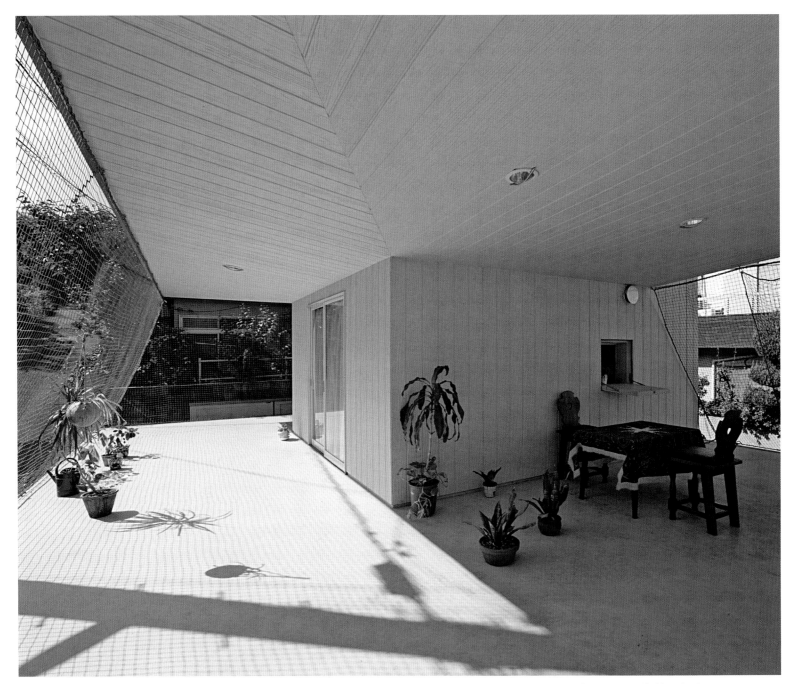

↑ | **Garden,** surrounded by plastic net

Between

Takarazuka

This is a two-family home with a garden on the first floor, sandwiched between residential zones. By shifting each floor, a large asymmetrical balcony appears. The site was too small to put a garden on grade next to the building, so the architect chose to locate it on a reinforced concrete podium, with a separate wooden structure overhead. A kitchen and dining area is on the same level as the garden. The semi-open garden is often used for baseball practice by the grandchildren, and sometimes as a place for an outdoor tea ceremony. The garden is a spacious yard, which commands an extensive view of the Osaka bay area.

PROJECT FACTS

Address: Takarazuka, Japan. **Client:** Tsuyoshi Watanabe. **Completion:** 2009. **Gross floor area:** 121 m². **Number of apartments:** 2. **Number of rooms:** 7. **Main materials:** wood, reinforced concrete. **Situation:** detached building in urban context.

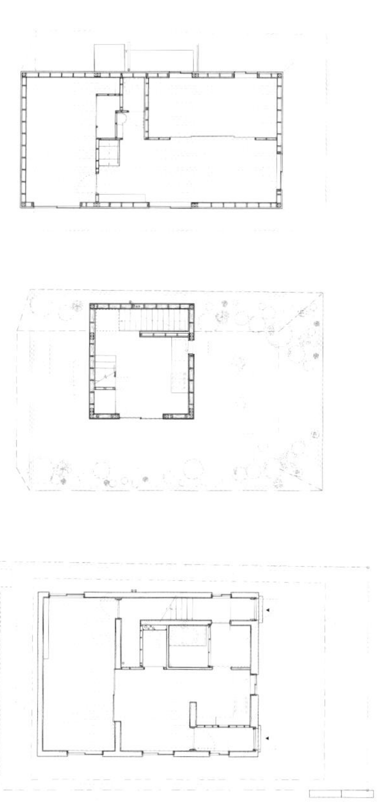

↗ | **Ground, first and second floor plans**

↑ | **Outdoor area on first floor**

↓ | **Entire building,** garden on first floor

GAAGA

↑ | **Exterior,** view from west
→ | **Façade,** carved with horizontal stripes

Stripe House

Leiden

Stripe House is a small, mixed-use house located in Leiden, the Netherlands. It takes its name from the horizontal stripes carved into the façade. The house resides in a new urban planning area where clients can develop their own houses. Despite its limited size, the plot is not entirely built on. One quarter of the plot is reserved for a small, enclosed garden, creating a soft transition from public to private space. The ground floor houses the office space and the patio, the next level contains the kitchen, living and dining space, while two bedrooms and a bathroom are located on the upper floor. The large void along the north façade is the focal point in the house. The large window at the top offers an abundance of natural light. The huge exterior walls are made tangible and appealing by means of horizontal grooves in the plaster. The grooves, with a total length of approximately 7,000 meters, are handmade and carved into a semi-hardened plaster.

PROJECT FACTS

Address: Wattstraat 8, 2316 SK Leiden, the Netherlands. **Client:** Arie Bergsma, Esther Stevelink. **Completion:** 2012. **Gross floor area:** 206 m². **Number of rooms:** 4. **Additional use:** office. **Main materials:** striped plaster. **Situation:** semi-detached building in suburban context.

↑ | **Interior,** bedroom
← | **Kitchen,** with large window

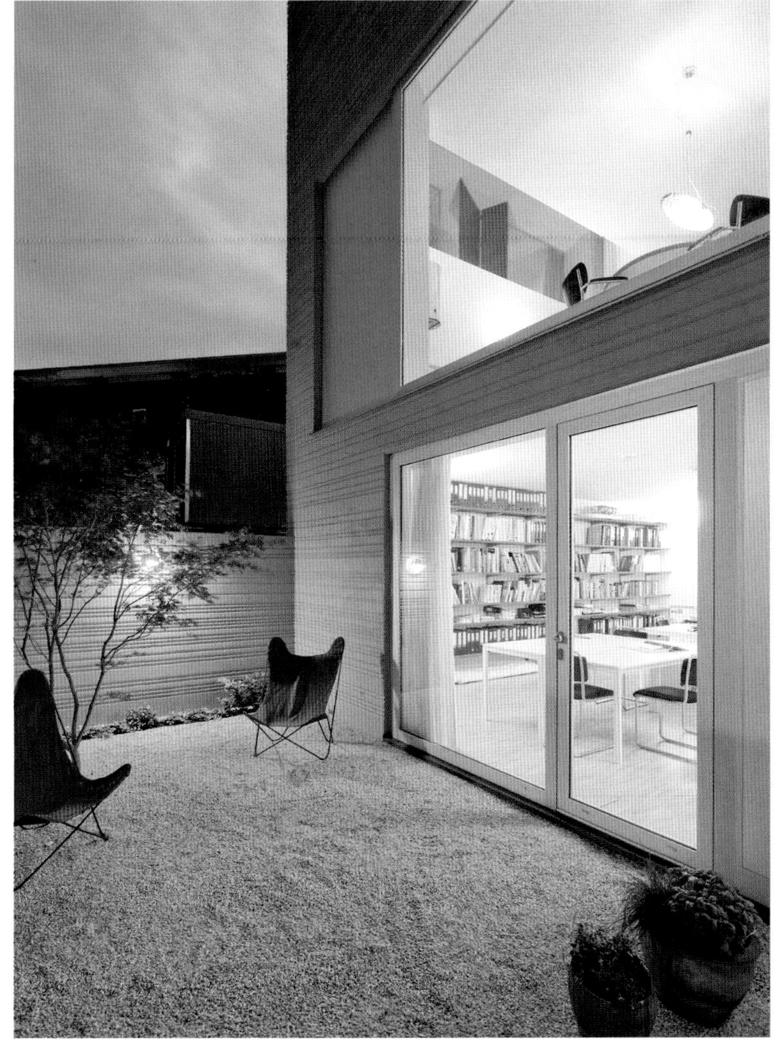

← | **Patio,** view to office space

↓ | **Ground to third floor plans**

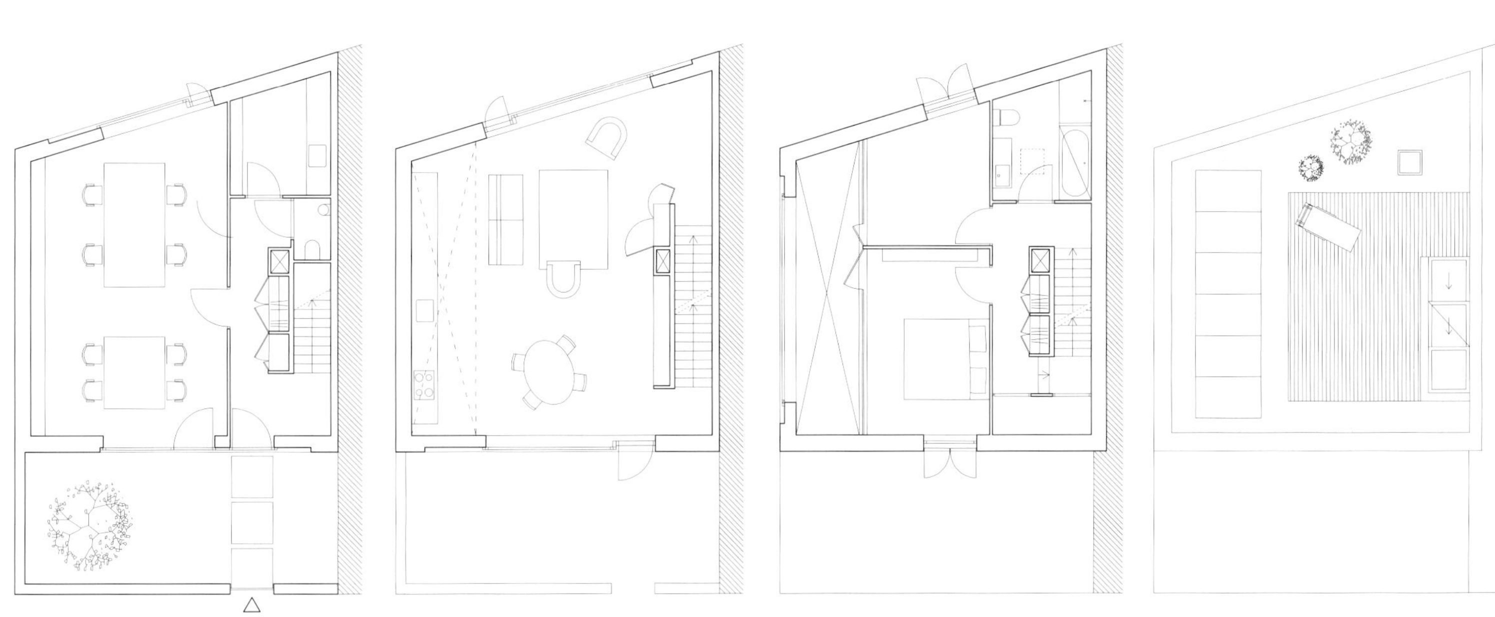

↑ | **Entrance from Rheinfelderstrasse**
→ | **Interior,** and view of loggia

Living in Wettsteinpark

Basel

These two residential apartment blocks were designed to protect the special character of this historical park-like area. The two compact apartment blocks have been added directly on to the existing estate. They develop a discrete physiognomy, while at the same time ensuring that a maximum of green areas and trees have been preserved. The building transforms the linear structure of the existing apartment blocks. The stairwell is lit from above and is positioned centrally, providing easy access to all the apartments. Each apartment has a large open balcony cut into the building volume. Both buildings vary in appearance. On the other hand both are featuring mineral roughcast plaster and resin bound plaster, what gives the desired unity and a character engaged in a dialogue with the surrounding buildings.

PROJECT FACTS

Address: Wettsteinallee 20, Rheinfelderstrasse 29, 4058 Basel, Switzerland. **Client:** CMS Christoph Merian Stiftung, Basel. **Completion:** 2011. **Gross floor area:** 2,700 m^2. **Artist:** Jeannette Mehr, Basel. **Number of apartments:** 20. **Number of rooms per apartment:** 2.5-3.5. **Main materials:** concrete, masonry, wood and metal windows, smoked oak flooring. **Situation:** existing development in urban context.

↑ | **Building,** surrounded by greenery
← | **Interior**

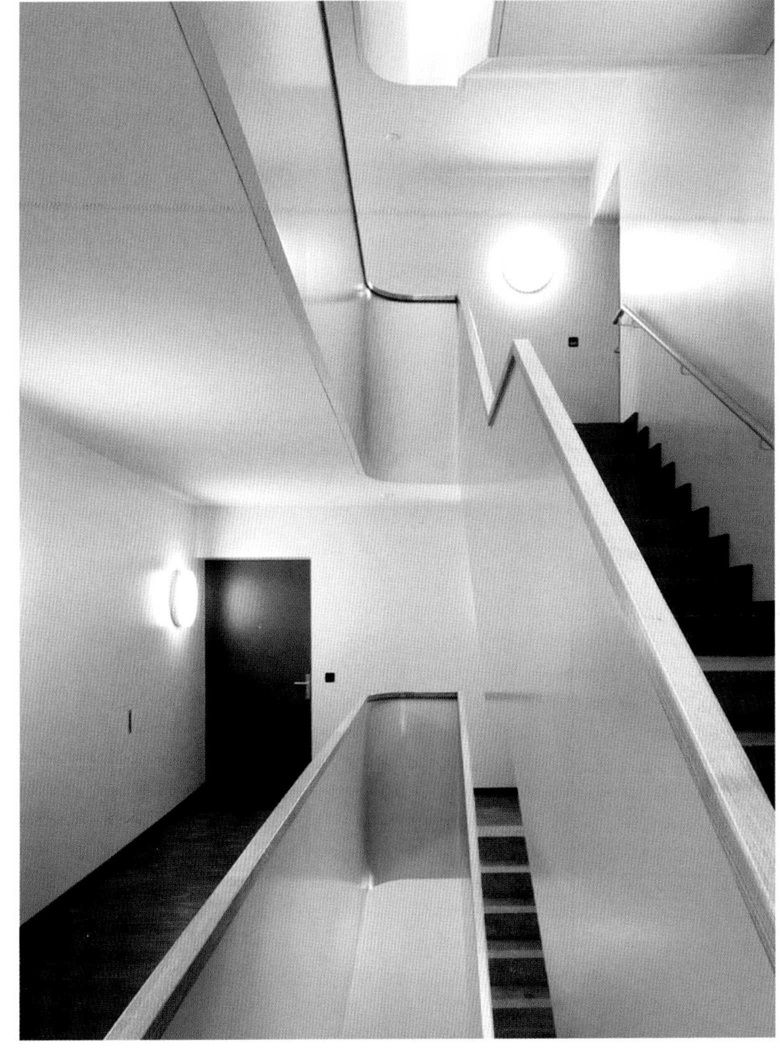

← | Staircase
↙ | Site plan
↓ | First floor plan

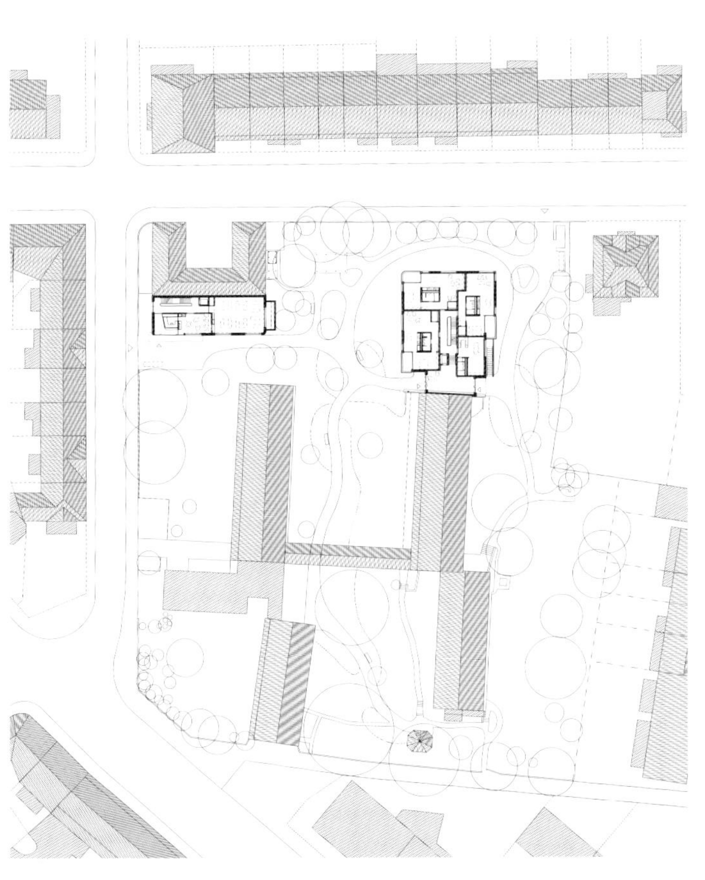

S+Na. Sanuki + Nishizawa architects

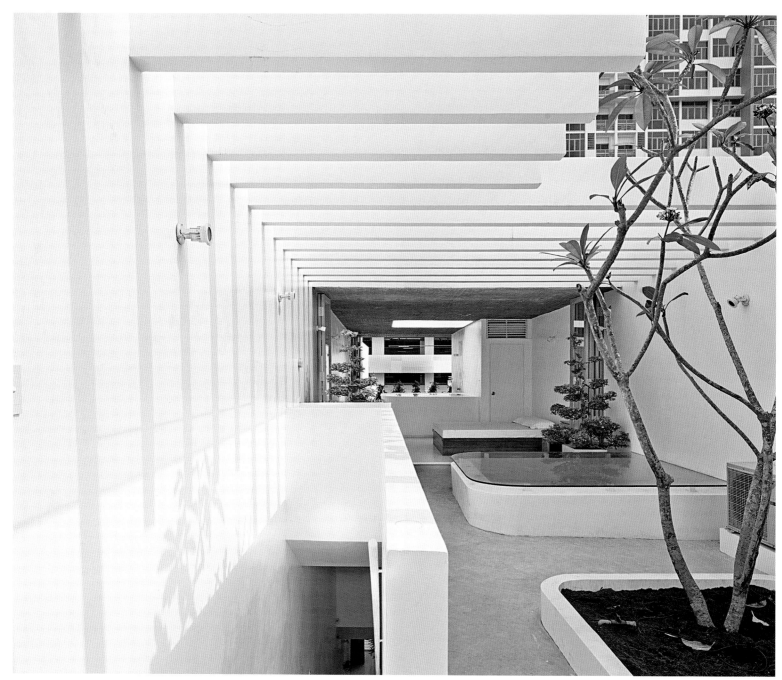

↑ | **Terrace,** third floor

Anh House

Ho Chi Minh City

Located in Ho Chi Minh City, this house is built on a plot just four meters wide and 21 meters long. The house is designed with four solid thick slabs and no fixed partition walls. Each slab has several voids that guide natural light from the skylight, façade and rear into the house. Furthermore, fixed partition walls have been replaced by light, movable and translucent partitions that separate the various spaces, adjusting the balance between privacy and fluency of the design. This sustainable and ecological proposal is considered as a re-definition of traditional Vietnamese architecture. The architects have designed this house as an example of alternative living in Vietnam.

PROJECT FACTS

Address: District 2, Ho Chi Minh City, Vietnam. **Client:** confidential. **Completion:** 2013. **Gross floor area:** 332 m². **Number of rooms:** 7. **Main materials:** concrete. **Situation:** detached building in suburban context.

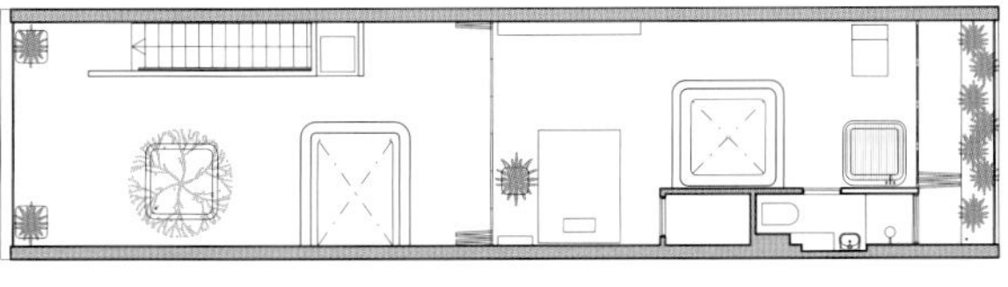

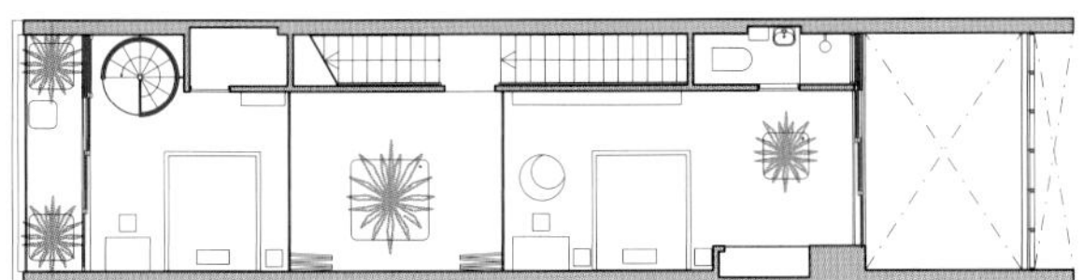

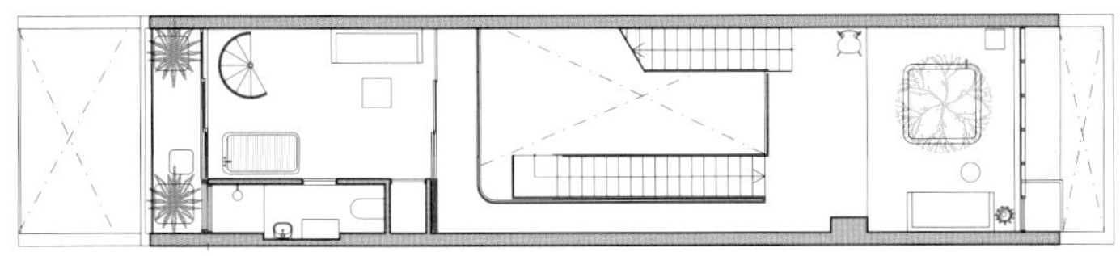

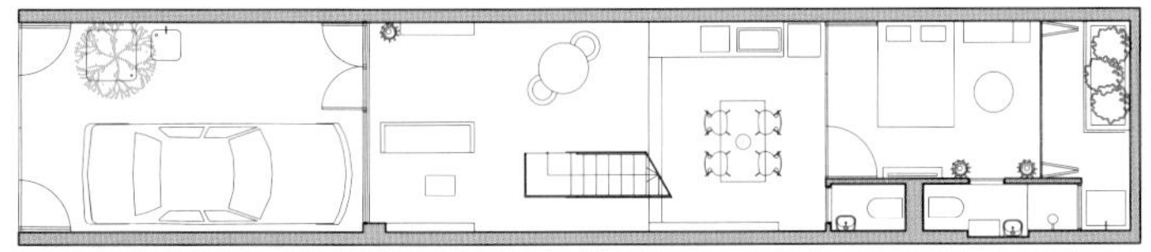

↑ | **Ground, first, second and third floor plans**

↓ | **Front view,** entrance area

↑ | **Interior with greenery**

↓ | **Ground floor,** view to entrance

Ahad Architekten

↑ | **Exterior view,** from St.-Leonhards-Garten
↗ | **Interior,** roof terrace in background
→ | **Rear of houses,** view from east

St.-Leonhards-Garten Townhouses

Brunswick

This site once housed a light rail depot and is a valuable plot of land that offered the perfect opportunity to build a row of elegant residential houses. The design is the result of a competition, which determined the materials, together with the desired building height. The new residential quarter offers families a good alternative to living in the suburb. The individual houses were built, based on three different floor plans: number 14 is a small house for two people; number 15 is a compact house for a large family; and number 16 is a house with office space. The volumes are structured to accommodate private terraces and roof gardens. The courtyard functions as a communal play and leisure area.

PROJECT FACTS

Address: St.-Leonhards-Garten 14–16, 38102 Brunswick, Germany. **Client:** Upper Eastside building group. **Completion:** 2011. **Gross floor area:** 252 m², 198 m², 180 m². **Number of apartments per building:** 3. **Number of rooms per building:** 6–7. **Additional use:** office. **Main materials:** wood, brick, fair-faced concrete, finery. **Situation:** part of new development in urban context.

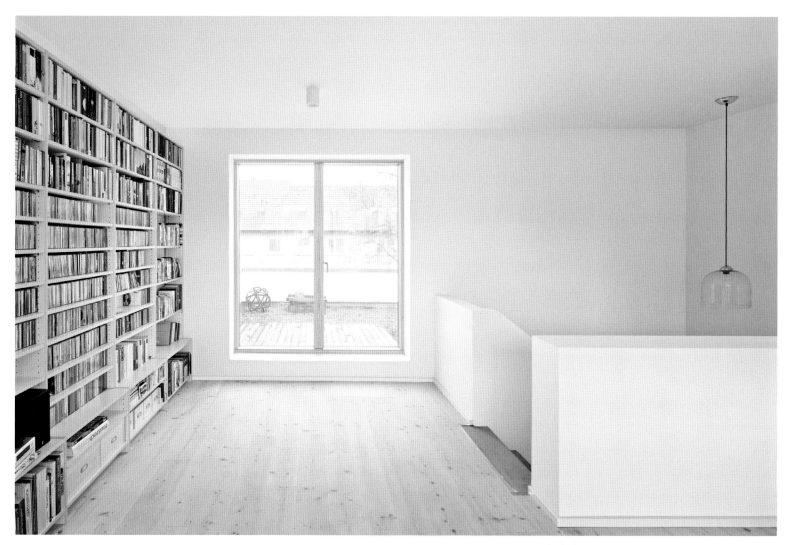

↑ | **Living area,** house 14
← | **Sketch**

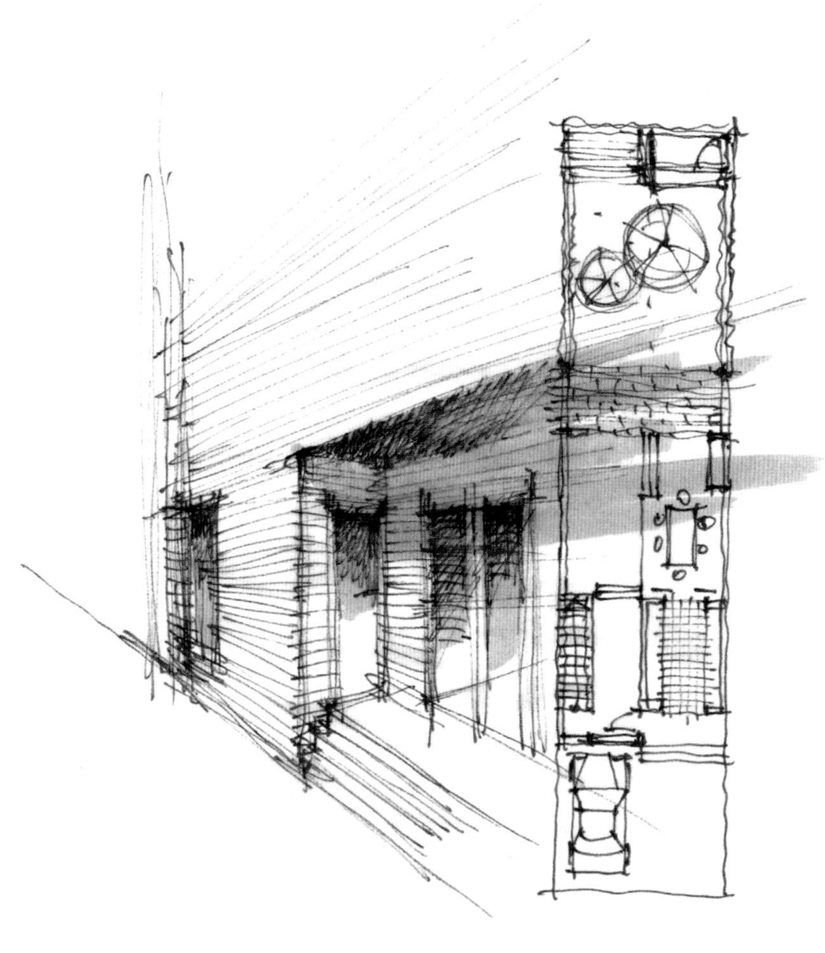

← | **Ground to third floor plans**
↙ | **Stairs to second floor,** house 14
↓ | **Cooking and dining area,** with balcony

Rebelo de Andrade Architectural & Design Studio

↑ | **General view**
→ | **Stairs downwards,** roof terrace

House in Travessa do Patrocínio

Lisbon

This house is located on a small plot of land in Lisbon. The constraints of the site presented the architects with a number of challenges. A courtyard at the center of the house draws an abundance of light into the interior, enhancing the main entrance and blurring the boundary between interior and exterior. The technical areas and garage have direct access to the street. The first floor houses the private living areas, while the social areas are located above on the second floor. The striking green façade transforms the wall into a cascade of living plants and foliage. The vertical garden comprises around 4,500 plants and covers over 100 square meters.

PROJECT FACTS

Address: Travessa do Patrocínio 5, 1350-233 Lisbon, Portugal. **Client:** BWA - Buildings With Art. **Completion:** 2012. **Gross floor area:** 248 m². **Planning partners:** ADN-Garden Design. **Number of rooms:** 4. **Main materials:** wood, concrete. **Situation:** semi-detached building in urban context.

← | **Exterior,** façade

← | Staircase
↓ | Section

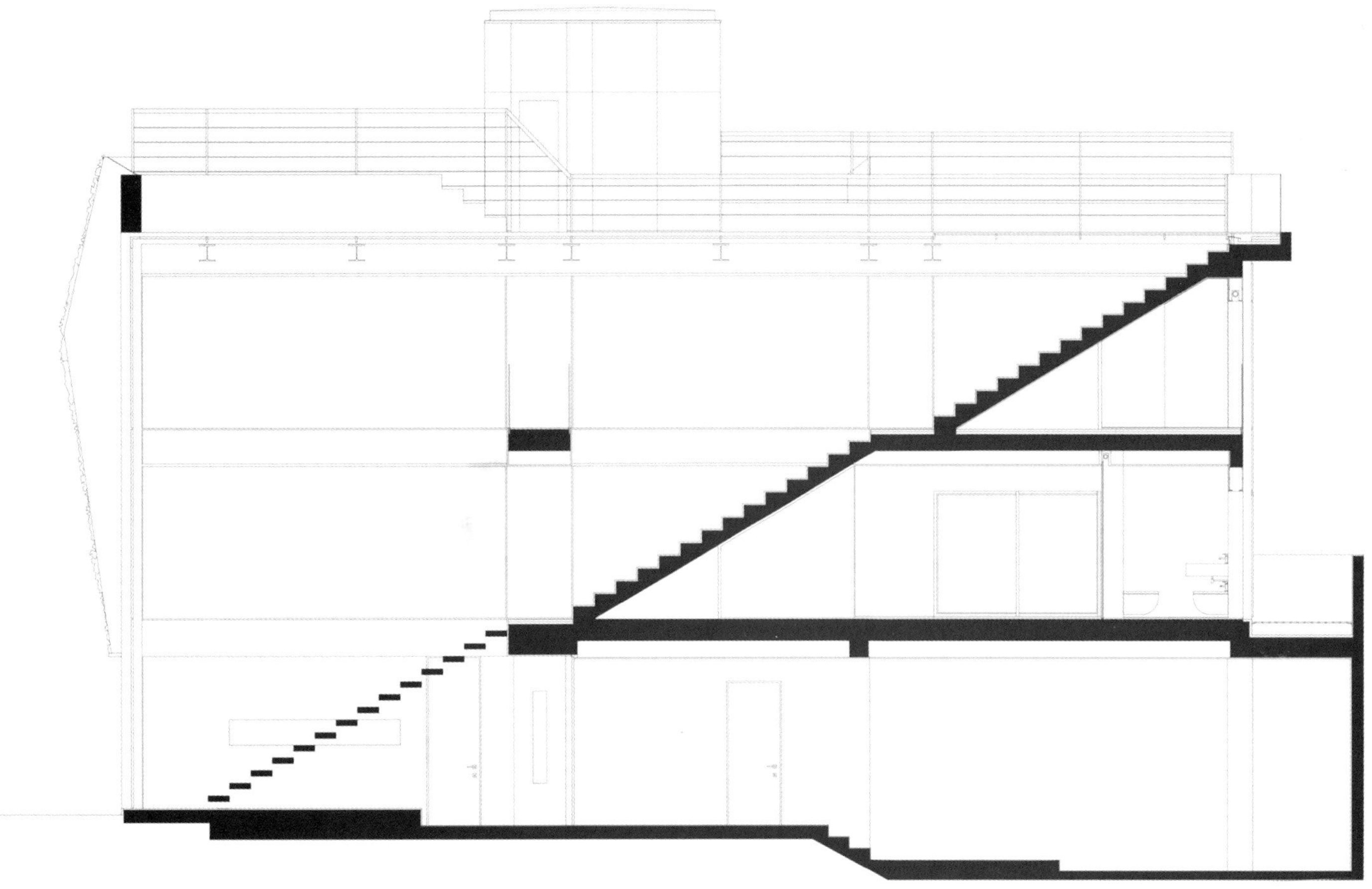

Atelier Norisada Maeda

↑ | **Swimming pool,** second floor
→ | **Street façade,** illuminated at night

Plastic Moon

Tokyo

A mold was used to form the shape of this building. Four casting molds were used to shape each space. The volume is perforated with void-like atria that flood the rooms with light. Finally, the four molds were stacked on top of each other creating a dynamic and unique townhouse. The thick alternating bands give the house a more lightweight appearance, which is emphasized by the glass façade sections and the incision cut into the top floor. Inside, an abundance of light, combined with clear lines and shapes creates a modern, bright and welcoming interior.

PROJECT FACTS

Address: 158-0081 Hukazawa, Setagaya, Tokyo, Japan. **Client:** confidential. **Completion:** 2009. **Gross floor area:** 206 m². **Number of rooms:** 5. **Additional use:** dental practice. **Main materials:** steel, mosaic tiles. **Situation:** detached building in urban context.

↑ | **Interior,** bathroom and swimming pool
← | **View from street**

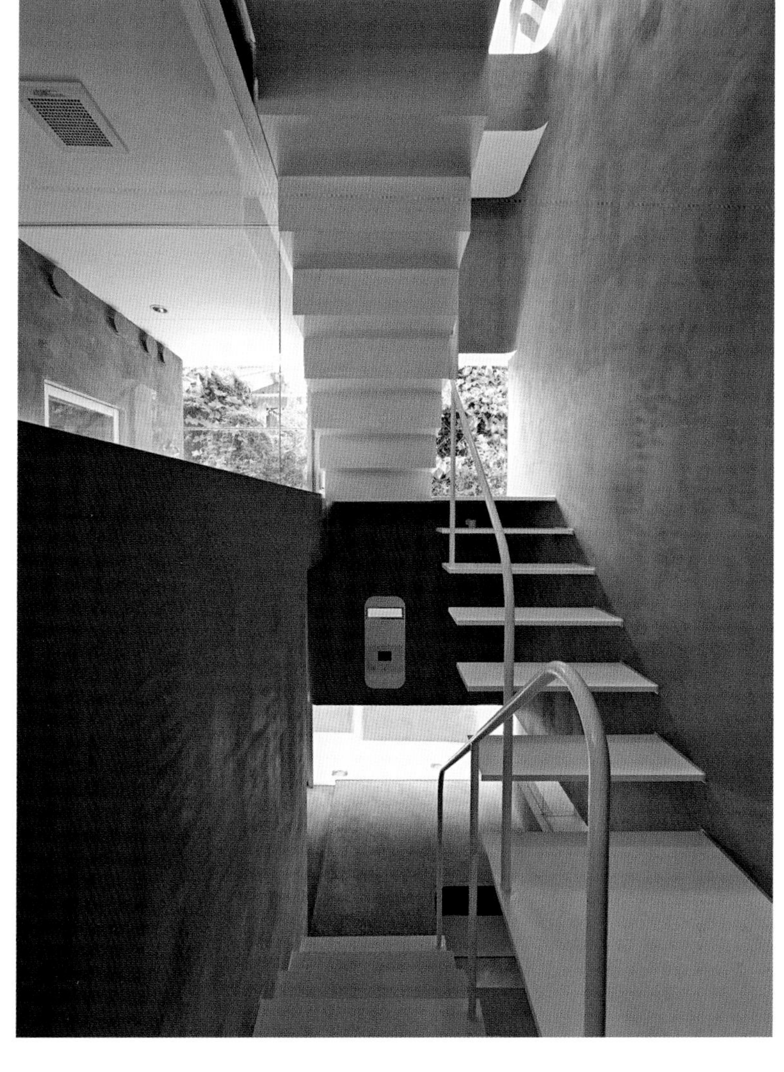

← | Staircase

↓ | Ground, first and second floor plans

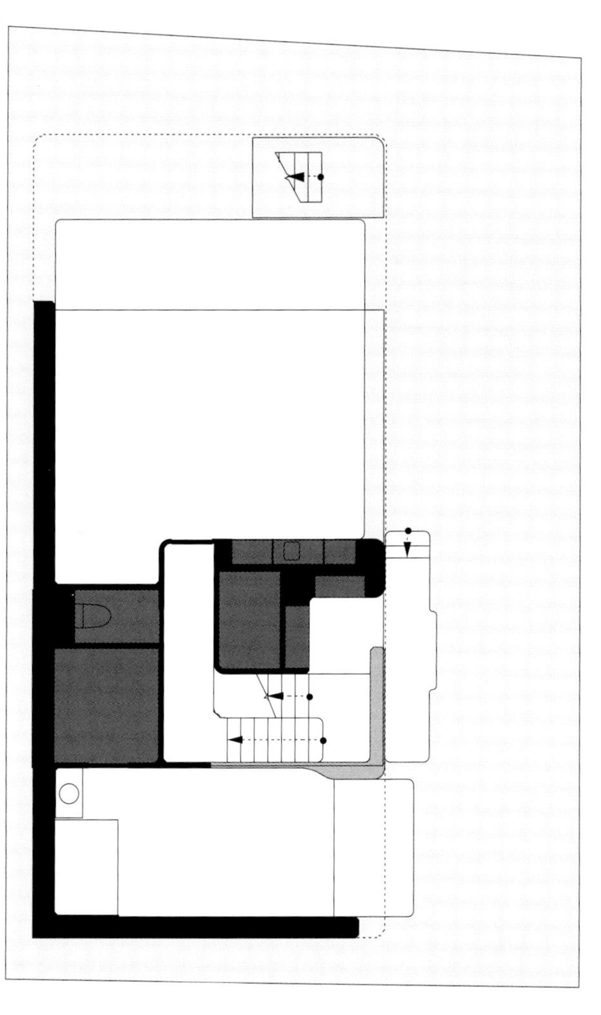

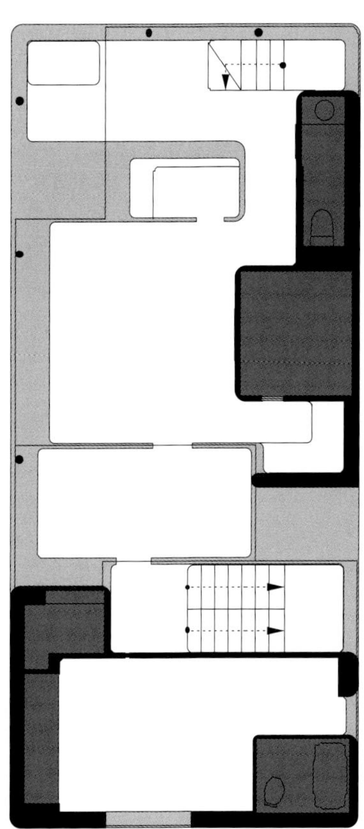

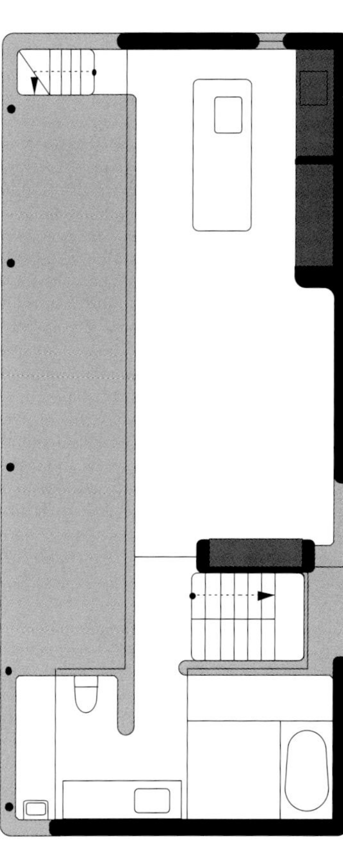

Sue Architekten

↑ | Balconies
→ | Front yards

Dense Identity on the Old Meadow

Vienna

This site is 150 meters long, with a width of between 17 and 34 meters and accommodates 40 apartments in two different building types. A row of 18 houses is located between the two apartment blocks along the adjacent streets. The houses are connected, an arrangement that allows a high level of living and open space, despite the building density. The buildings facing the streets are more open towards the south, with floor-to-ceiling glazing facing the balconies. The balconies and sloping roofs give the building complex the necessary structure. In contrast, the north façade has open and closed façade sections, giving it an almost pixelated appearance.

PROJECT FACTS

Address: Zachgasse 12/Benjowskigasse 35–37, 1220 Vienna, Austria. **Client:** wvg Bauträger Ges.m.b.H. **Completion:** 2011. **Gross floor area:** 3,760 m². **Number of apartments:** 40. **Total number of rooms:** 120. **Main materials:** concrete, wood. **Situation:** new development in suburban context.

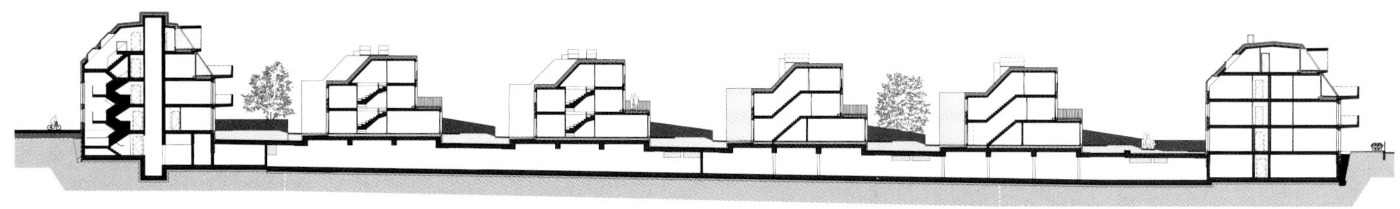

↑ | Site plan and section
← | Passage between houses

← | Garden side
↓ | Street view

24H > architecture

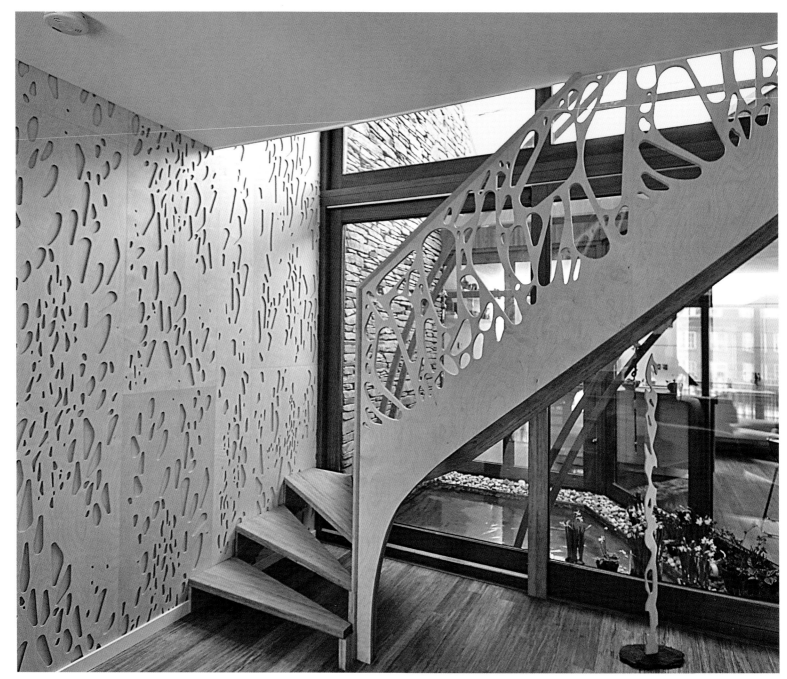

↑ | **Stairs**, detail
→ | **View of entire building**

2 Private Houses

Leiden

MVRDV's urban plan for Nieuw Leyden comprises 18 houses, designed by different architects. 24H > architecture designed two ecological houses. The half-sunken parking garage is situated at the center of the building block, giving the houses a split-level arrangement, resulting in a high-density area with narrow car-free streets. The houses in the building block are organized following a back-to-back principle, the general layout of the design is arranged in such a way that the use of daylight is maximized. A so-called canyon has been introduced to provide residents with maximal daylight during the day. A solar water heating system is used in combination with district heating. Together with insulated HR++ glass and highly insulated walls, this results in an overall energy performance which is far more ambitious than the requirements stated in the Dutch building regulations.

PROJECT FACTS

Address: Wattstaat, 2316 SK Leiden, the Netherlands. **Client:** family Van Dam-Lock, family Blansjaar-Visser. **Completion:** 2011. **Gross floor area:** 200 m², 180 m². **Number of houses:** 2. **Number of rooms per building:** 4, 5. **Main materials:** corten steel, jatoba wood, bamboo. **Situation:** part of new development in urban context.

← | Staircase

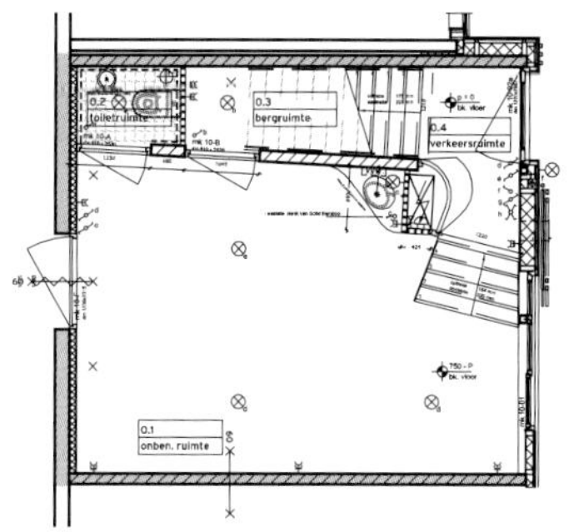

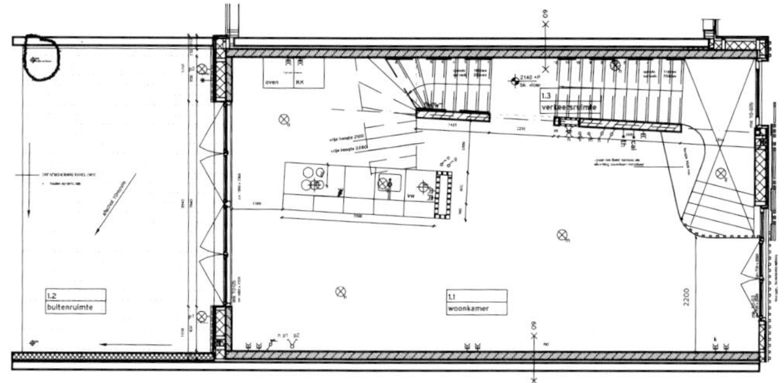

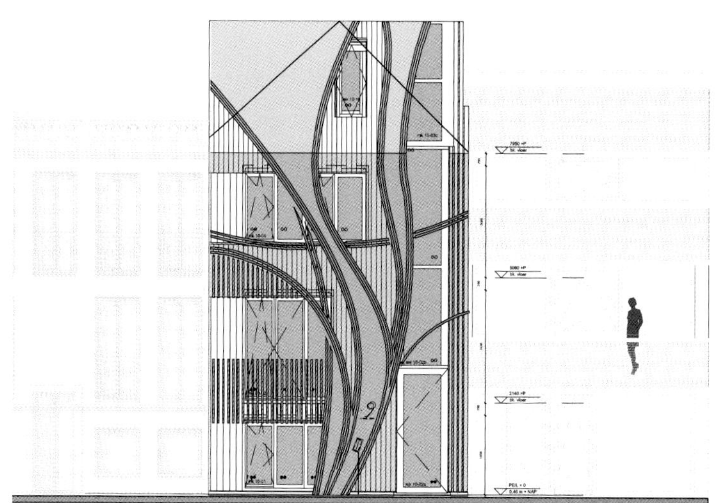

↖ | **Ground and first floor plans**
↑ | **Front elevation**
← | **Façade detail,** living area in background

Form/Kouichi Kimura Architects

↑ | **Narrow house,** in context
→ | **Interior areas,** connected by long corridor with window at end

Promenade House

Shiga

This project involved the construction of a house for a young couple on a small site just four meters wide. The building itself is just 2.7 meters wide and 27 meters long. A long narrow corridor connects all of the rooms and eventually ends in a study, where a large window not only draws light inside, but also makes the most of the views. On the second floor, the end of the hallway functions like a bridge; the ladder installed there connects the upper and lower spaces. The corridors laid out throughout the house act like promenades and emphasize the shape of the site.

Address: Shiga, Japan. **Client:** confidential. **Completion:** 2013. **Gross floor area:** 124 m². **Number of rooms:** 5. **Main materials:** concrete. **Situation:** detached building in city center.

↑ | House in context
↓ | Ground and first floor plans

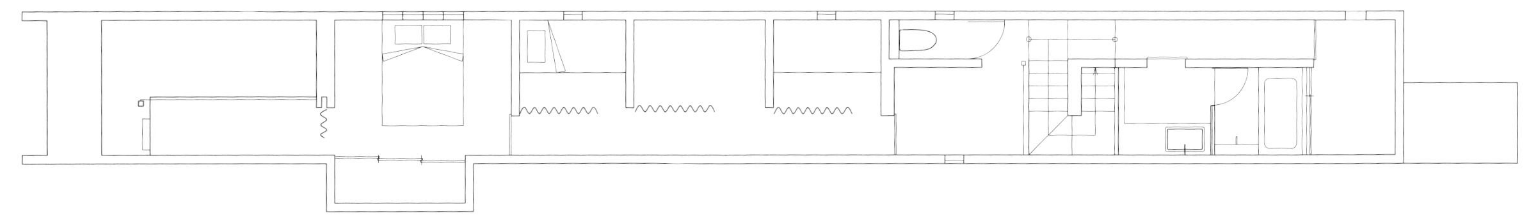

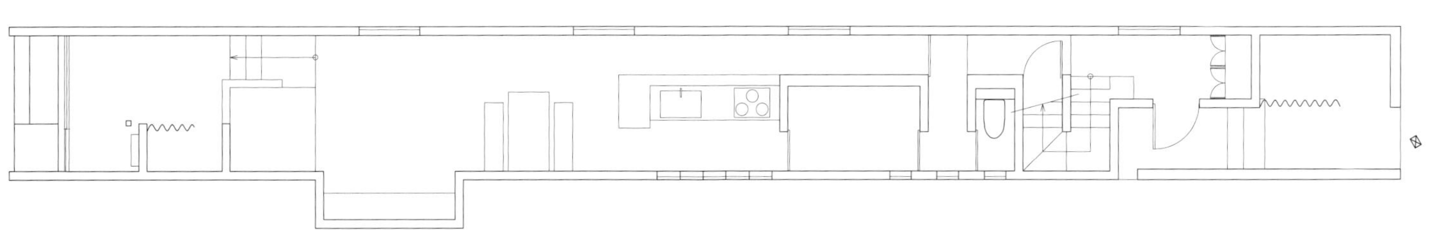

↖ | **Site plan**
↓ | **Large window,** draws light into house and frames views of the surroundings

Tiago do Vale Arquitectos

↑ | **Kitchen,** facing the block's interior plaza
→ | **Main elevation,** west

The Three Cusps Chalet

Braga

The Three Cusps Chalet is a Portuguese structure influenced by Brazilian traditions. The intent was to recover the construction's identity, lost in 120 years of small, unqualified interventions, in order to clarify the building's spaces and functions while simultaneously making it fit for modern life. A studio is located on the ground floor, while the top floors house the living areas. The open-plan loft is filled with light and dividing walls are kept to a minimum, in order to enhance the size and openness of the space. The use of white paint and a strict selection of natural wood and stone gives the home character, transforming a small dwelling into a comfortable and fresh 21st century home.

PROJECT FACTS

Address: Rua Dom Frei Caetano Brandão 121, 4700-031 Braga, Portugal. **Client:** Tiago do Vale. **Completion:** 2013. **Gross floor area:** 165 m². **Number of rooms:** 8. **Additional use:** office. **Main materials:** wood, yellow granite, yellow pine, marble, tiles. **Situation:** part of existing development in city center.

← | **Bedroom,** over living and dining room

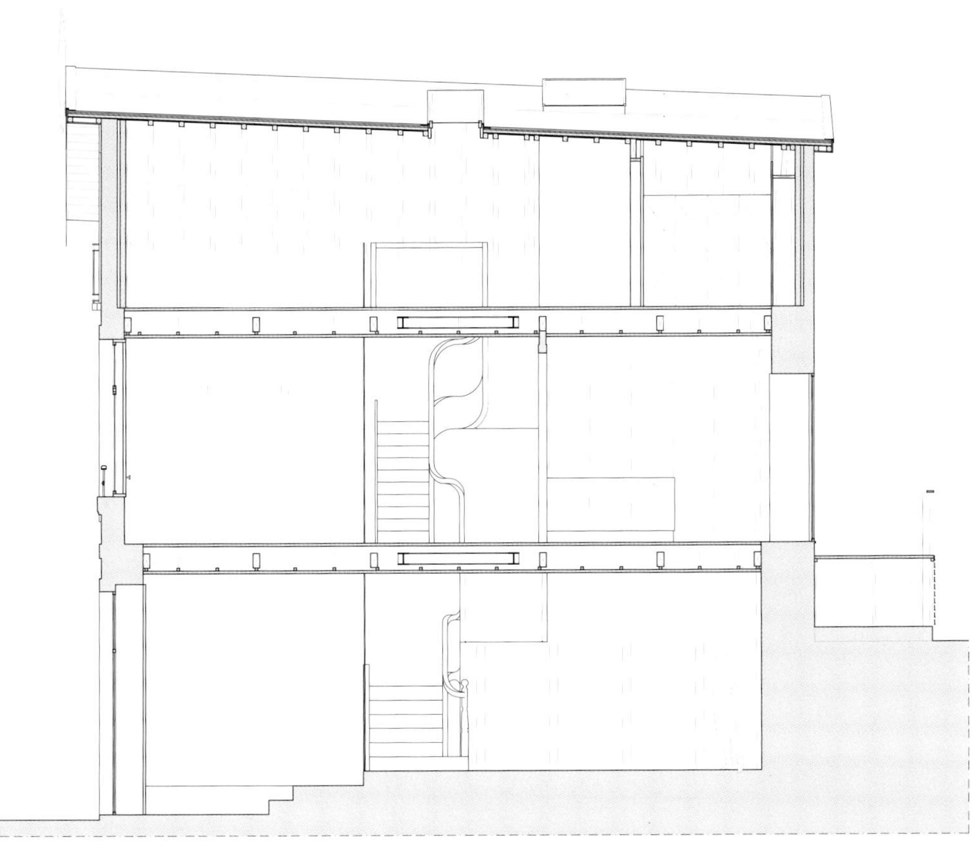

↖ | **Section**
↓ | **Office**, ground floor

Carl Turner Architects

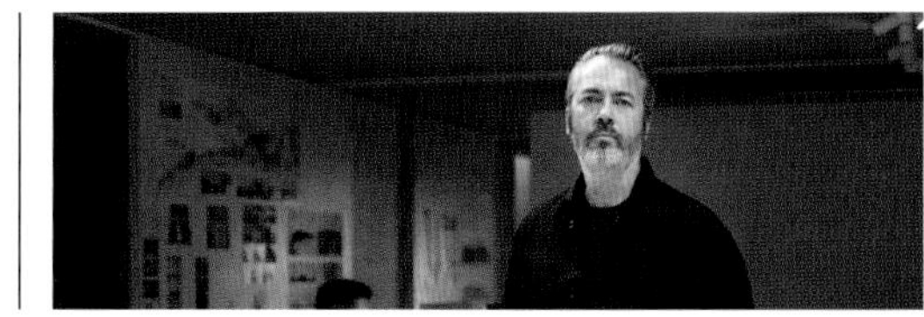

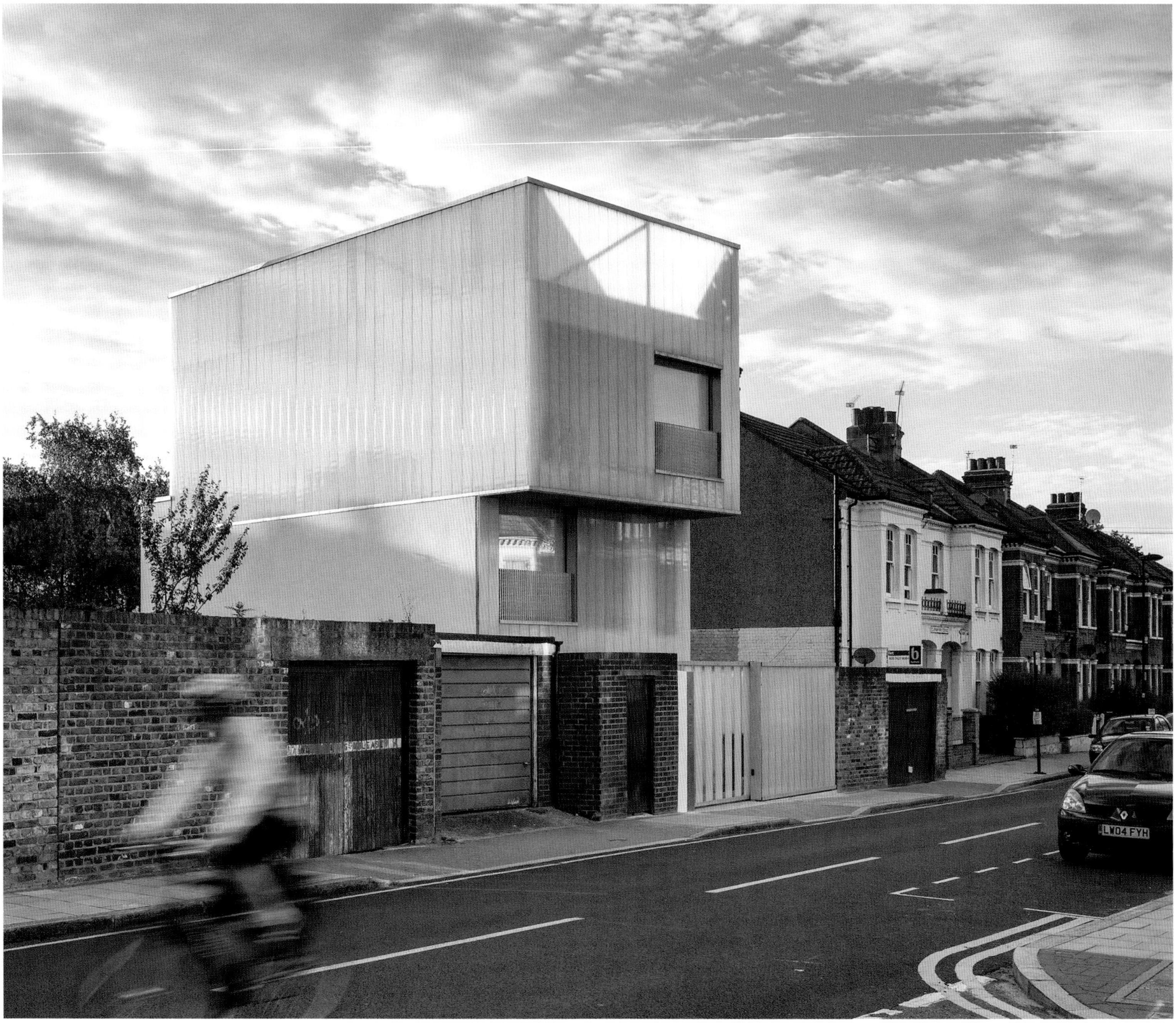

↑ | **Exterior,** street view
→ | **Elevation**

Slip House

London

Occupying one of four plots (a gap in a Brixton terrace), Slip House was built in the bottom of the garden of a derelict house. Three simple 'slipped' orthogonal box forms break up the bulk of the building and give it its striking sculptural quality. The top floor is clad in milky, translucent glass panels which continue past the roof to create a high level enclosure for a private roof terrace. Designed to code for Sustainable Homes Level 5, Slip House features energy piles which use a solar assisted ground source heat pump integrated into the pile foundations, photovoltaics, a green roof, rain water harvesting, mechanical ventilation with heat recovery and underfloor heating.

PROJECT FACTS

Address: 16 Clapham Park Terrace, Lyham Road, SW2 5EA London, UK. **Client:** Carl Turner. **Completion:** 2012. **Gross floor area:** 192 m². **Number of rooms:** 4. **Additional use:** workspace. **Main materials:** steel, glass. **Situation:** detached building in urban context.

↑ | Roof terrace
← | Kitchen with lighting from above

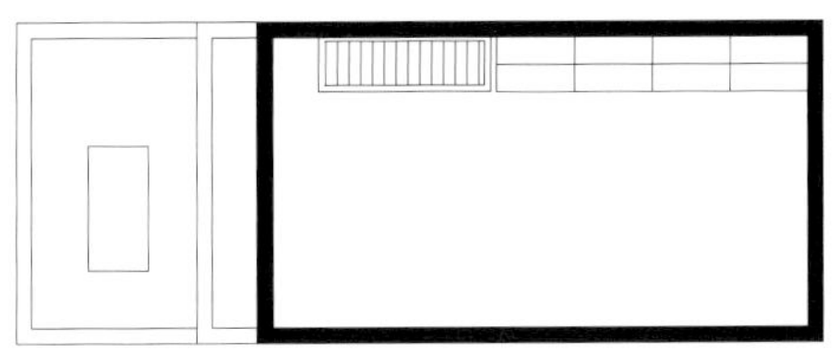

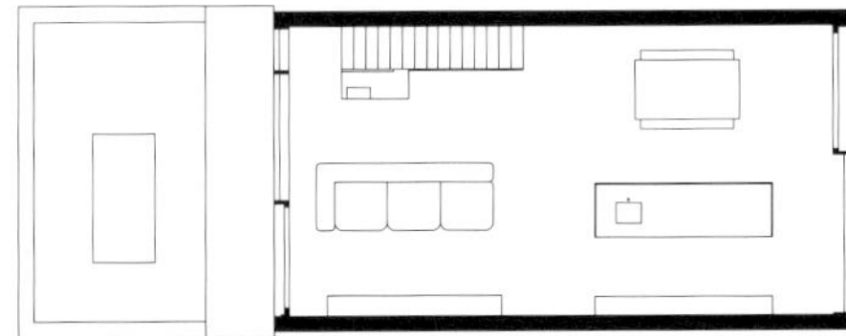

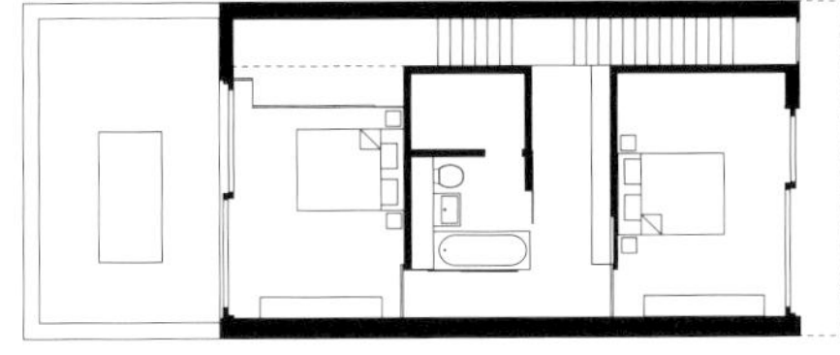

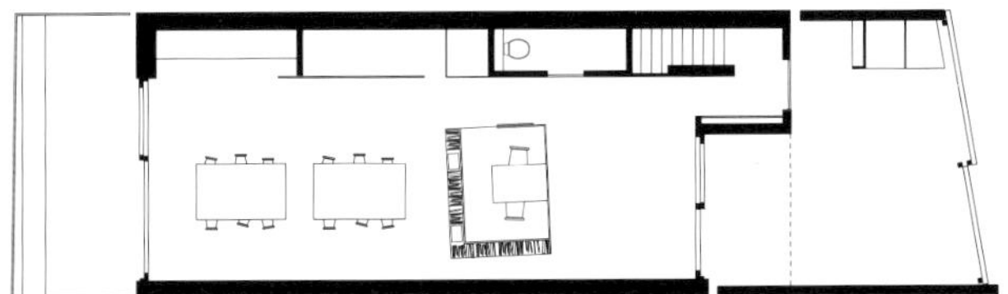

← | Ground to roof floor plans
↓ | Living area

Yasutaka Yoshimura Architects

↑ | **Interior,** view from bedroom
→ | **Entire building,** east façade

Window House

Miura

This weekend house faces Sagami Bay and offers stunning views of Mount Fuji and Enoshima. The site is just three by eight meters and three stories in height. The building volume needed to be raised in order to protect it from storm surges. The large windows compensate slightly for blocking the view of the houses behind. They also have the added advantage of drawing light deep into the house, making the interior bright and welcoming.

Address: Miura, Japan. **Client:** confidential. **Completion:** 2013. **Gross floor area:** 33 m². **Number of rooms:** 1. **Main materials:** reinforced concrete, wood. **Situation:** detached building in suburban context.

↑ | **General view,** from sea
↙ | **First and second floor plans**

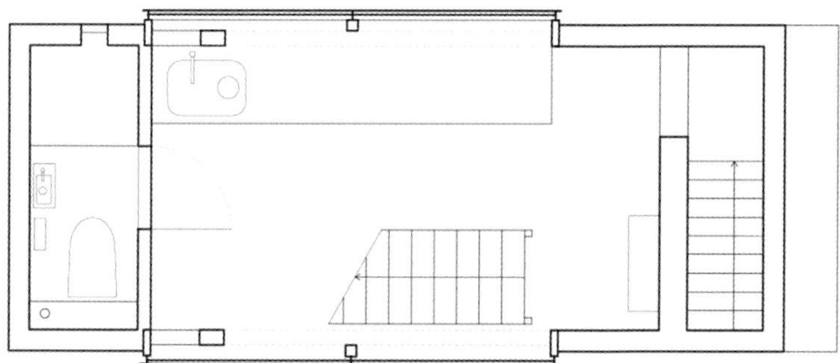

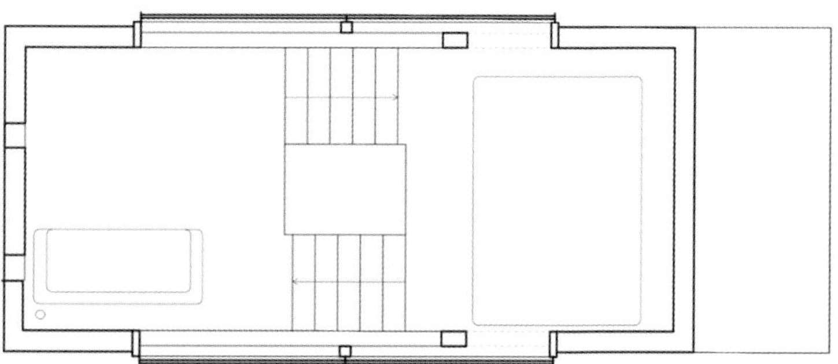

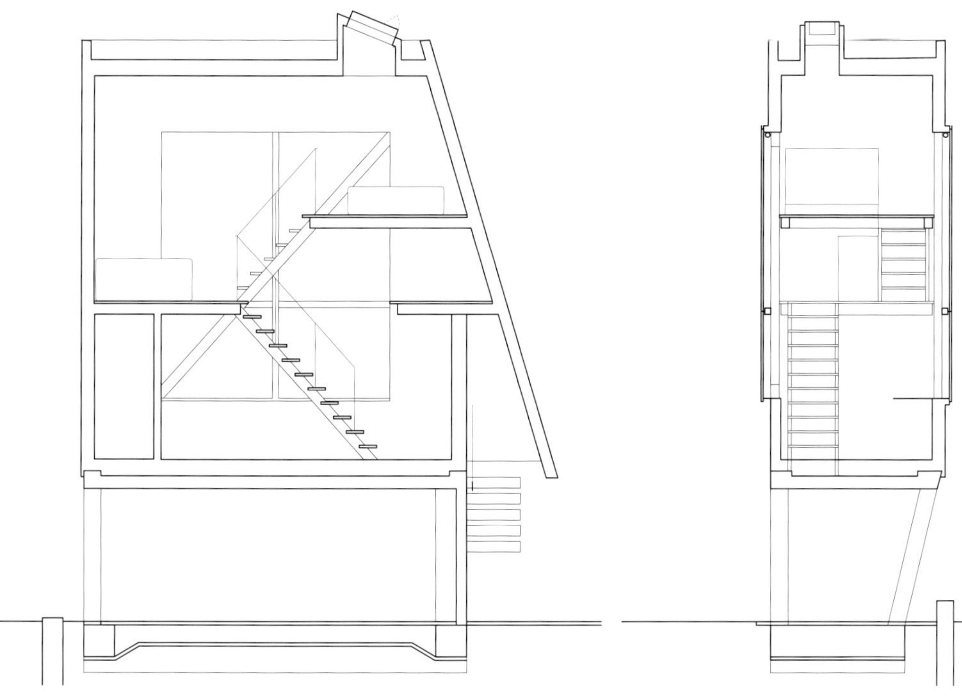

↖ | Sections
↓ | Interior

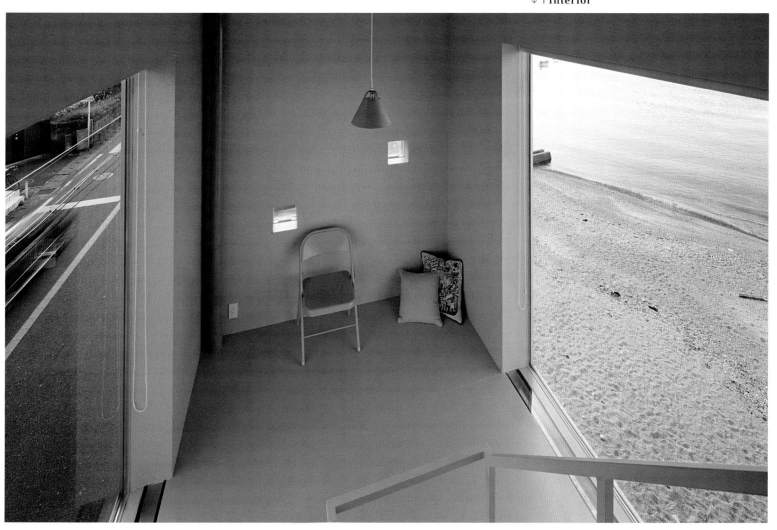

Helwig Haus und Raum
Planungsgesellschaft

↑ | **Street view,** building situated on slope
→ | **Interior,** stairs of fairfaced concrete

Am Hang und aus der Reihe

Neustadt an der Weinstraße

This residential house is well integrated into the surrounding neighborhood. The roof design is adapted to respond to the situation and the house also has a typically high base. The house has an individual character and stands out from its neighbors. The design uses the position of the sloping site to its advantage, making the most of views over the city center. Furthermore, it also accentuates the views of the historical hillside vineyards. The functional rooms are located on the slope-side, while the living room can be found on the upper floor. From the living room, a staircase leads up to the gallery, providing access to the terrace and garden.

PROJECT FACTS

Address: Im Meistental 55, 67433 Neustadt an der Weinstraße, Germany. **Client:** Helwig Bauausführungen GmbH, Lorsch. **Completion:** 2012. **Gross floor area:** 300 m². **Number of rooms:** 9. **Main materials:** fairfaced concrete, plaster, wood. **Situation:** detached building in suburban context.

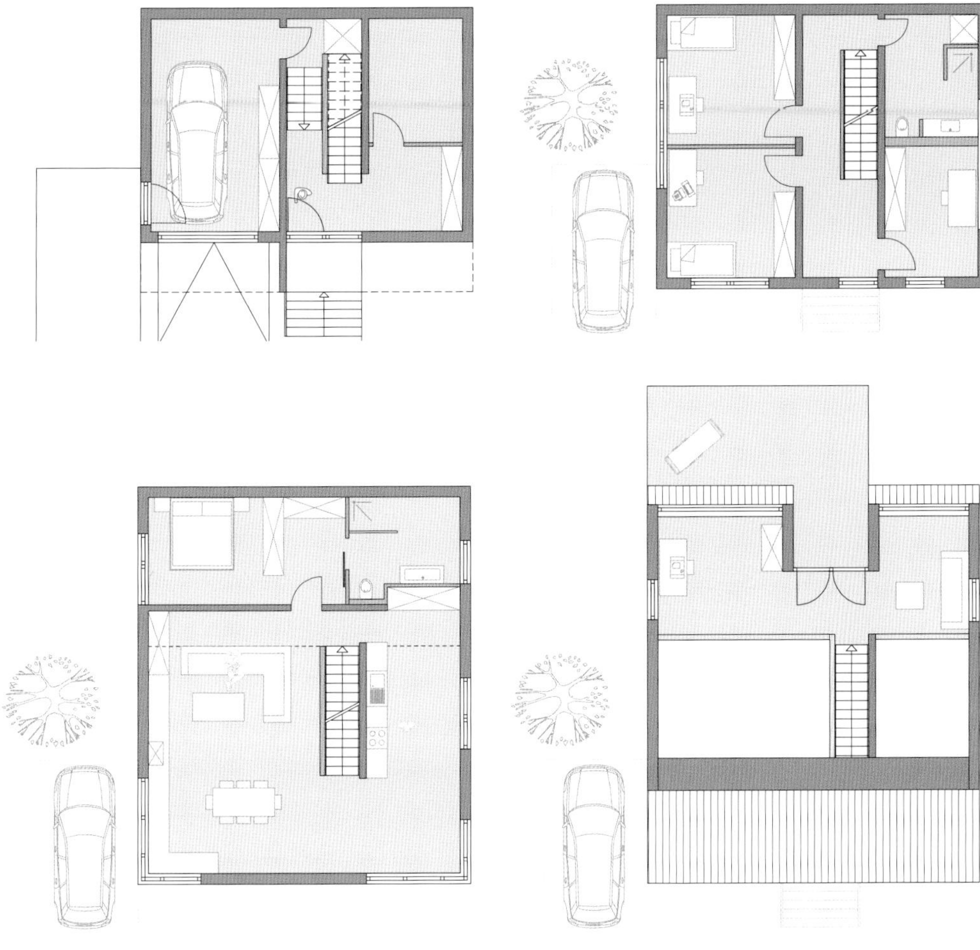

← ← | **Building in context**
↖ | **Ground to third floor plans**
↓ | **Interior,** attic

Gluck+

↑ | **Dining room,** garden in background
↘ | **First floor plan**

→ | **Vertical library,** lights cascading down stairwell

Urban Townhouse

New York City

By radically reconfiguring the organization and façade of the building, open loft living finds privacy from the street behind a four-story vertical library. The conventional plan and section were redefined with the stair and elevator core pushed up against the street façade, instead of running along one of the party walls. As a result, loft-like spaces run fluidly the entire length of the 11.5-meter-deep building, rather than being divided into small front and back rooms. The front façade engages the street with a custom water-cut aluminum rainscreen, with brick-shaped openings relating to the solid bricks of its neighbors. The rear façade is all glass; a full-height, full-width curtain wall that extends the materials of the ground floor open living and dining area out into the garden.

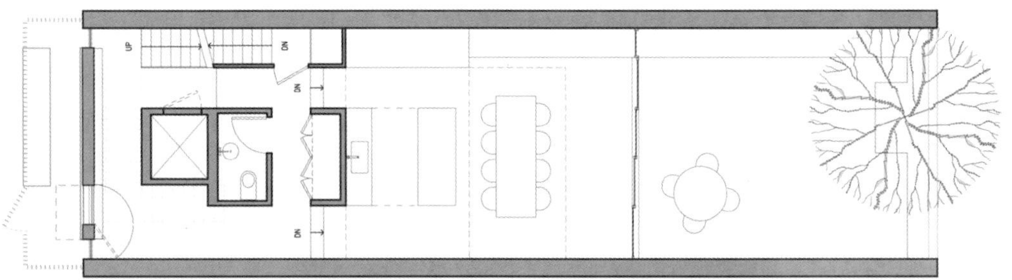

PROJECT FACTS

Address: New York City, NY, USA. **Client:** confidential. **Completion:** 2009. **Gross floor area:** 344 m². **Number of rooms:** 7. **Main materials:** structural light gauge metal framing, structural steel, aluminum curtain wall system, aluminum rainscreen. **Situation:** part of existing development in urban context.

← | Street façade at dusk
↓ | Mezzanine and third floor plans

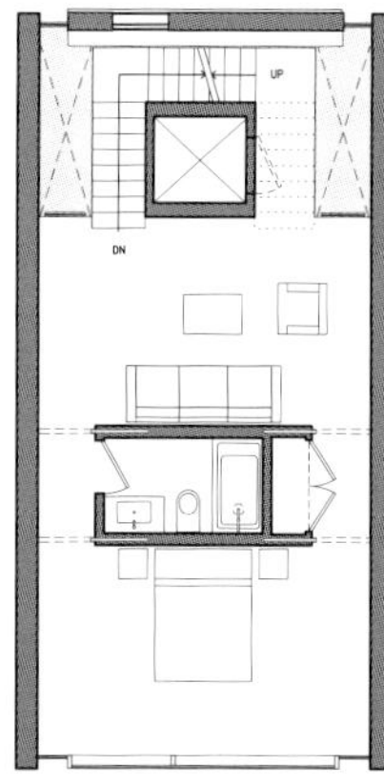

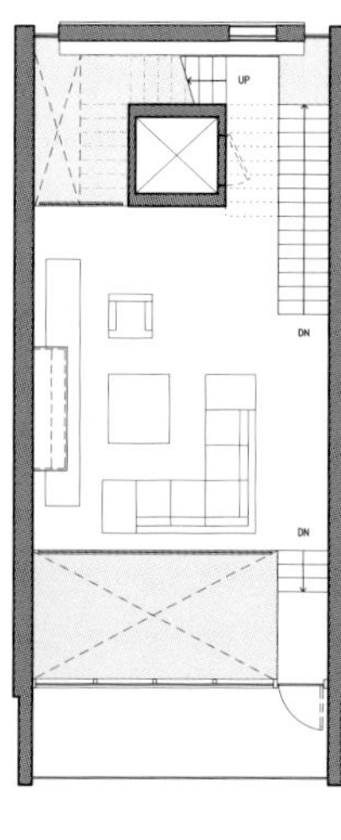

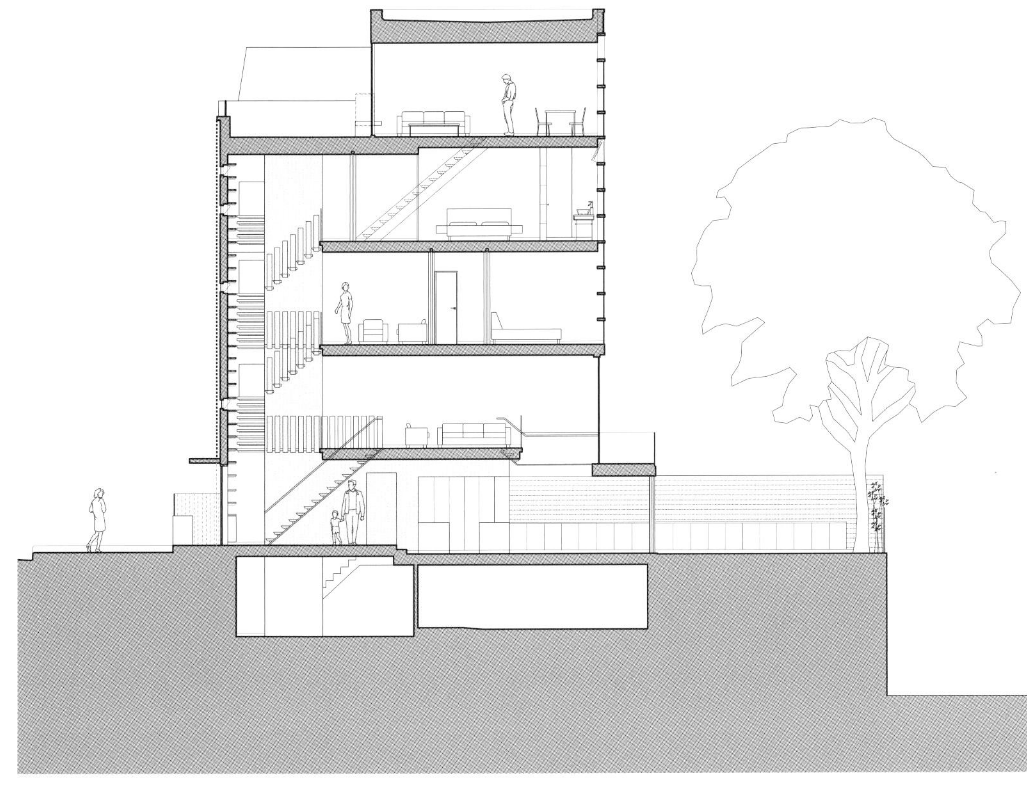

↖ | Section
↓ | Street façade during the day

Marie-Theres Deutsch Architekten

↑ | Living room
↗ | Seating in oriel
→ | Library in attic story

Paradiesgasse 13

Frankfurt/Main

This house is located on a 143-square-meter site on Paradiesgasse; a narrow street that leads to the nearby ford through the river Main that gave the city its name. This six-story residential house picks up on the medieval typology of the immediate surroundings. Subdivided by a glazed intersection, the five-meter-wide oriels push out over the street. The rooms behind these oriels are 2.74 meters high. Minimal exterior insulation gives the building a slim appearance. This, combined with hidden inside insulation allows the house to meet Low Energy House requirements. The interior spaces are extremely flexible, and various units can be easily joined together with minimal intervention.

PROJECT FACTS

Address: Paradiesgasse 13, 60594 Frankfurt/Main, Germany. **Client:** home owner association Paradiesgasse 13. **Completion:** 2012. **Gross floor area:** 567 m². **Number of apartments:** 6. **Number of rooms per apartment:** 2–3. **Situation:** part of existing development in city center.

← | **Street façade**

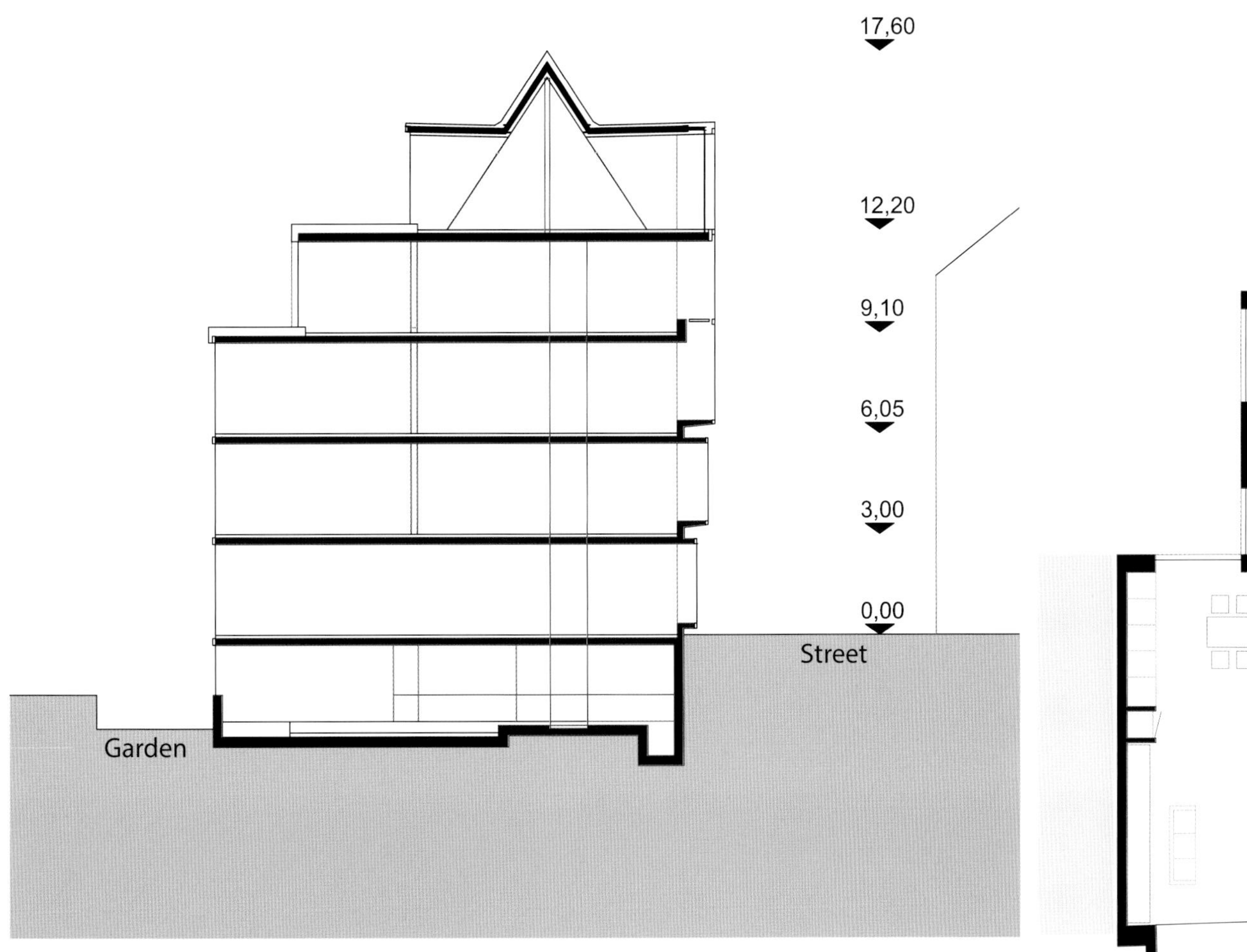

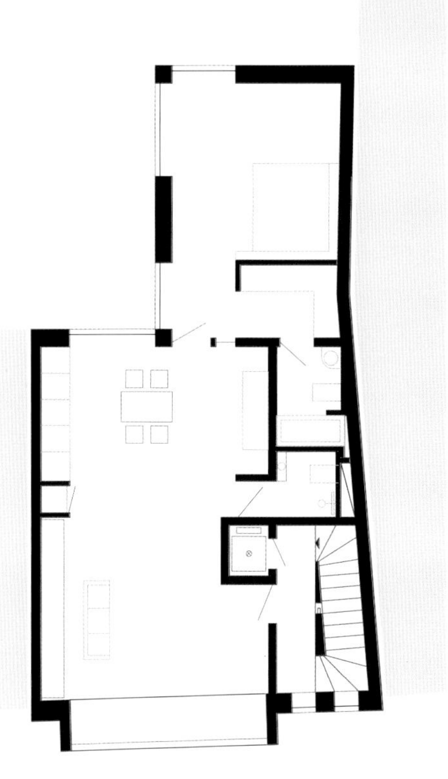

↑ | **Section and first floor plan**
← | **Rear façade,** view from garden

Rintala Eggertsson
Architects

↑ | **Prototype,** building was temporarily located in courtyard of Maxxi Museum in Rome
→ | **Façade detail**

Cabinet Home

Rome

On the ground floor of this house, the kitchen and dining spaces open up towards a garden with a fountain. The bright white exterior creates a deliberate contrast to the cool dark interior, which serves as a retreat, a tranquil space in which to relax and get away from the heat outside. The whole house comprises three container-sized units, which could be transported by road to their final location. The design of the house deliberately tries to move away from the perceived ideal of having a large expensive house. All the power for the house is provided by solar panels, which is not only extremely environmentally friendly but also significantly reduced costs.

Address: Maxxi Museum, Via Guido Reni 4A, 00196 Rome, Italy. **Client:** Maxxi Museum, Rome. **Completion:** 2010. **Gross floor area:** 20 m^2. **Number of rooms per building:** 3. **Situation:** detached building in urban context.

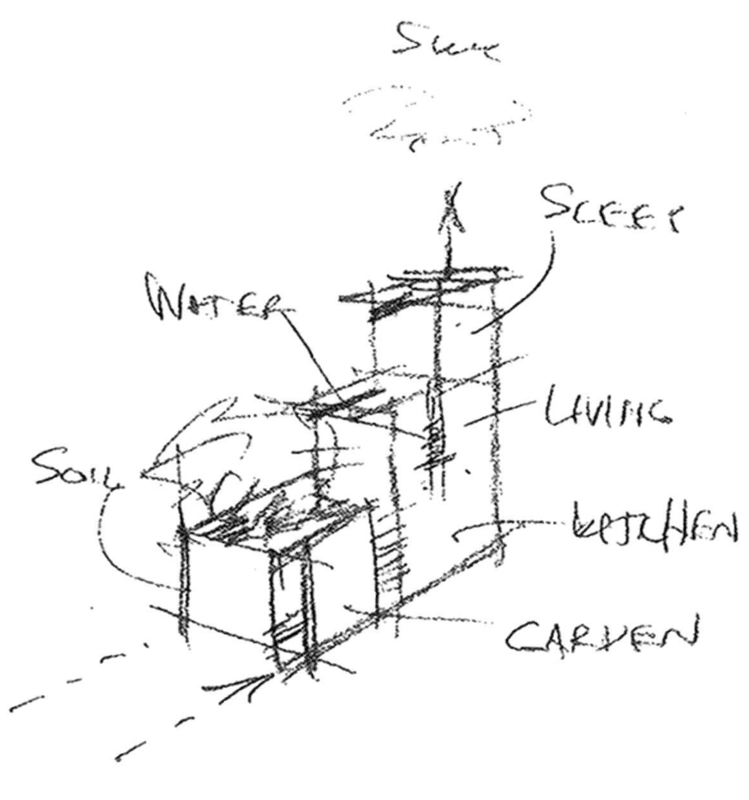

↑ | Sketch
↓ | Courtyard from inside

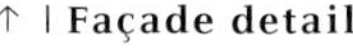

↑ | Façade detail
↓ | Design uses simple materials

Moussafir Architectes

↑ | **Front view at night**
→ | **Interior,** play of light and shadow

Maison Escalier

Paris

Built on the site of an old house in the heart of a well-preserved block in central Paris, the Maison Escalier has a tree-like structure delimited on three sides by original masonry walls. Only the glazed south façade belies the total reconstruction of the building and provides a glimpse of its complex interior space. The best metaphor for the project is that of a gigantic stairway: its core houses the wet rooms, while its landings form the various living zones. The client's request for a home with no partitions enabled total spatial continuity from basement to roof terrace. Cantilevered floors are borne by the central core and partly dissociated from the outer walls onto which have been grafted concrete boxes acting as built-in furniture. The central core, the floors and the ceilings are clad in wood, whose color and pattern contrast with the texture and whiteness of the outer walls.

PROJECT FACTS

Address: 22, rue Jacob, 75006 Paris, France. **Client:** Eric de Rugy. **Completion:** 2011. **Gross floor area:** 153 m². **Number of rooms:** 1. **Main materials:** steel, wood. **Situation:** part of existing development in urban context.

←←| **Exterior,** transparent frontage
↑ | **Interior,** stairs
↙ | **Basement to third floor plans**

Architekturbüro Schmid

↑ | **Interior with fireplace,** ground floor
→ | **Exterior**

Hybrid

Berlin

These townhouses were built using composite construction; the dividing walls and ceilings are built of stone and concrete, while the building shell, façade and roof are timber with a curtain façade. This makes optimal use of the advantages of each material, including: flexible floor plan design, heat storage, sound insulation, and insulated outer walls. The client was able to choose between the incorporation of geothermal energy or solar panels. The project was carried as a collaboration between the architects, construction managers and the client. This allowed the concepts, processes and structures to be smoothly bundled together.

Address: Dietzgenstraße 3a–3f, 13156 Berlin, Germany. **Client:** ARTE-Bau GmbH, holz & raum. **Completion:** 2011. **Gross floor area:** 230 m². **Co-architect:** Anna Borgmann. **Number of apartments:** 6. **Number of rooms per building:** 8. **Main materials:** wood, concrete, stone. **Situation:** new development in urban context.

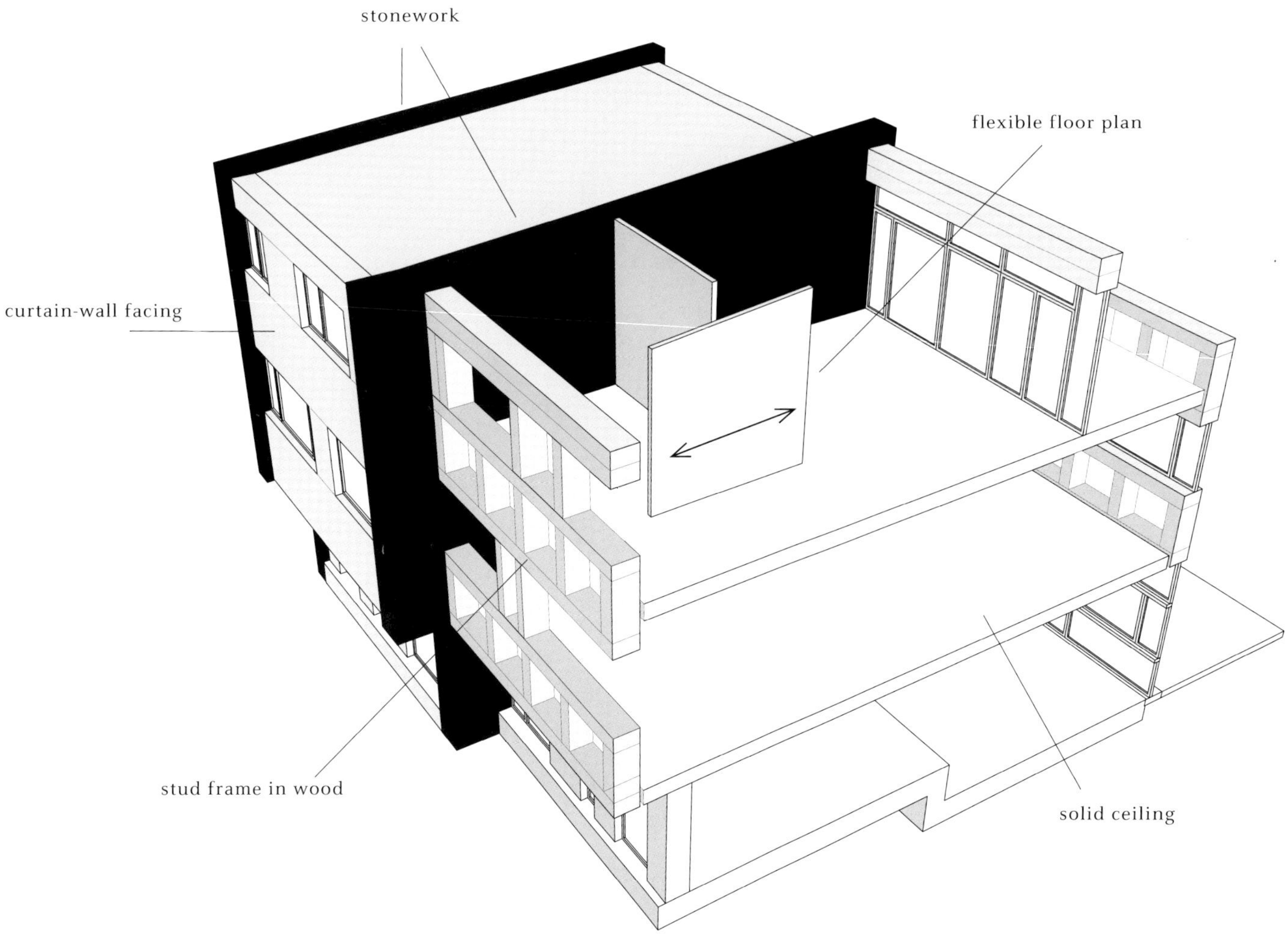

stonework

flexible floor plan

curtain-wall facing

stud frame in wood

solid ceiling

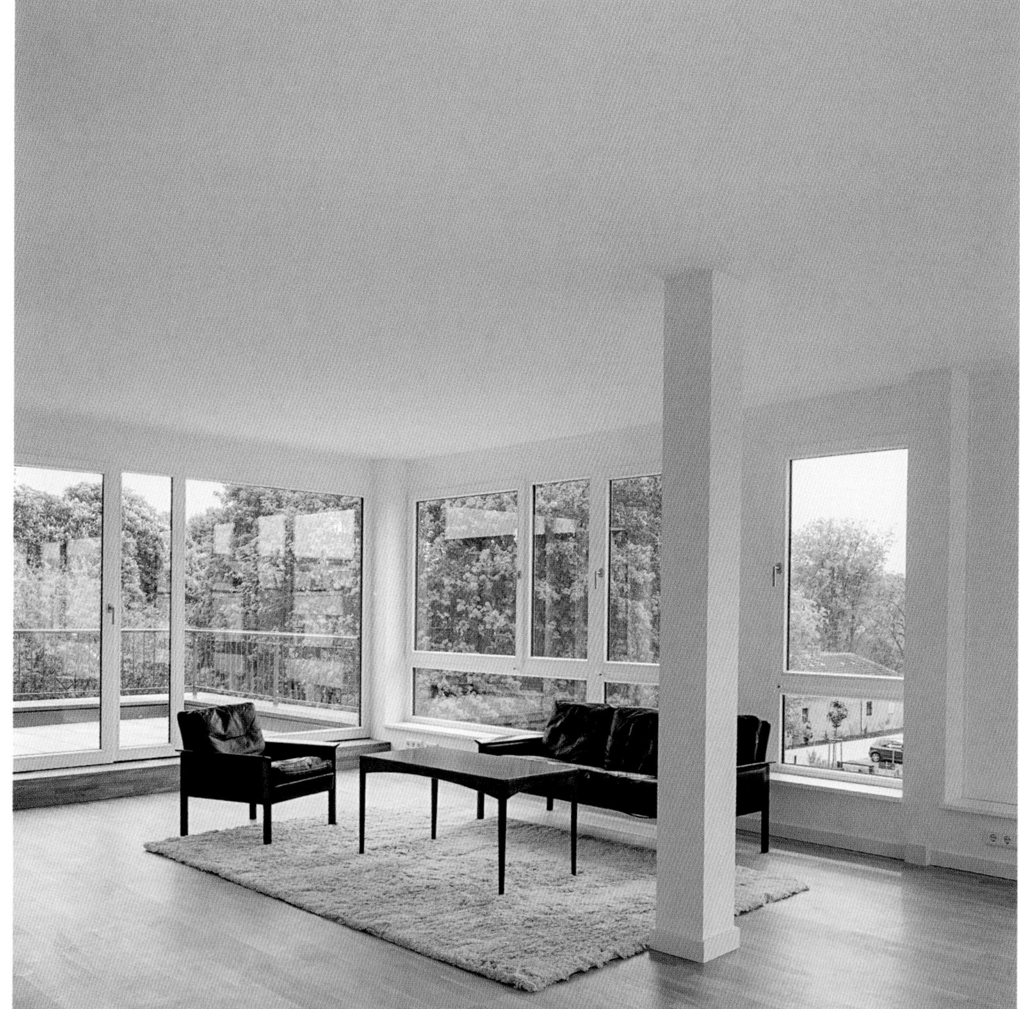

↑ | **Axonometry**

← | **Living area,** terrace in background

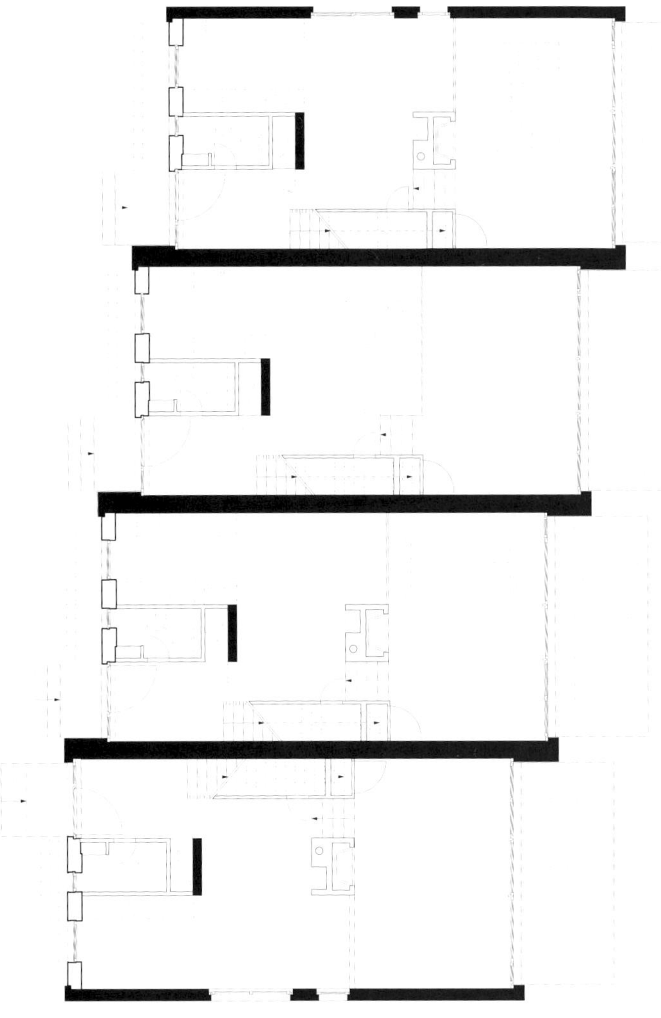

← | Ground floor plan

↓ | General view

Bottega + Ehrhardt Architekten

↑ | **Street view**
→ | **Large windows,** open house up to garden

K2 House

Stuttgart

K2 House is a compact single-family home in a residential area in Stuttgart. The polygonal floor plan follows the boundaries of the site. The uppermost level retreats behind the line of the building, forming a small roof terrace. Facing the street, a two-story element with large panorama windows projects out over the entrance area below. The open-plan arrangement unites cooking, dining, and living and helps to forge a connection between the interior and the surrounding environment. The children's bedrooms are located on the first floor, while the remaining bedrooms, and a living area with access to the roof terrace are all located on the second floor. The dark gray Eternit cladding gives the house a homogeneous appearance.

Address: Leibnizstraße 14 A, 70193 Stuttgart, Germany. **Client:** confidential. **Completion:** 2011. **Gross floor area:** 325 m². **Number of rooms:** 6. **Main materials:** wood, Eternit. **Situation:** detached building in city center.

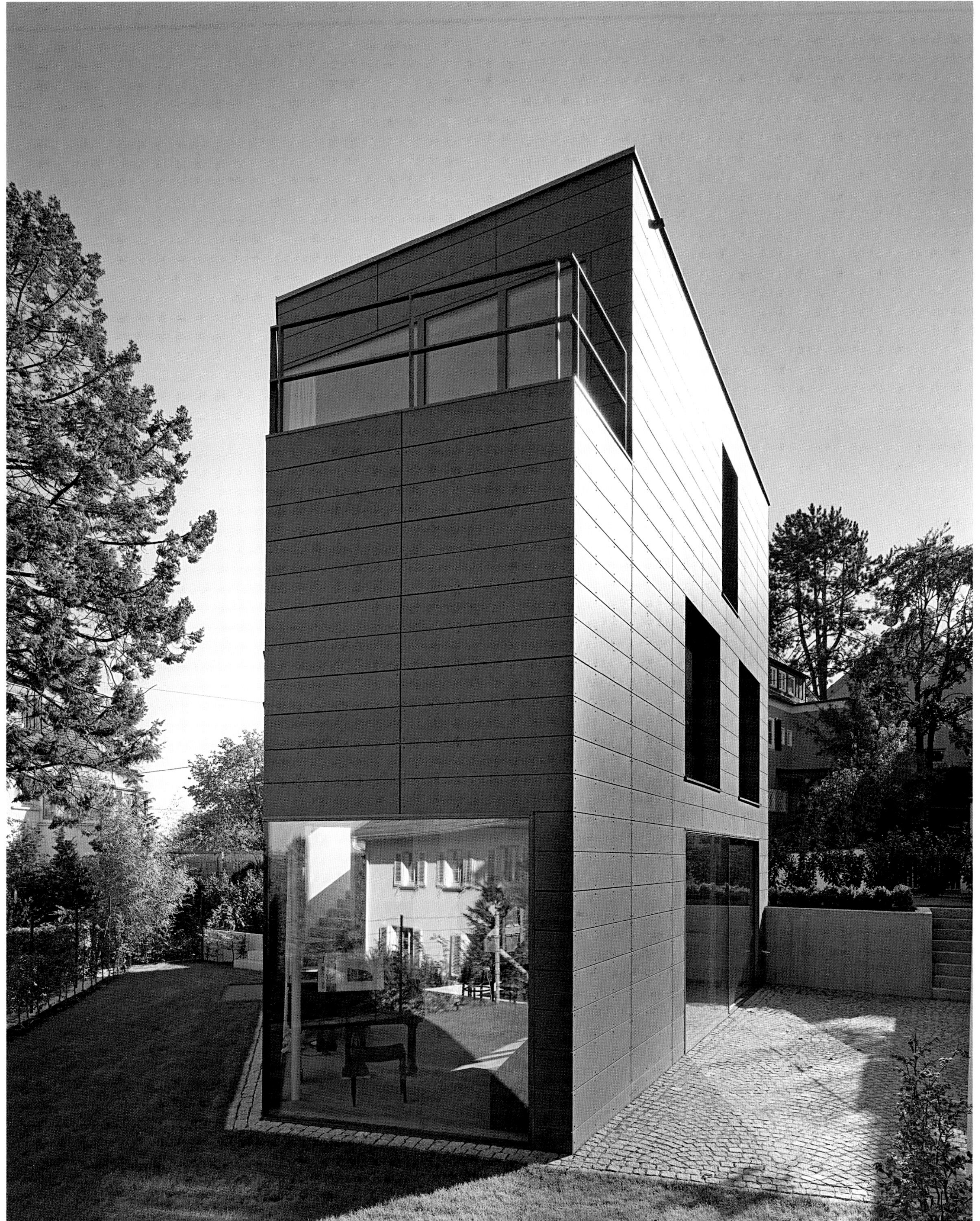

↑ | Reading room and terrace
↙ | Ground floor plan

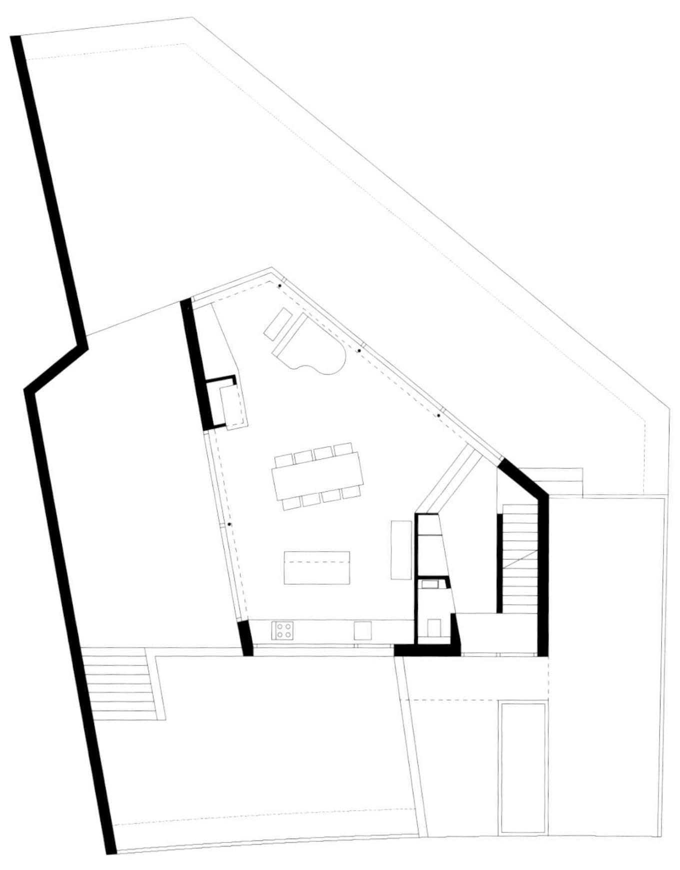

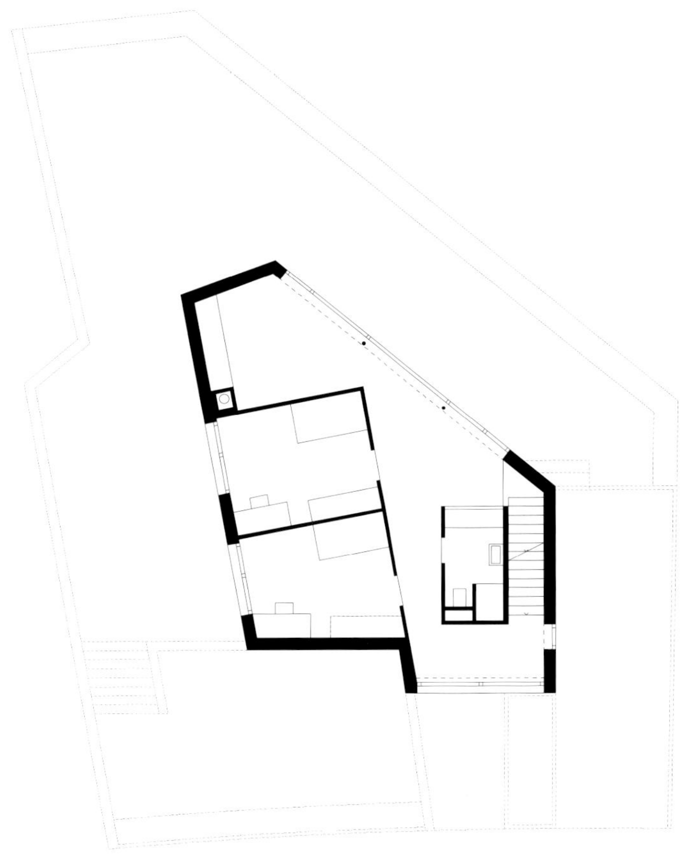

↖ | First floor plan

↓ | Light-filled, bright interior

P8 Architecten

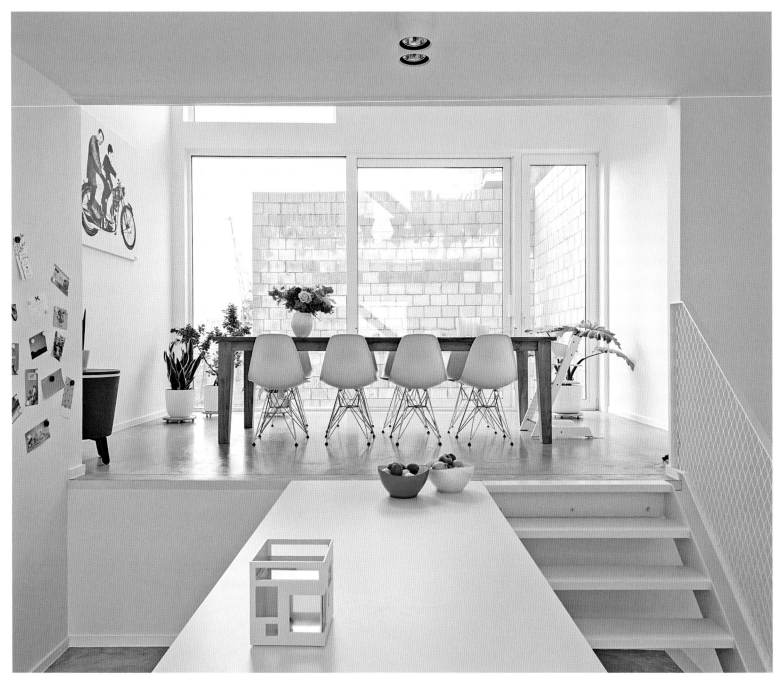

↑ | **Dining area**
→ | **Split level,** first and second floor

House BRZ

Antwerp

This house is located in the former 't Eilandje harbor area in Antwerp, Belgium. Creating a contemporary townhouse in this area dominated by warehouses and apartment blocks was the main intention of this project. There are no new single-family houses to be found in the immediate vicinity and also the new building regulations are mainly tailored to apartment construction. To obtain a maximum of outside space on this small plot, the architects raised the house off the ground and turned the ground level into a partly covered garden. The stairs were moved to the front of the house so they have only a small impact on the flexibility of the plan. This way the stairs become a playful design element visible from the outside, appearing and disappearing behind the different windows.

PROJECT FACTS

Address: Braziliestraat, 2000 Antwerp, Belgium. **Client:** Hansi Ombregt, Sophie Janssens. **Completion:** 2012. **Gross floor area:** 200 m². **Number of rooms:** 9. **Main materials:** aluminum, polished concrete, steel. **Situation:** semi-detached building in urban context.

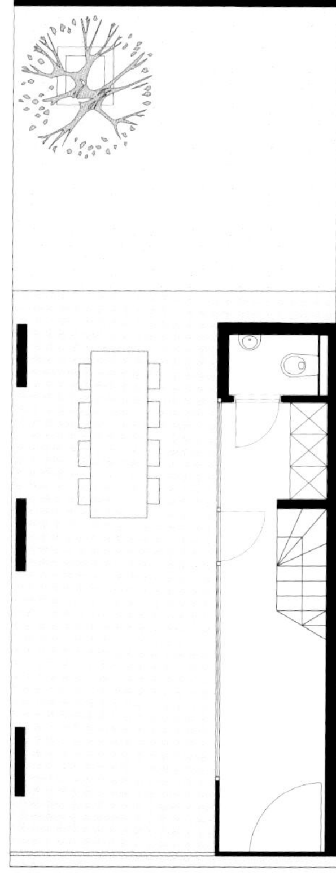

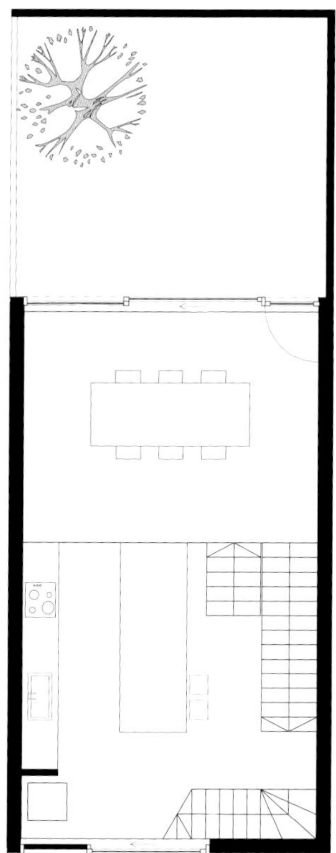

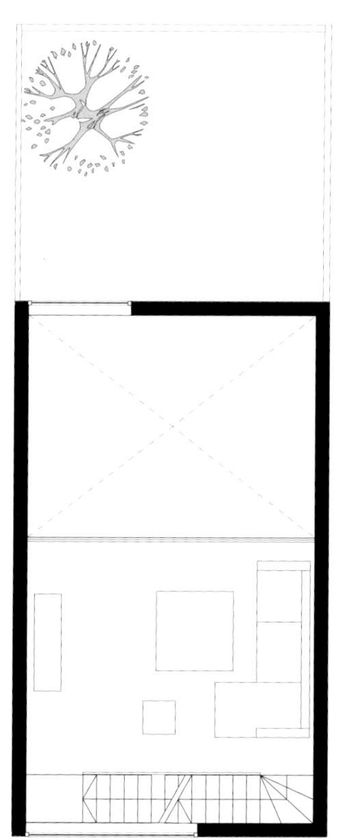

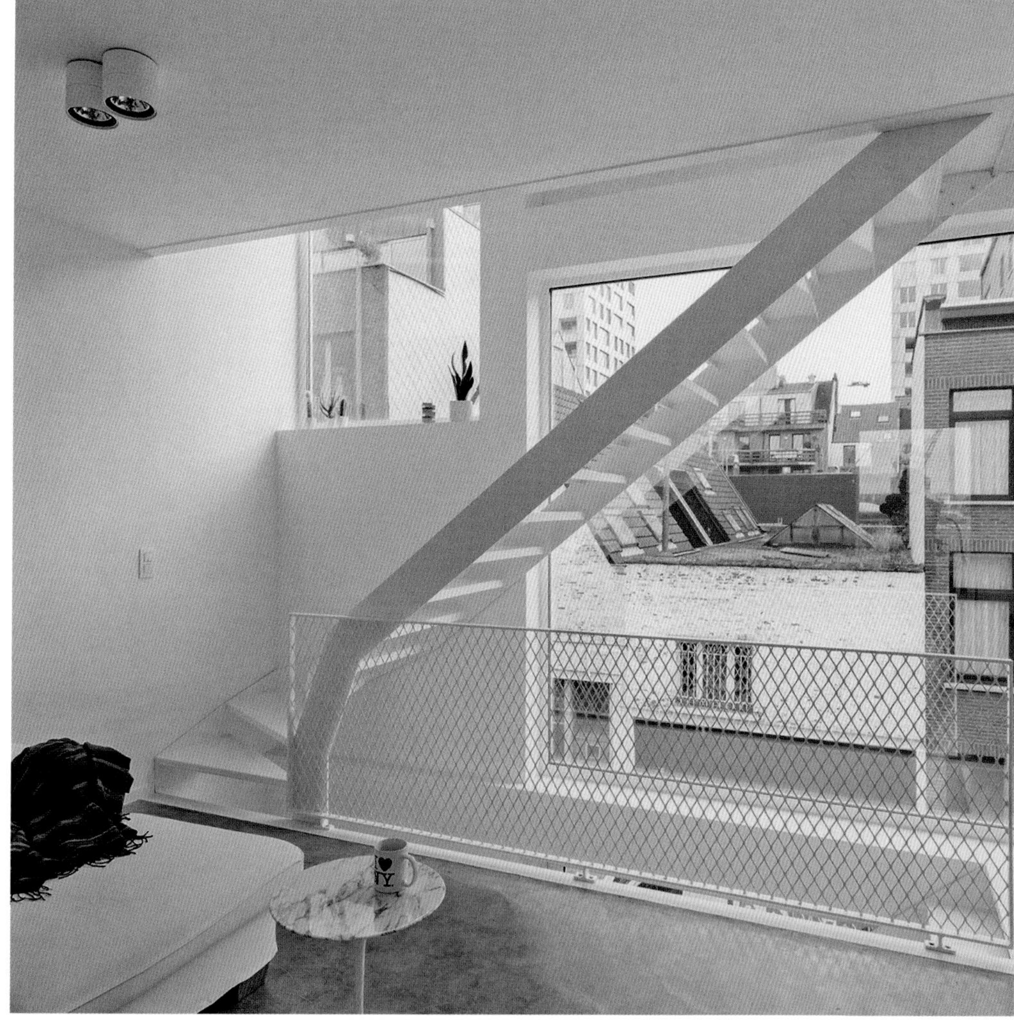

↑ | **Ground, first and second floor plans**
← | **Living area,** view towards façade

← | Front façade
↓ | Third, fourth and fifth floor plans

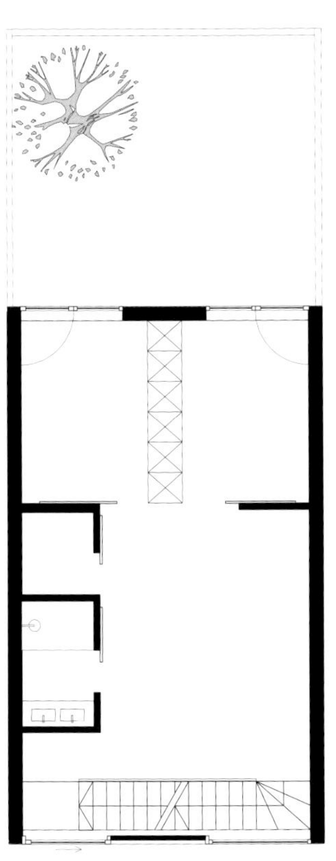

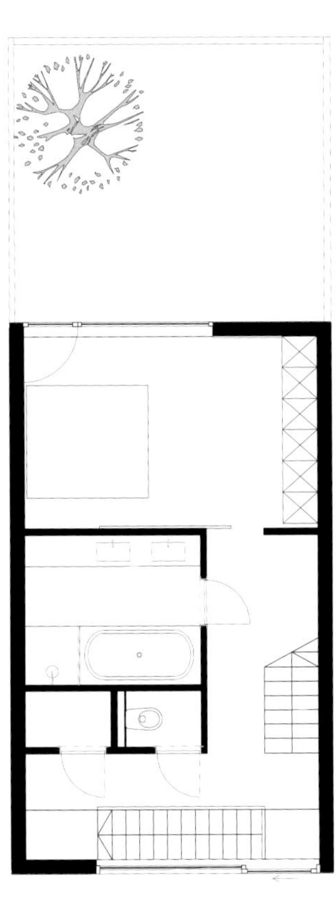

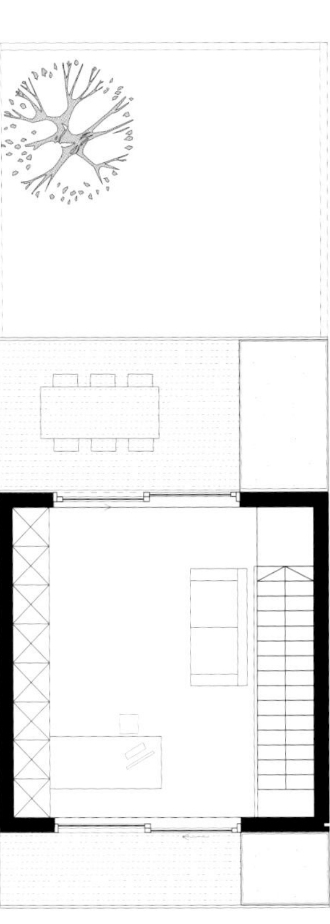

pool Architekten

↑ | Front façade
↗ | Terrace
→ | Living area

Blue Notes

Richterswil

Seen from above, the flat roofs of these 14 houses are long, narrow and dark, which makes the upper floor volumes and the terraces between them look like the keys on a piano. In order to give the arrangement a rhythm, the rows have incisions in three places that reach down to the building base. Thanks to the sloping site, each house has a forecourt, a garden on the sloping side and flexible exterior spaces. The building floors vary, which permits a range of uses and arrangements and is therefore open to a number of different interpretations. The façades of the neighboring houses protect the terraces and create protected and private individual areas.

Address: Chrumbächliweg, 8805 Richterswil, Switzerland. **Client:** Halter AG | Entwicklungen. **Completion:** 2010. **Gross floor area:** 3,950 m². **Number of apartments:** 14. **Number of rooms per building:** 4–5. **Main materials:** plaster, ceramic tiles, wood, metal. **Situation:** new development in suburban context.

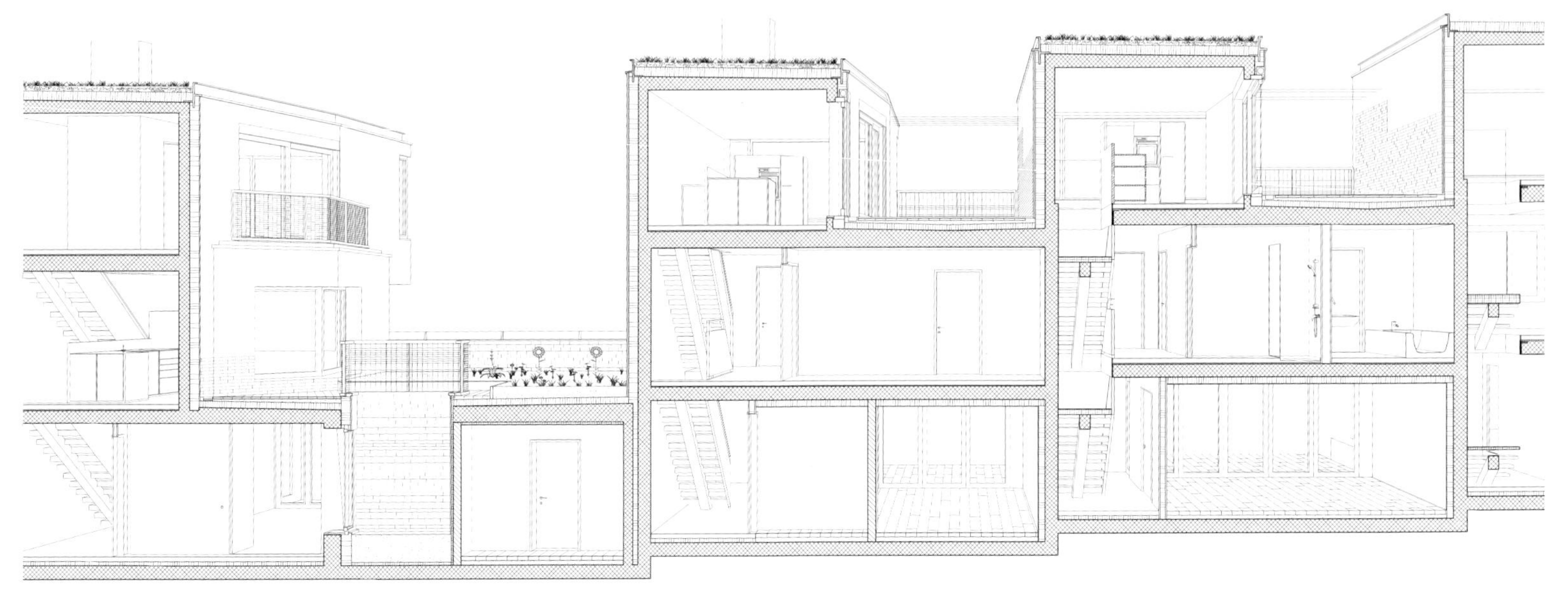

↑ | **Section**
← | **Front view**

← | **Interior,** dining area
↓ | **Ground, first and second floor plans,** with section

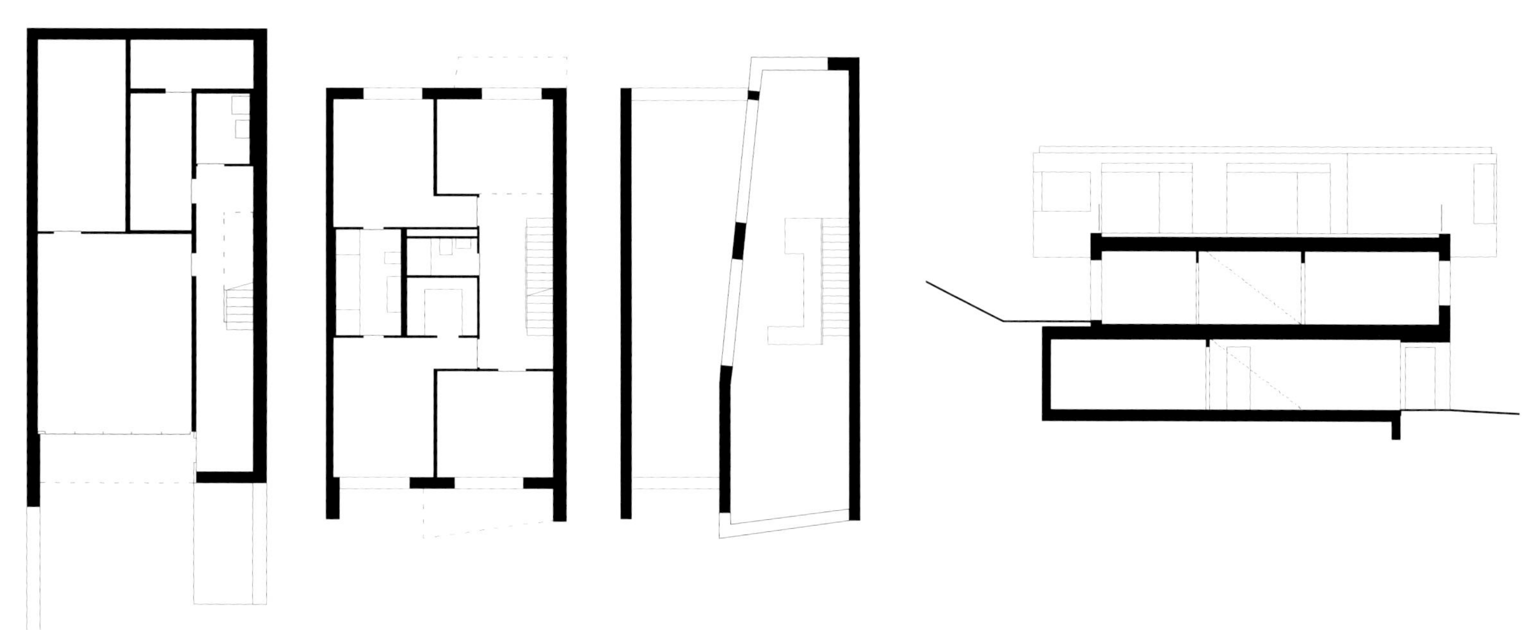

Paul Archer Design

↑ | **Façade,** timber and glass box
→ | **Entire view,** from backyard

Power House

London

Power House, Paul Archer Design's refurbishment of a private house in Highbury North London, takes the modernization of a typical London Victorian terraced house in a new direction with a highly sculptural timber clad rear extension. The focal point of the new house is a spacious double height kitchen and dining area at the rear of the property. A structural glass box allows direct sunlight to penetrate deep into the house. The upper floors of the extension are clad with a skin of Douglas fir battens, which run both inside and out as exterior cladding and interior wall lining, emphasizing the interplay between volumes. A whole new ground floor level has been created beneath the original house. Wood is put to striking effect and is abundant in all aspects of the scheme.

PROJECT FACTS

Address: Highbury North London, United Kingdom. **Client:** confidential. **Completion:** 2012. **Gross floor area:** 230 m^2. **Number of rooms:** 11. **Main materials:** wood, glass. **Situation:** part of existing development in urban context.

←←| **Interior,** kitchen and stairs
← | **Front view,** red front door
↓ | **Lower and upper ground and first floor plans**

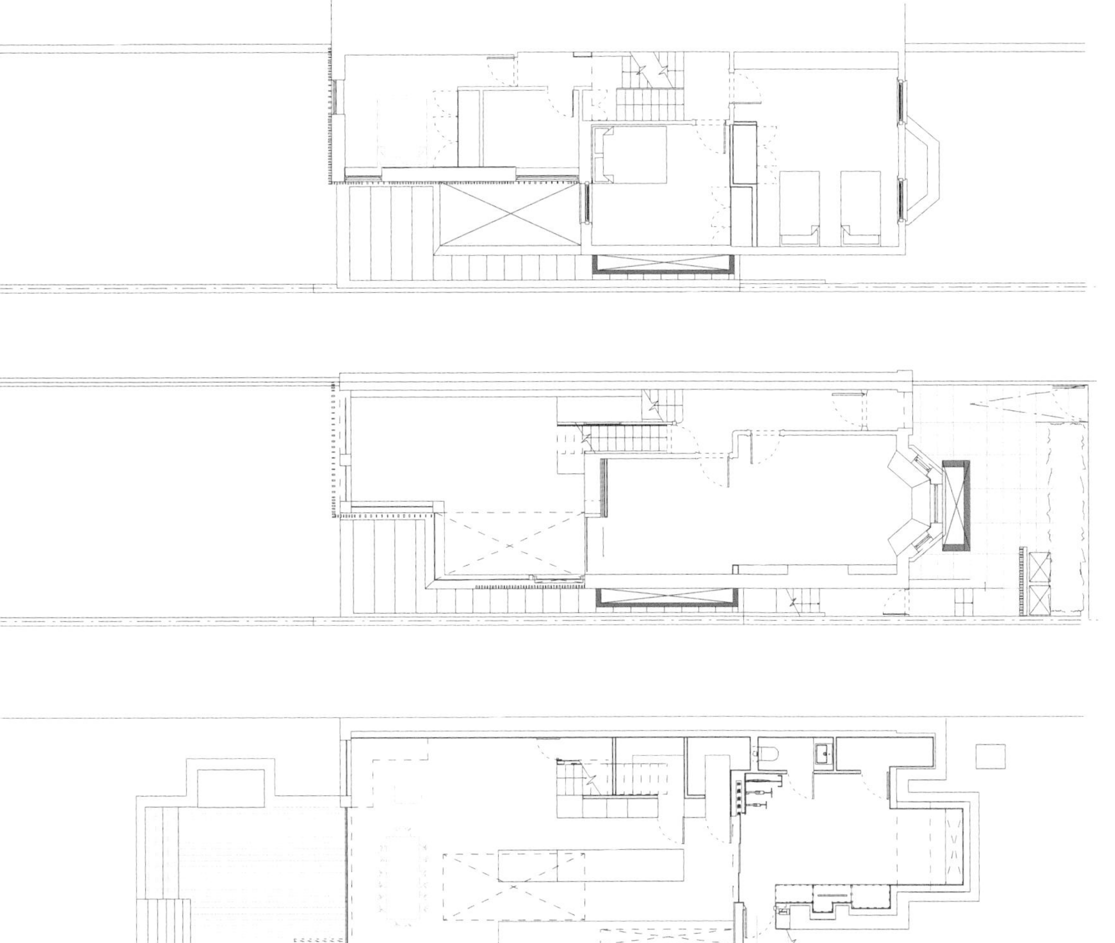

dma deckert mester architekten

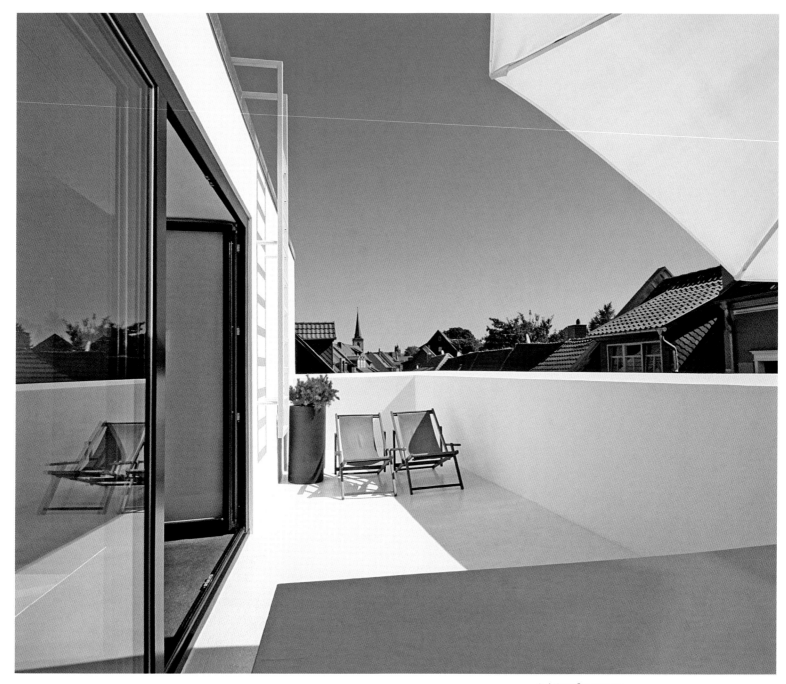

↑ | Roof terrace
→ | Façade at dusk

Haus zur Rose

Erfurt

This new townhouse has been built in place of the medieval Haus zur Rose, constructed on a 60-square-meter plot of land supposedly unfit for development in the center of Erfurt. It was considered unsuitable for development because of the firewalls on three sides, which offer excellent insulation but mean that light can only enter from the street side. The typical horizontal bands of windows have been used, although these are frameless and don't show the traditional structuring. A dome above the stairway draws light deep into the house and also aids ventilation. The irregular pattern of roses in the golden aluminum cladding on the ground floor pays homage to the name of the original house and allows filtered light into the garage, guest rooms and entrance area.

PROJECT FACTS

Address: Pergamentergasse 2, 99084 Erfurt, Germany. **Client:** Prof. Joachim Deckert. **Completion:** 2009. **Gross floor area:** 210 m². **Number of rooms:** 5. **Additional use:** engineering room. **Main materials:** concrete, aluminum, glass. **Situation:** part of existing development in city center.

←← | **Staircase**

↑ | **Living area,** kitchen

↙ | **Ground, first, second and third floor plans**

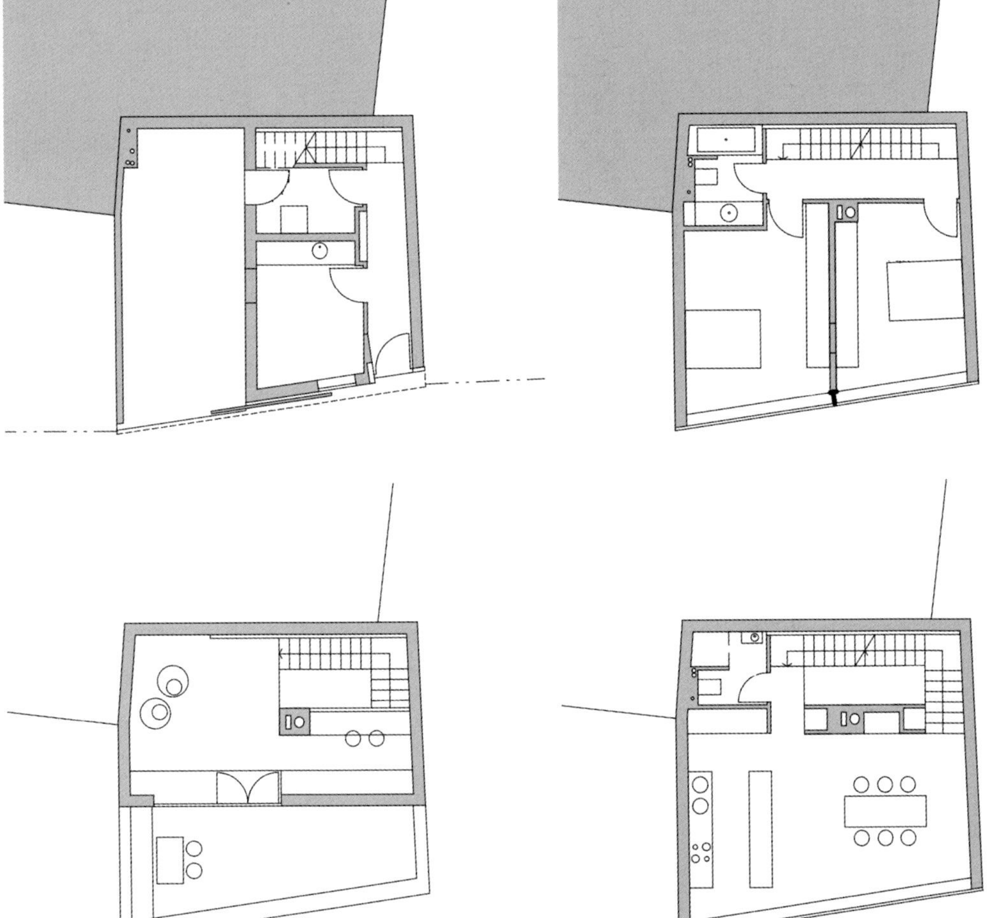

_naturehumaine

↑ | Living room
→ | Exterior view

8th Avenue

Montreal

This intervention transformed a residential two story duplex in Rosemont into a single dwelling unit by completely reorganizing the interior and constructing a large extension to the rear. The extension includes a master bedroom on the second floor and a family room that joins onto an intimate garden at ground level. While little work was done to the front façade, this extension was designed in contrast, with bright colors, an angled form, and generous glazing. Work on the interior focused on exposing and highlighting the beauty of existing wooden structural walls and beams and supporting them with a more subtle pallet of materials. Natural daylight is brought into the core with a large skylight and glass floor placed at the center of the house.

PROJECT FACTS

Address: 8th Avenue 5626, H1Y2L6 Montreal, Canada. **Client:** confidential. **Completion:** 2013. **Gross floor area:** 152 m². **Number of rooms:** 6. **Main materials:** brick, painted fiber cement panels. **Situation:** part of existing development in city center.

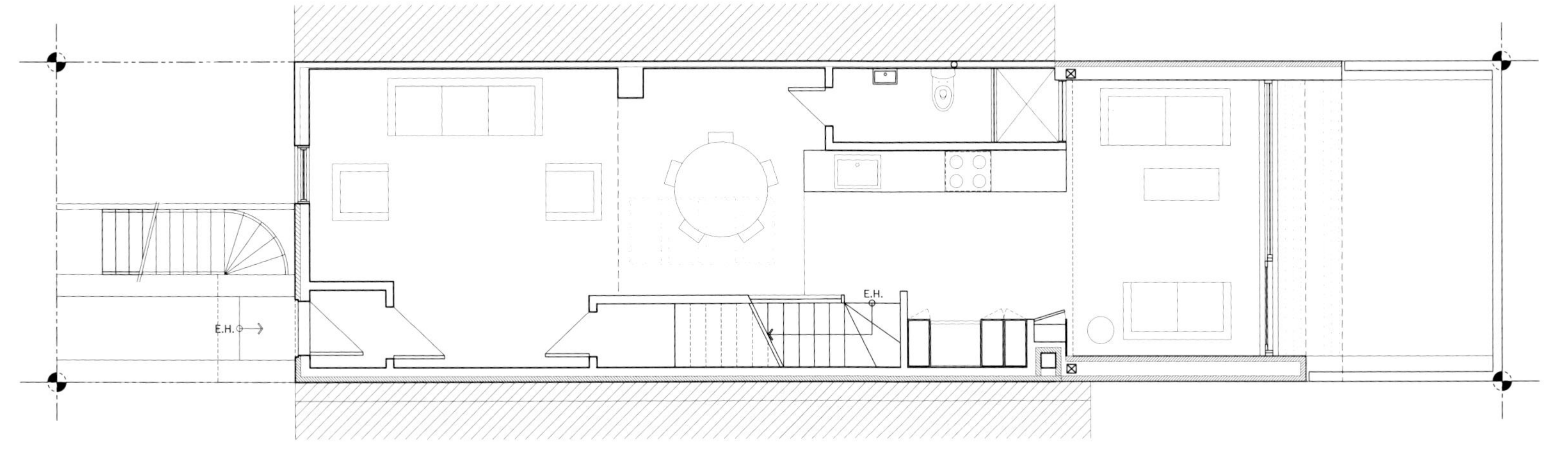

← | **Light-filled modern interior**
↑ | **Ground floor plan**
↓ | **Glass floor,** from below

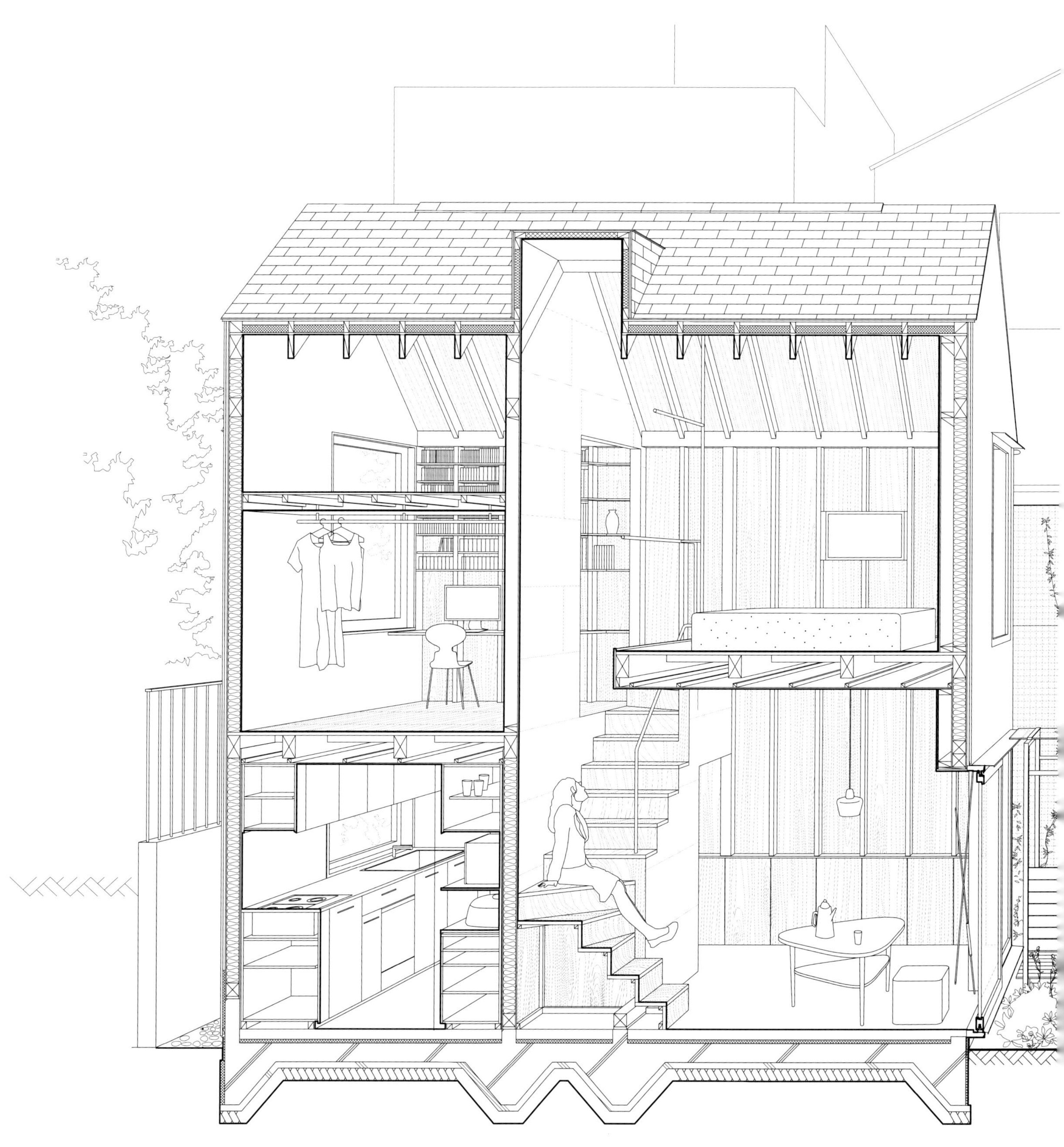

SUBTLE

Atelier Reza Aliabadi [rzlbd]

↑ | **Main elevation at dusk**
→ | **Interior,** totem and staircase

Totem House

Toronto

The totem in Totem House is a vertical gallery that exhibits the clients' souvenirs from around the world. Each piece has been carefully measured and placed in a designated niche inside the tower. An open wooden staircase connecting the three stories of the house gently circulates around the totem. The totem becomes the focal point in the house. The exterior of the house is a monolithic charcoal brick mass. Two small blocks on the north and south façades of the volume have been extracted and surfaced with wood. The small wooden corner creates an interesting deception where one imagines the wood to be the core material of the brick mass, like a bitten apple exposing the color of its flesh.

PROJECT FACTS

Address: 317 Lumsden Avenue, Toronto M4C 2K5, Canada. **Client:** Robert Langton, John Farrauto. **Completion:** 2013. **Gross floor area:** 151 m². **Number of rooms:** 8. **Main materials:** wood, aluminum, brick. **Situation:** detached building in urban context.

↑ | **Master bedroom,** open ensuite
← | **Kitchen and dining area**

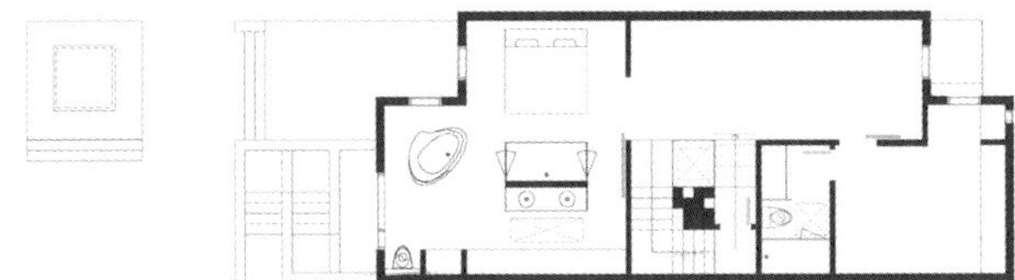

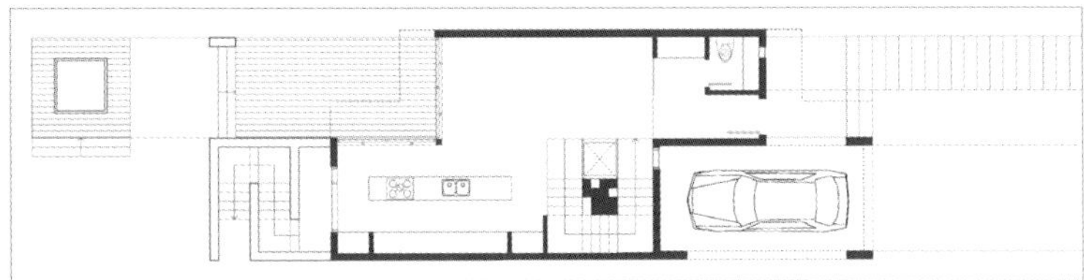

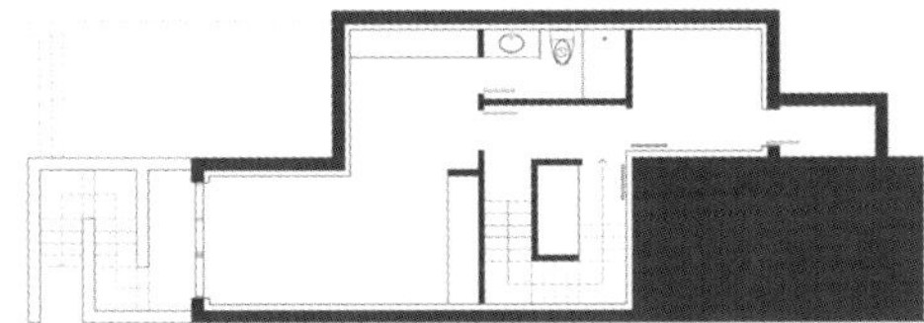

← | **Basement, ground and first floor plans**
↓ | **Interior,** living area

Apollo Architects & Associates

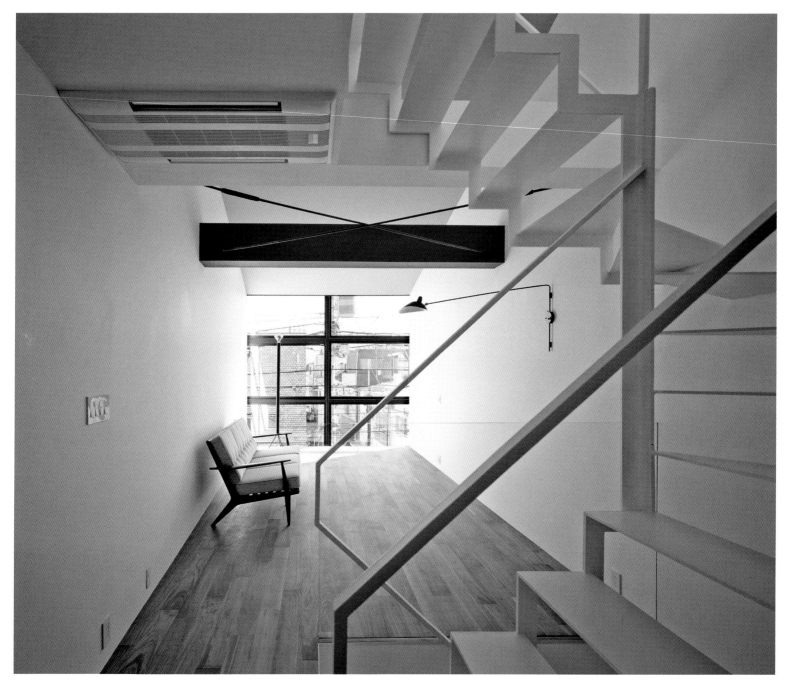

↑ | **Interior,** view of city
→ | **Living area,** lower floor

Flag

Tokyo

This urban residence is located in a commercial district, not so far from the city Shinjuku. The plot is narrow on the street side and deeper towards the rear. The façade comprises large openings arranged in a regular grid. The gallery on the first floor opens to the busy street with glazed storefront. Even though the house is compact, it can also be used as a shop. In order to cater to the client's photography hobby, a dark room has been created on the first floor, along with the study space on the same floor. An open room adjacent to the stairwell functions as a reception room for guests. The third floor is arranged as one open space with double height ceiling.

PROJECT FACTS

Address: Nakano ward, Tokyo, Japan. **Client:** confidential. **Completion:** 2013. **Gross floor area:** 105 m². **Number of rooms:** 5. **Main materials:** walnut floor, steel, concrete. **Situation:** part of existing development in urban context.

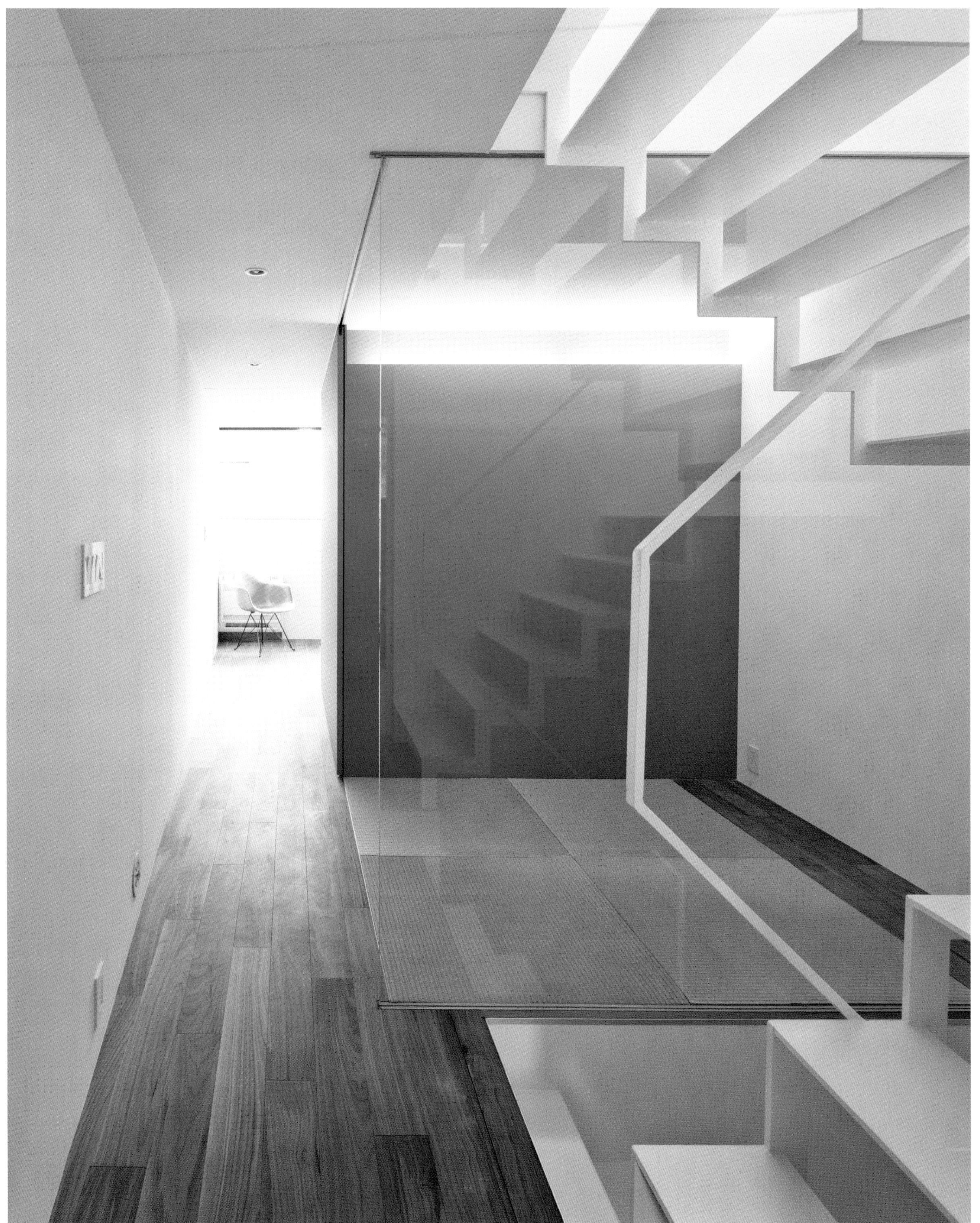

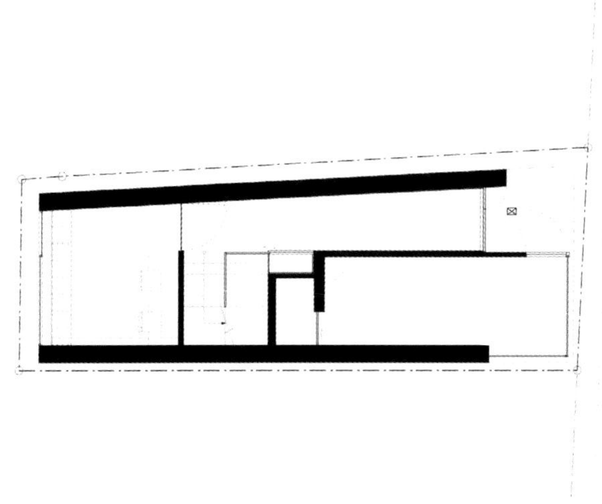

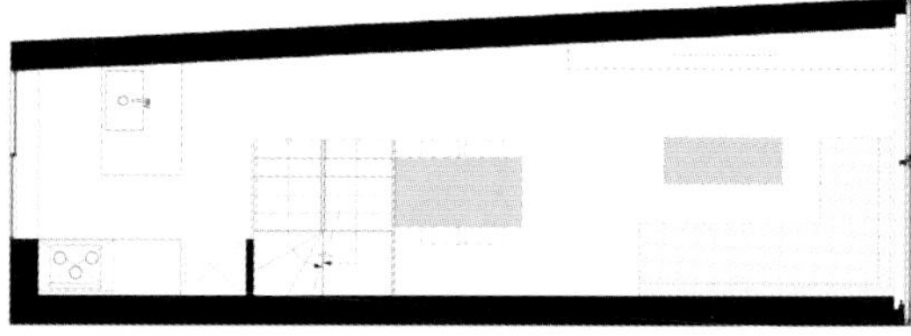

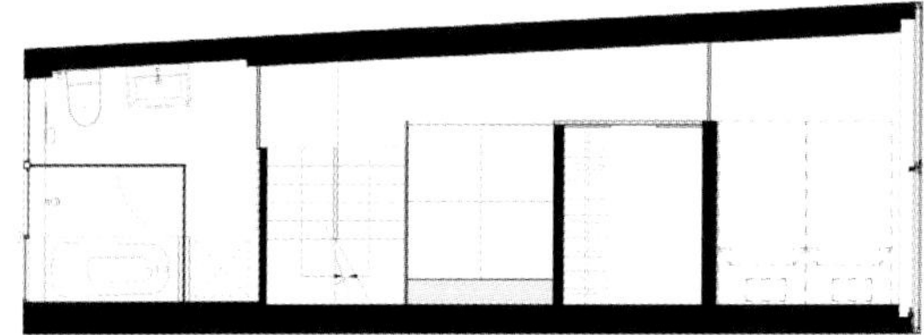

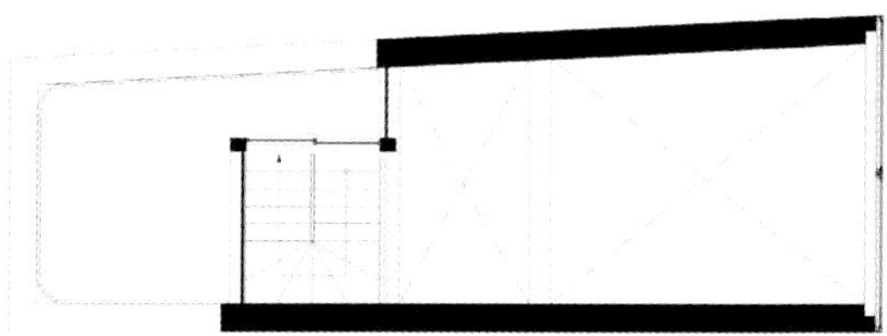

↑ | **Ground, first, second and roof floor plans**
← | **Entire building,** in the evening

← | **Volume on roof top,** third floor
↙ | **Sections**

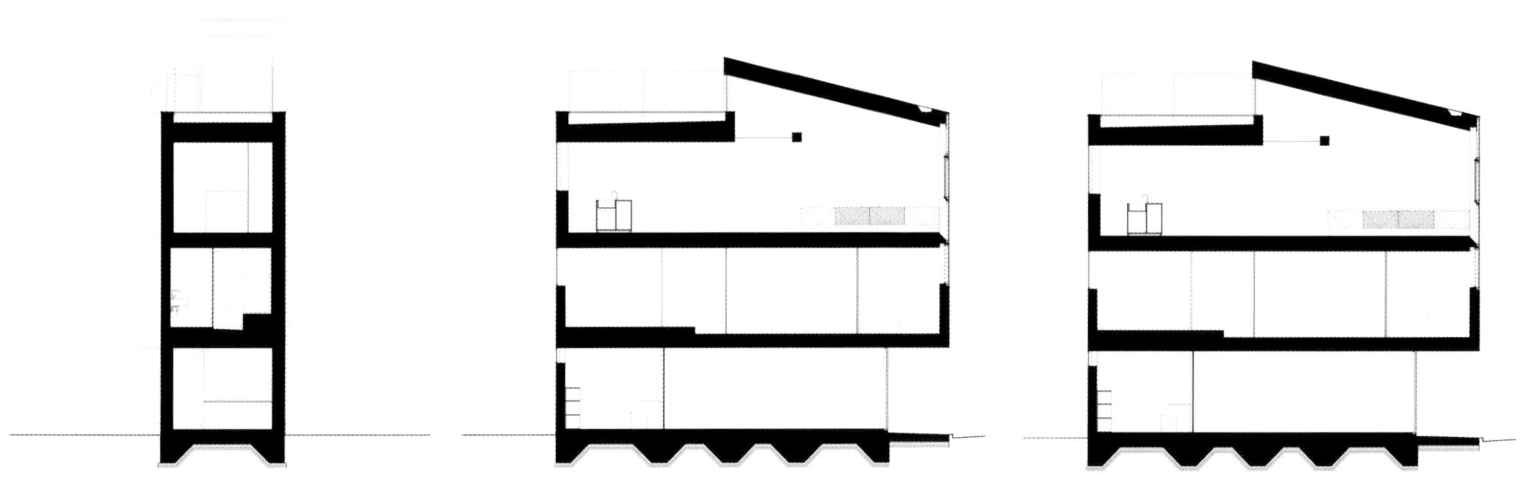

Atelier Bow-Wow

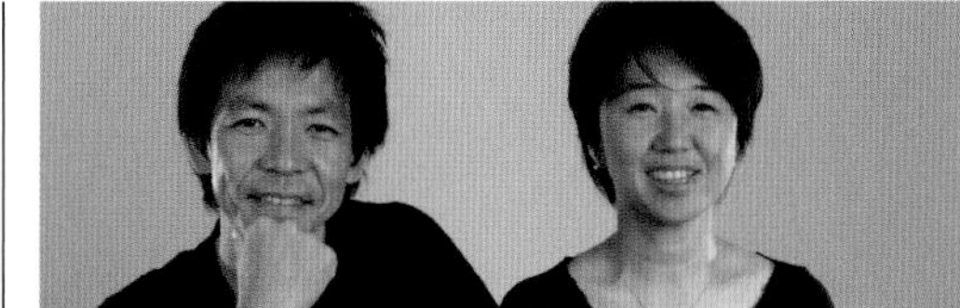

↑ | Rear of house with garden

Split Machiya

Tokyo

The new generation "Machiya" (townhouse) is situated on a typically long and narrow plot in Tokyo. The house is split into two volumes, separated by a courtyard. Inside, the repetition of exposed beams and columns gives the interior a dynamic rhythm. The courtyard is a key part of the design. A large bench and a corridor connects the two parts of the house. The integration of an open space into the design of the house is unusual in Tokyo and gives the city dwelling an almost suburban feel.

PROJECT FACTS

Address: Shinjuku, Tokyo, Japan. **Client:** confidential. **Completion:** 2010. **Gross floor area:** 54 m². **Number of rooms:** 7. **Main materials:** wood. **Situation:** part of existing development in urban context.

↑ | **Front façade,** large window

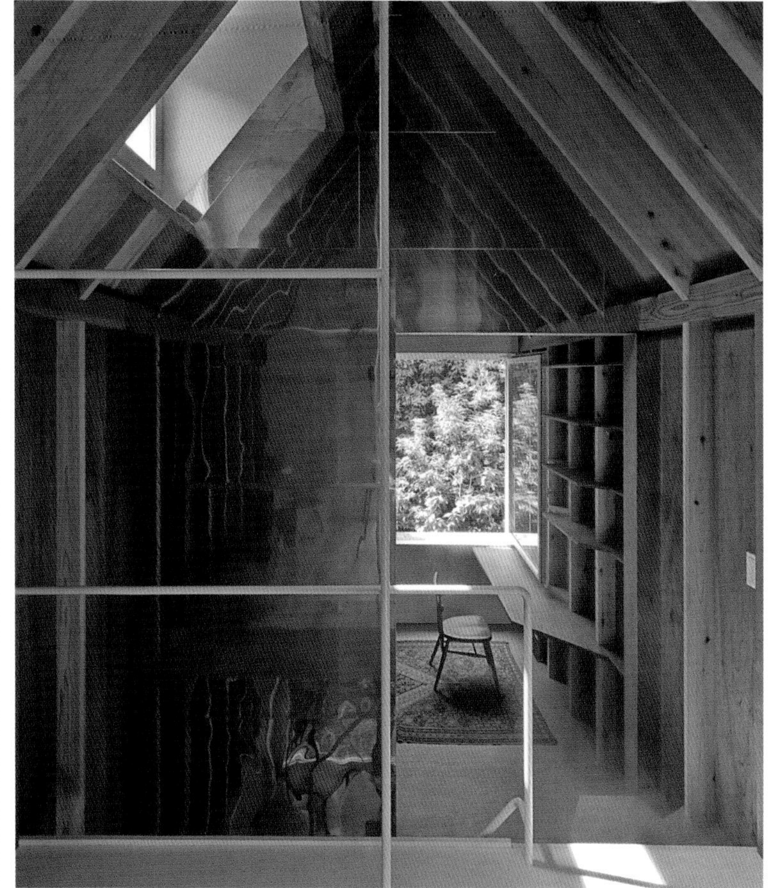

↑ | **Interior,** view from bedroom

↓ | **Section**

Barcode Architects

↑ | **Interior view,** second floor
→ | **Staircase,** ground floor

Markthuis

Maasdijk

Barcode Architects' design for Markthuis is driven by the desire to optimize the amount of daylight in the house and the wish of the client to reserve a prominent place for his large collection of art and hunting trophies. In order to maximize the spatial experience, most of the interior walls have been removed to leave just one open living space extending over the first two floors of the villa. Downstairs are comfortable spaces for receiving guests while the upper first floor houses more intimate and private areas with an open plan kitchen, study, and lounge area. A large atrium connects the two layers and provides space for an exclusive, double-height exhibition wall for displaying artifacts. A glass element separates the kitchen and the entrance lobby from the rest of the house and creates an exciting play of light and shadow.

PROJECT FACTS

Address: Maasdijk, Belgium. **Client:** confidential. **Completion:** 2013. **Gross floor area:** 350 m². **Number of rooms:** 1. **Main materials:** wood, glass. **Situation:** part of existing development in city center.

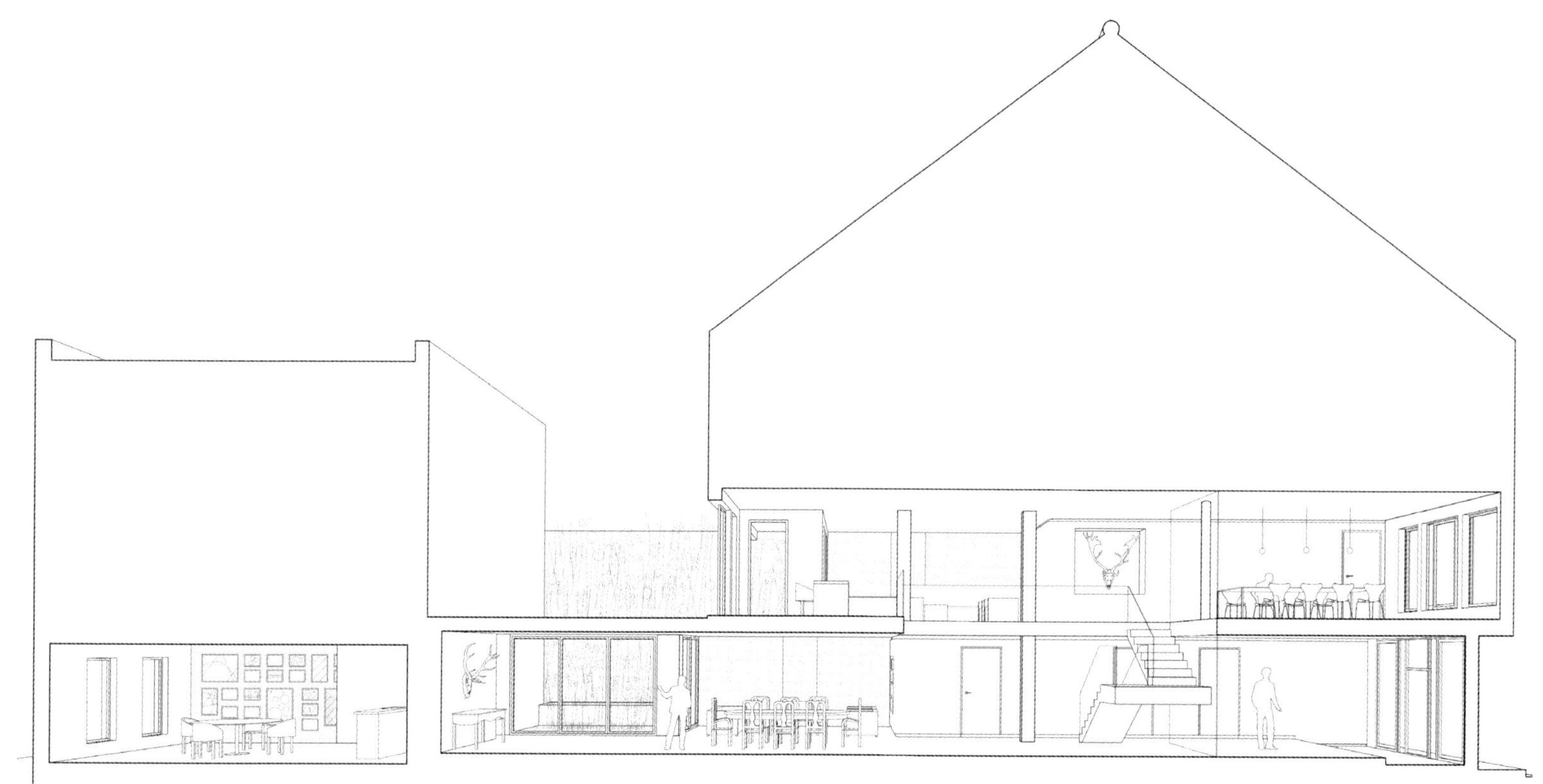

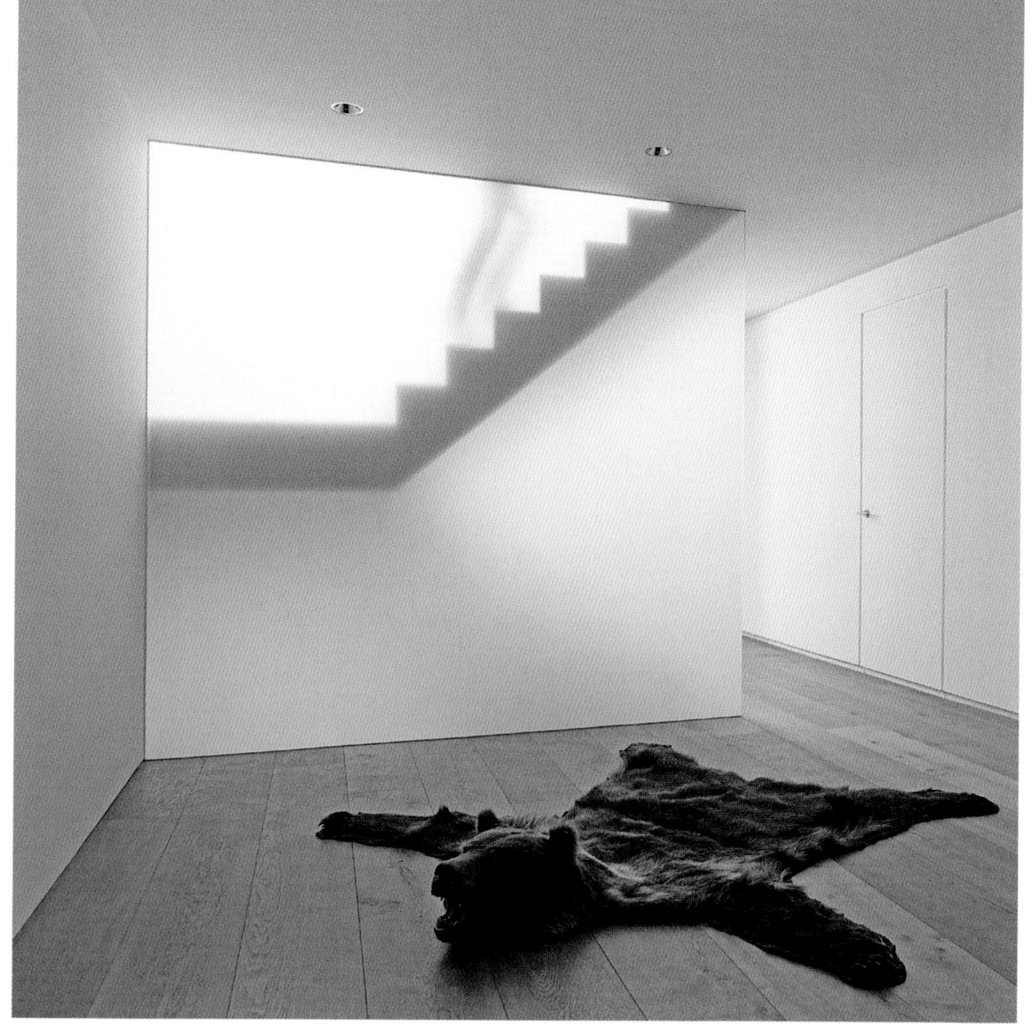

↑ | **Section**
← | **Bearskin rug,** stairs in background

↑ | Living area
↙ | Ground and first floor plans

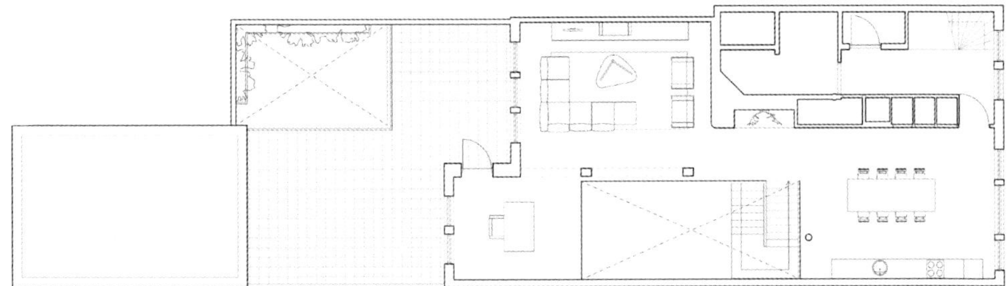

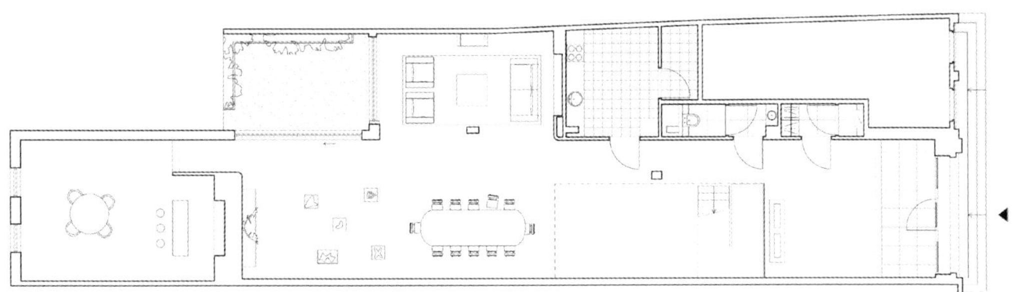

ANA Architects

↑ | **Interior,** living area

House JB

Amsterdam

House JB is built on the edge of the new suburban housing area IJburg, near Amsterdam. The house has a small garden on the waterside of the IJlake. The design combines the extensive program demands with a wide sense of space. Typically under-sized spaces such as staircase, corridor or hallway are oversized. The staircase moves in one continuous motion from ground floor to the top floor where a skylight draws daylight deep into the heart of the home. The study area overlooks the living area to the fantastic view on the outskirts of Amsterdam.

PROJECT FACTS

Address: James Bradleystraat 36, 1086 ZM Amsterdam, the Netherlands. **Client:** confidential. **Completion:** 2009. **Gross floor area:** 238 m². **Number of rooms:** 6. **Main materials:** concrete, stone. **Situation:** part of existing development in suburban context.

↑ | **Continuous stairs**

↓ | **Ground, first and second floor plans**

↑ | **View from hallway to kitchen**

↓ | **Façade,** garden side

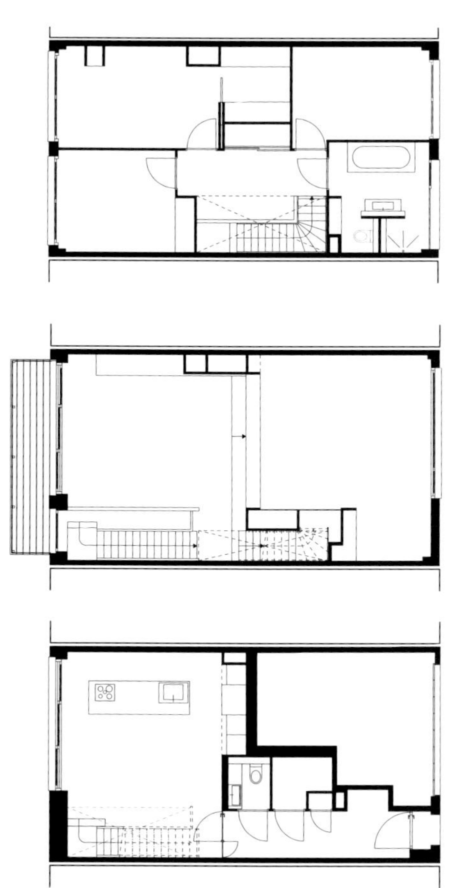

CBA Clemens Bachmann Architekten

↑ | **View into living area at dusk**
→ | **Entire building,** context

Holtmann House

Cologne

This roof extension has been added to a townhouse from the 1960s, located in the center of Cologne. The design is based on the concept "house on a house" and the extension is consequently an independent element that creates an exciting contrast to the house beneath. The contrasting façades also reinforce this – the original is plastered, the extension is clad with metal. A key element of the design is that it offers views of Cologne Cathedral. A large window has been integrated to serve this purpose, offering views not just of the cathedral but also of the surrounding city. Two large terraces have been cut into the level above, which also makes the most of the stunning views.

PROJECT FACTS

Address: Gereonswall 10, 50668 Cologne, Germany. **Client:** confidential. **Completion:** 2010. **Gross floor area:** 440 m². **Number of apartments:** 4. **Number of rooms:** 17. **Additional use:** office. **Main materials:** concrete, brick, wood, glass, steel. **Situation:** part of existing development in city center.

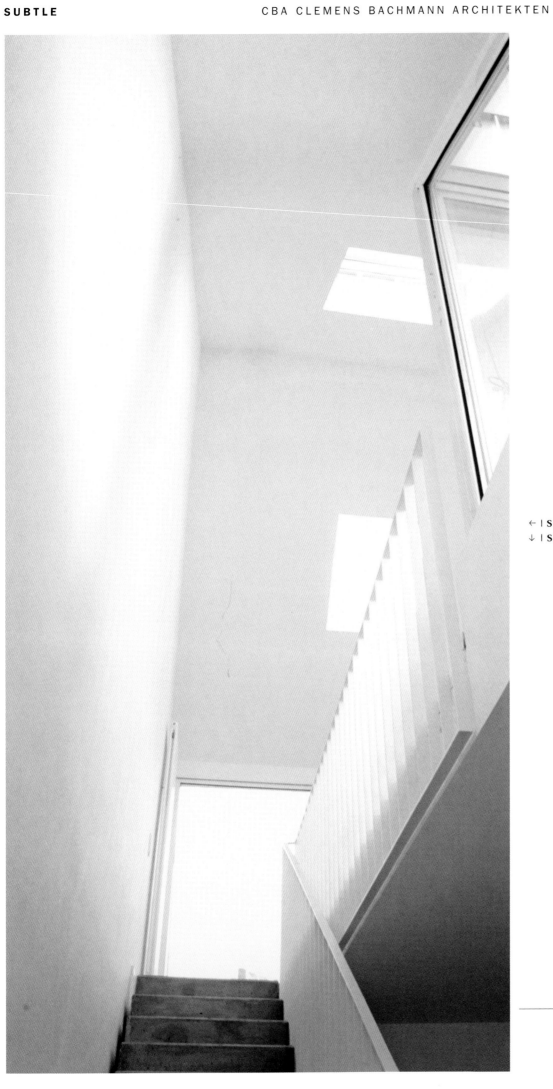

← | **Staircase**
↓ | **Section**

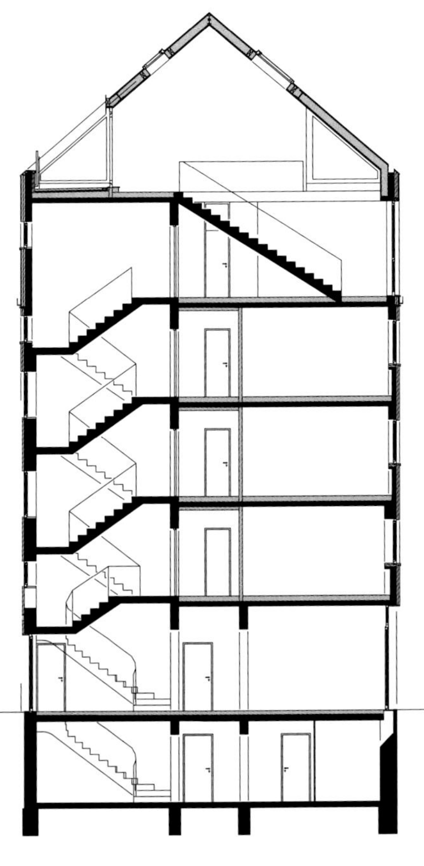

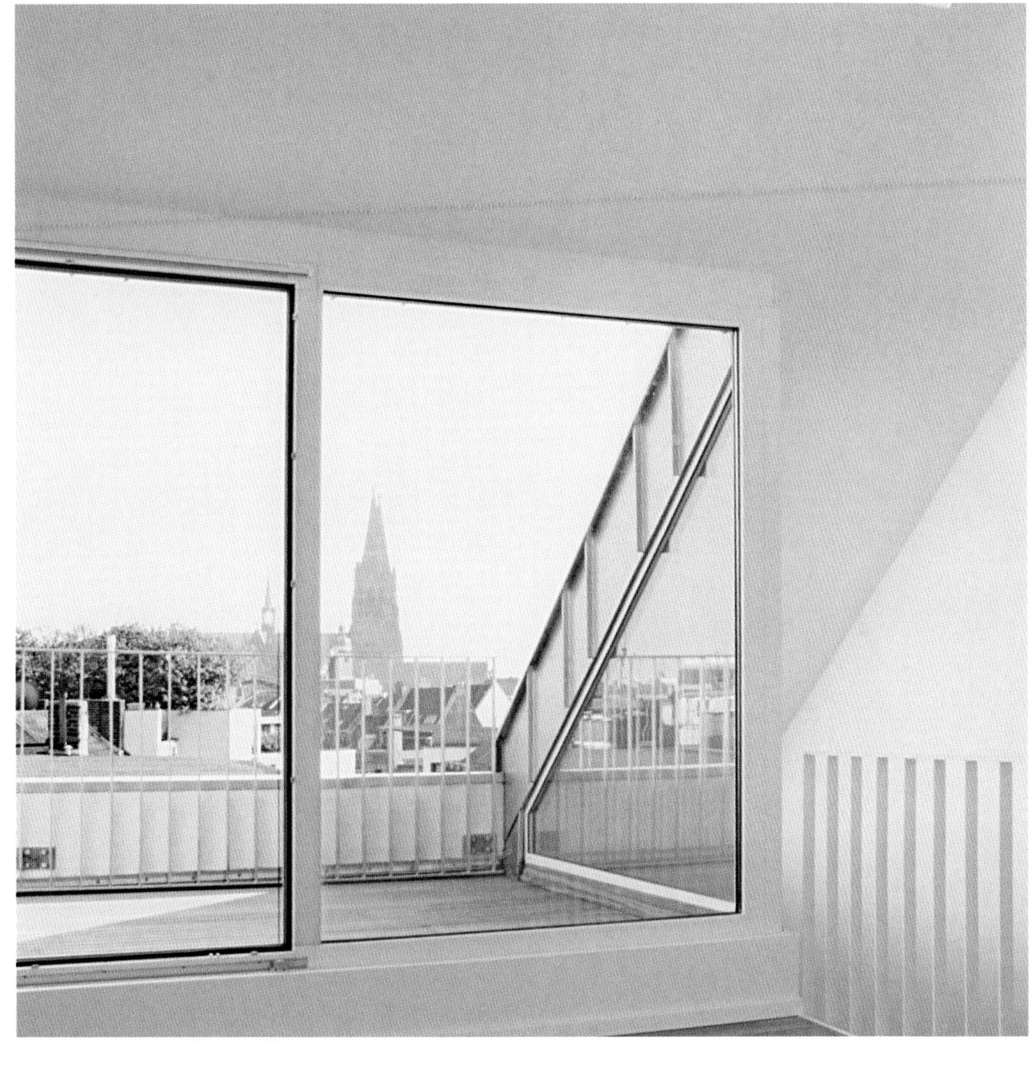

← | Roof terrace
↓ | Ground, typical, fourth and loft floor plans

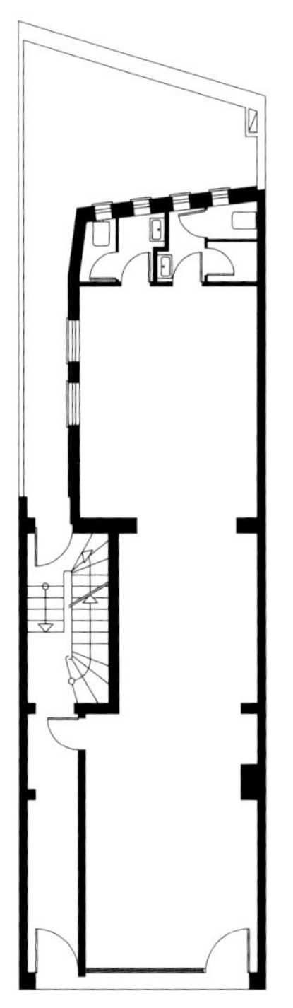

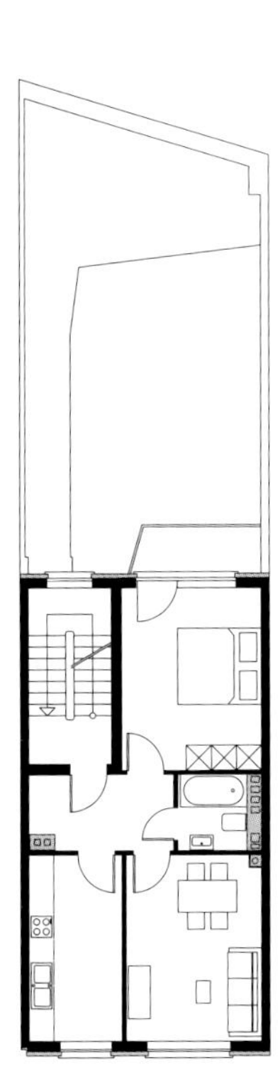

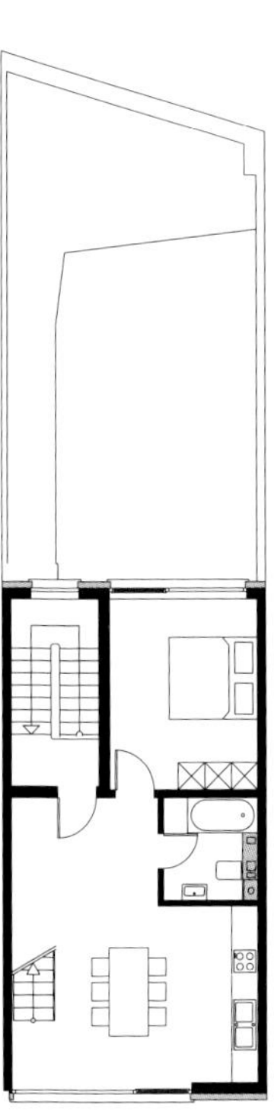

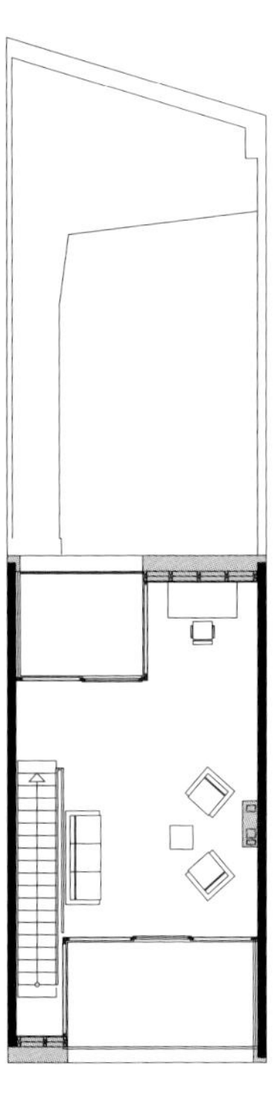

Guerrilla Office Architects

↑ | **Interior,** glass doors leading to garden
→ | **Double-height space at center of house**

House EVG

Ghent

This new townhouse has been built for a woman and her daughter on a narrow plot in the center of Ghent. Designed as a spatial knot, the house ascends towards the roof terraces. It is an open house that shares a dialogue with its surroundings. The house narrows towards the rear, but compensates for this with a double height room at the center. Despite its small size, the house is filled with light and appears much larger than it actually is.

Address: Tichelrei 104, 9000 Ghent, Belgium. **Client:** confidential. **Completion:** 2012. **Gross floor area:** 140 m^2. **Number of rooms:** 4. **Main materials:** concrete, concrete sheet panels. **Situation:** part of existing development in city center.

← | **Front façade**

← | Kitchen

↓ | Ground, first and second floor plans

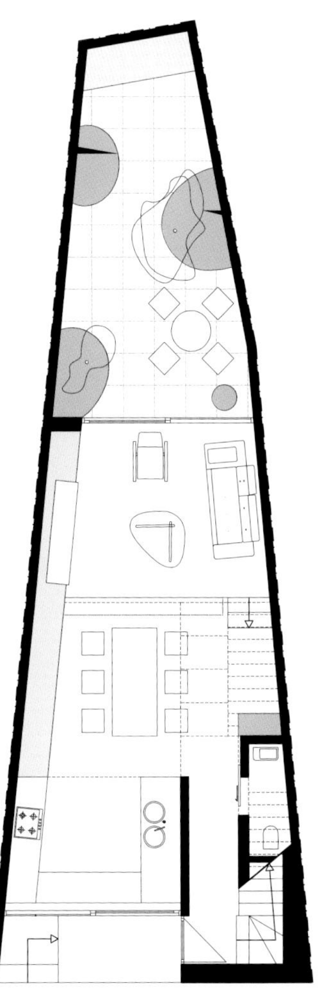

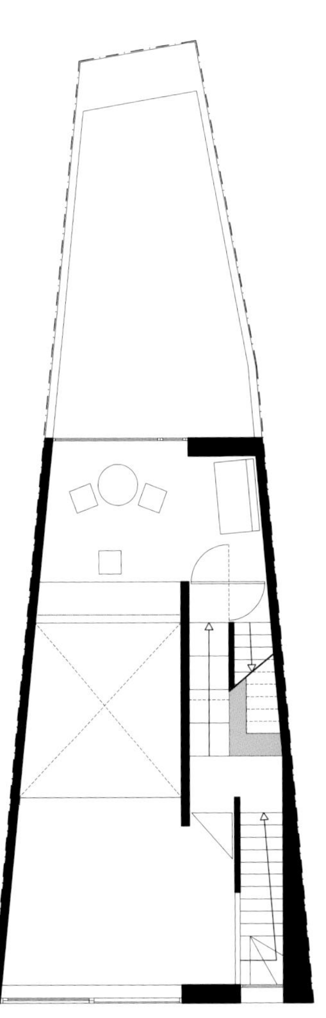

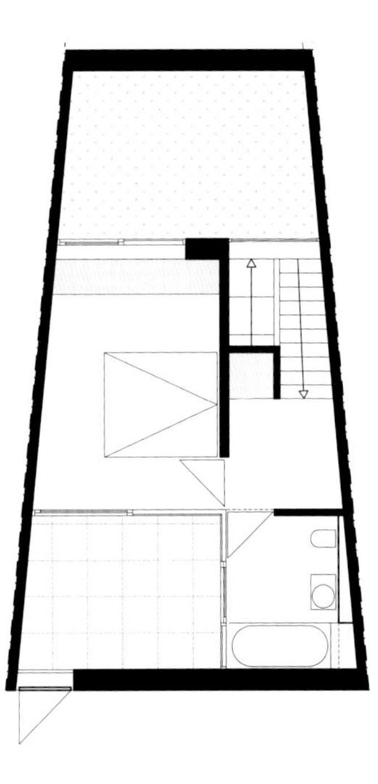

Atelier Reza Aliabadi [rzlbd]

↑ | **Interior,** kitchen and dining area
→ | **Main elevation,** dusk time

Whale House

Toronto

The Whale House is another spatial experiment by rzlbd, a monochromic contemporary manifesto that evolves around a central detached box painted in red standing free inside a foyer. The building appears to have swallowed the box, symbolizing the contemplation space inside the spacious jaw of the whale that swallowed Jonah. Upon entering the house the red box stands out and acts as a visual barrier between the home office at the front of the house and the more private domestic areas, kitchen and living room on the main floor. The circulation around the red box leads to the main floor and from there to the contemplation space on top of the box where one can overlook the spaces in the house as well as the outside view from the horizontal glazing on the front façade.

Address: 7 Doncaster Avenue, Toronto M4C 1Y4, Canada. **Client:** Brian D'Souza. **Completion:** 2012. **Gross floor area:** 163 m². **Number of rooms:** 9. **Additional use:** office. **Main materials:** wood. **Situation:** detached building in urban context.

↑ | **Building in context**
↙ | **Basement to roof plans**

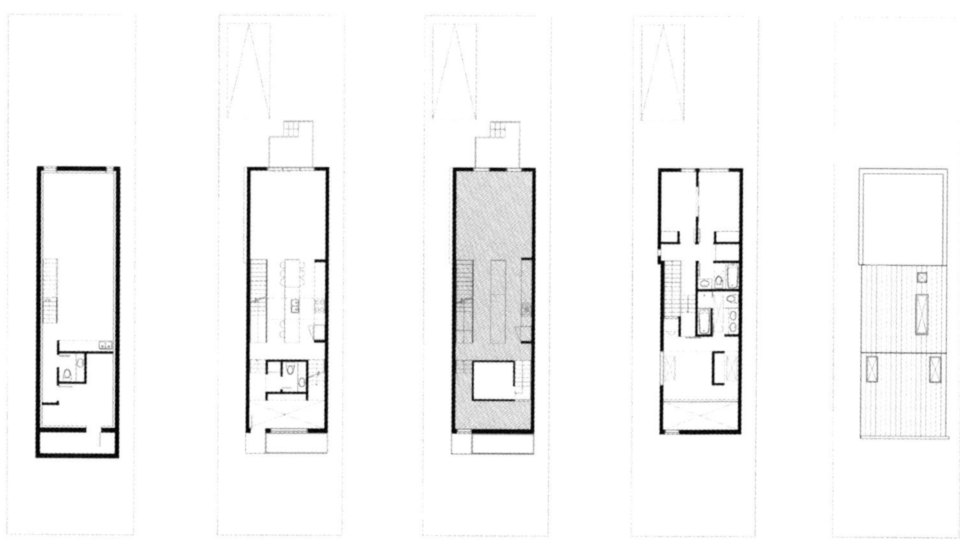

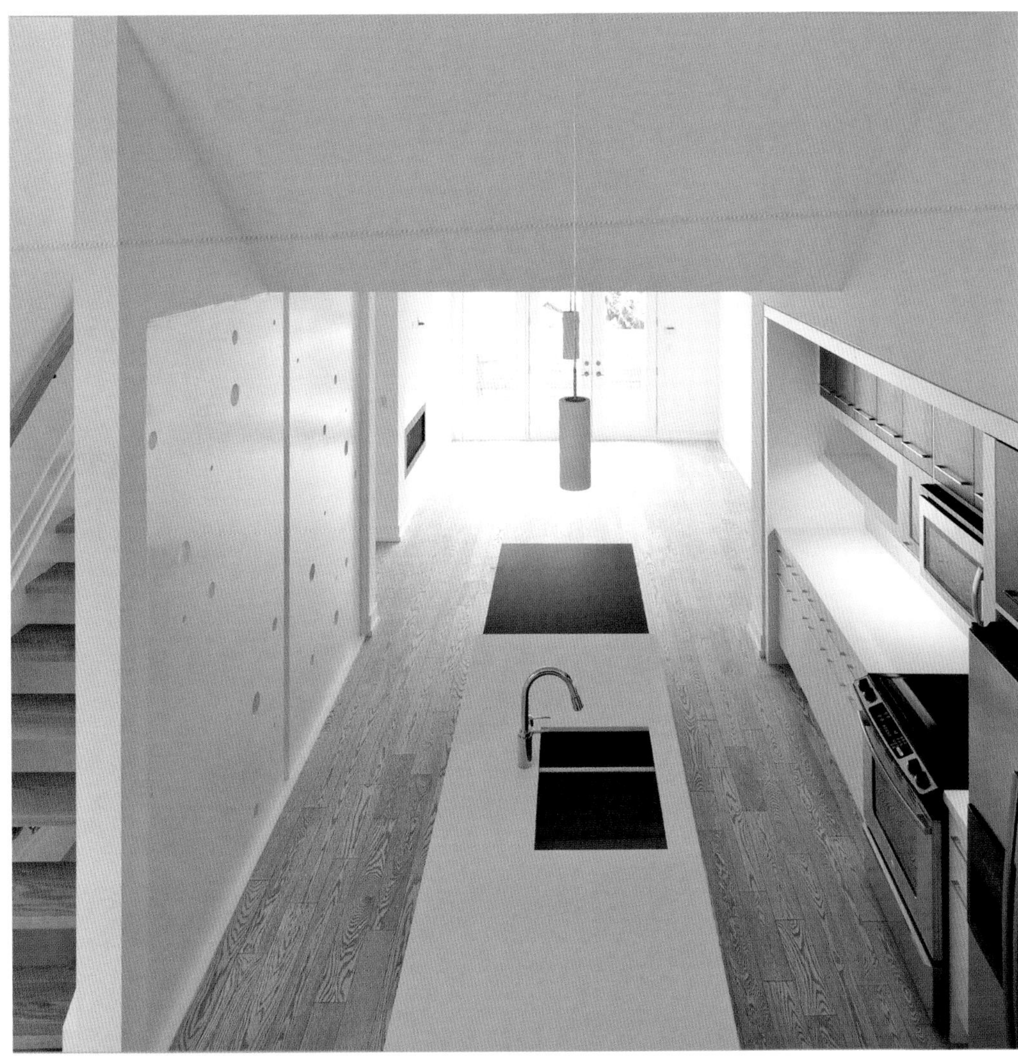

← | **Kitchen and living,** from loft

↓ | **Interior,** triple-height entry foyer

Atelier Bow-Wow

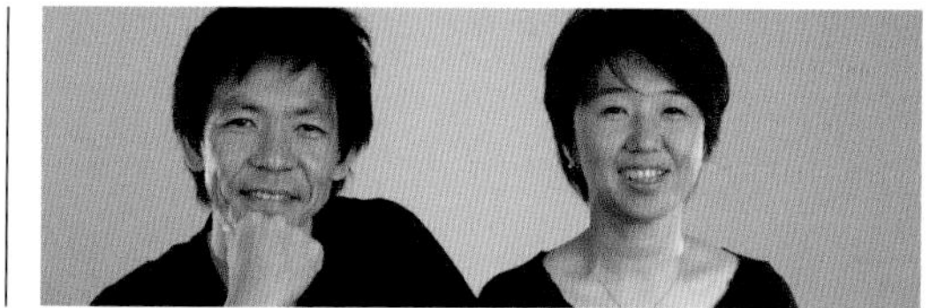

↑ | **Staircase,** landing

Tower Machiya

Tokyo

This house is built on a plot the size of a single-car garage and presented the architects with a lot of challenges. The clients are fervent practitioners of tea ceremony and hoped to have a house equipped with a tearoom and dreamed of teaching there in the future. The architects accepted the challenge and proposed a design similar to a "machiya" – a traditional wooden communal residence. As the size of the lot was severely limited, the machiya took the form of a tower that stretched upward. The architects placed the tearoom on the top floor facing the road. The small living space arose in fragments and was integrated through a rhythmic arrangement of steel beams and columns.

PROJECT FACTS

Address: Shinjuku, Tokyo, Japan. **Client:** confidential. **Completion:** 2010. **Gross floor area:** 58 m^2. **Number of rooms:** 6. **Main materials:** steel. **Situation:** part of existing development in urban context.

↑ | **Façade,** as seen from street
↓ | **Interior,** view from staircase to tea room

↑ | **Tea room**
↓ | **Section**

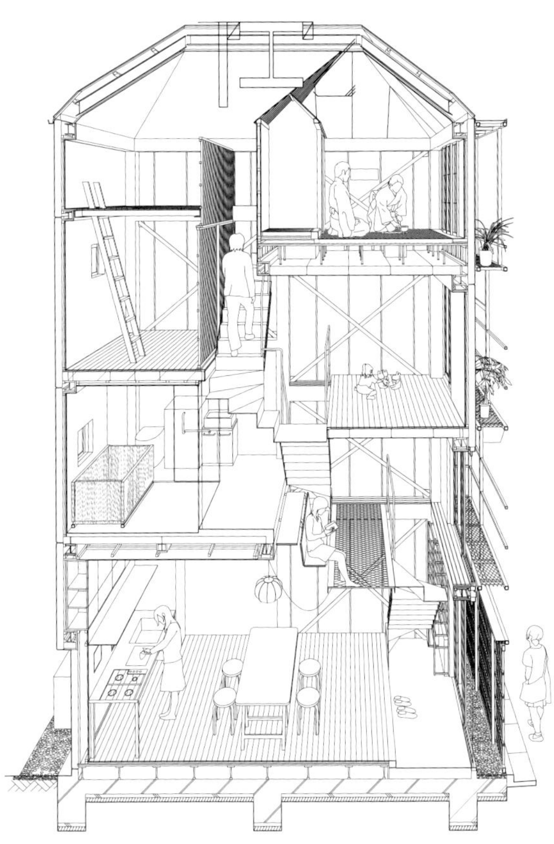

schöningmosca Architekten

↑ | **Detail window,** north side
→ | **Staircase**

Townhouse near the Berlin Wall Memorial Park

Berlin

This townhouse is oriented around a semi-public access route which can be reached via Strelitzer Straße and a park created in remembrance of the Berlin Wall. Conceived as a Passive House, it is developed from the trapezoid shape of the plot and is clearly oriented north to south. The site has been developed to form spaces of varying dimensions that increase inside towards the front of the house where the most daylight is drawn in through the large windows. The stairs are aligned under each other, which makes the small house appear larger than it is. The horizontal windows allow an abundance of light inside. This arrangement emphasizes the linear quality of the space, which is characterized by the play of sloping and straight surfaces and opens out towards the sky.

PROJECT FACTS

Address: Bernauer Straße 5a, 10115 Berlin, Germany. **Client:** Batrice Mosca, Wolfgang Schöning. **Completion:** 2010. **Gross floor area:** 240 m². **Number of rooms:** 5. **Situation:** part of new development in city center.

↑ | **Kitchen**
← | **View from first to ground floor**

← | South-west façade with large windows
↓ | Ground, first and second floor plans

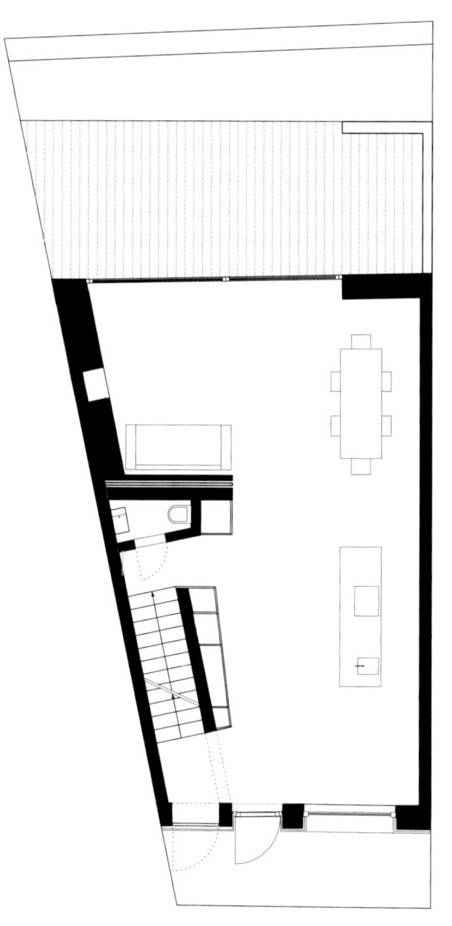

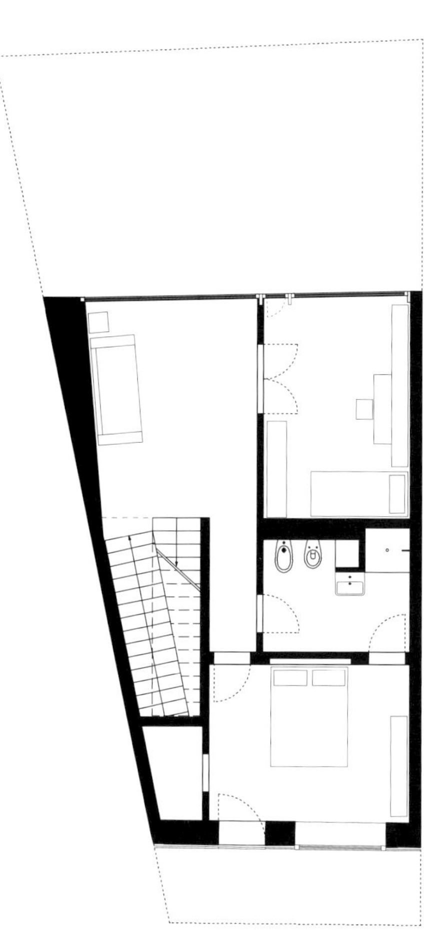

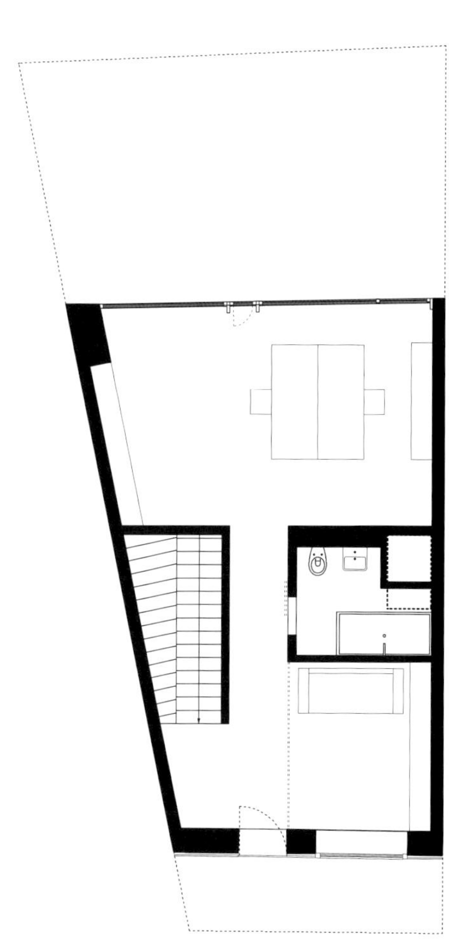

Apollo Architects & Associates

↑ | Entrance area at night
→ | Front view with surroundings

Lattice

Tokyo

This house is located in a densely populated residential area in eastern Tokyo. The façade of the house is entirely covered with wooden louvers. The front and rear of the house are loosely connected by the transparent stairs located at the center. Inside, the house has a split-level arrangement with an open ceiling, this draws light deep into the narrow house. The dark floors and light walls give the house a strikingly modern appearance, reinforced by the use of concrete as a main building material.

PROJECT FACTS

Address: Taito ward, Tokyo, Japan. **Client:** confidential. **Completion:** 2013. **Gross floor area:** 101 m^2. **Number of rooms:** 4. **Main materials:** reinforced concrete, wood. **Situation:** part of existing development in urban context.

↑ | View from street
↙ | Sections

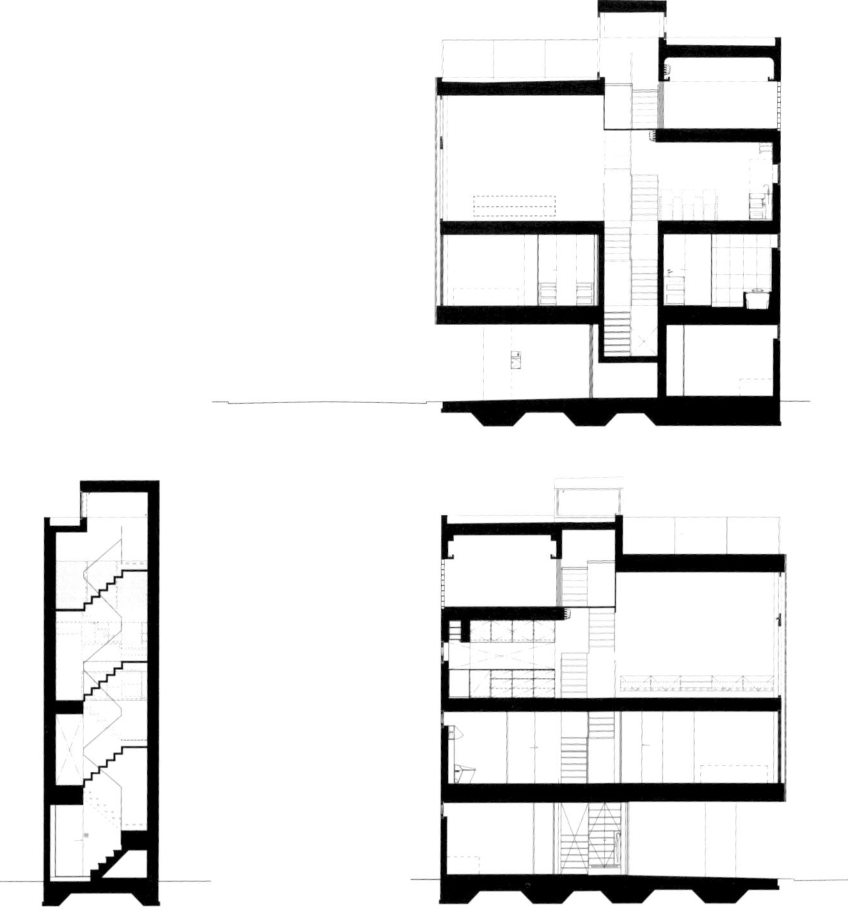

← | **Interior,** stairs
↓ | **Ground, first, second floor with loft and penthouse plans**

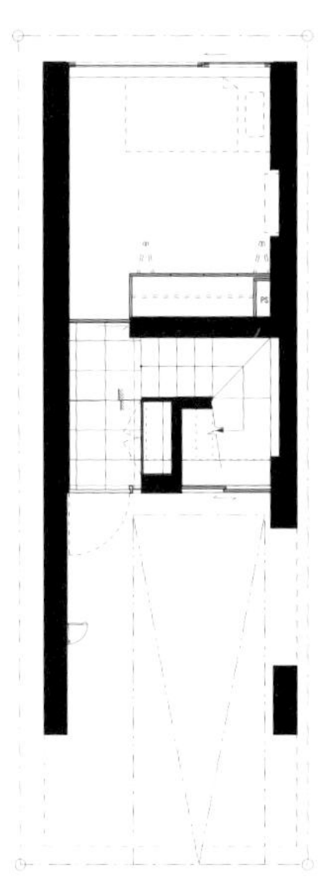
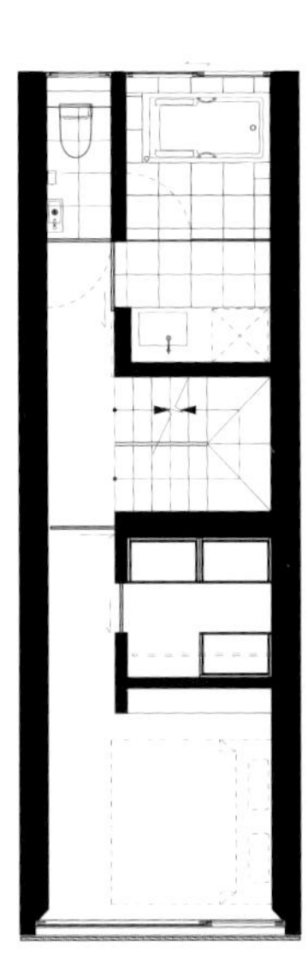
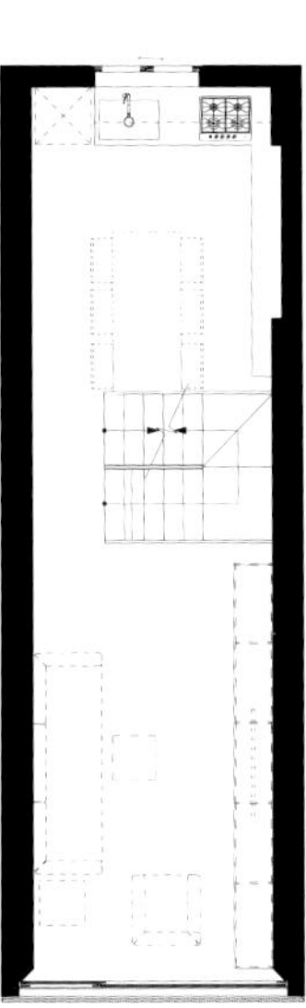
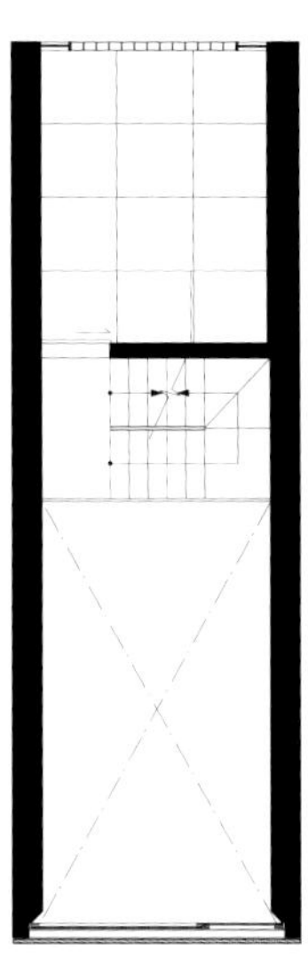
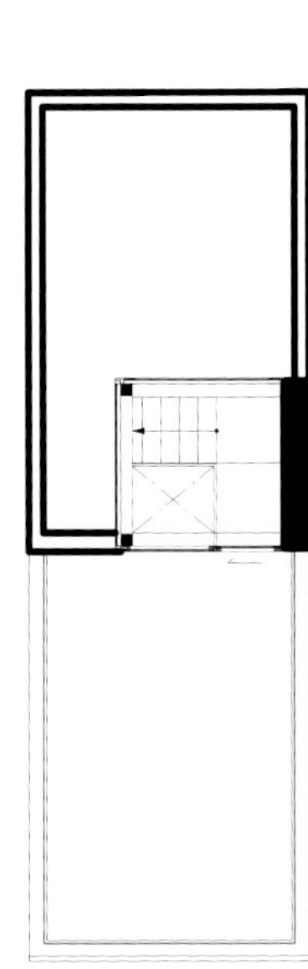

Endo Shuhei Architect Institute

↑ | **Interior,** natural light from above and through front façade

RooftectureOT2

Osaka

This house is designed for a couple and their three children. Located on a small site in the heart of Osaka, this is a busy, lively area and the house is surrounded by buildings on three sides. The client requested that while the façade should secure the necessary lighting and ventilation, it should be moderately closed from the outside. The house has a perforated metal steel sheet wall formation facing the street. This makes the house more private while allowing light and air inside. Air is also drawn deep into the house by a skylight above the stairs. During the evening, holes in the façade allow the light from the inside to shine out. Variations in the way the interior is illuminated gives the façade pattern more variety.

PROJECT FACTS

Address: Tenma, Kita-ku, Osaka, Japan. **Client:** confidential. **Completion:** 2012. **Gross floor area:** 127 m². **Number of rooms:** 4. **Main materials:** steel. **Situation:** part of existing development in city center.

↑ | **Bird's-eye view**

↑ | **Steel façade,** perforated and partly translucent

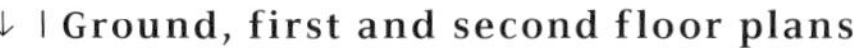

↓ | **Ground, first and second floor plans**

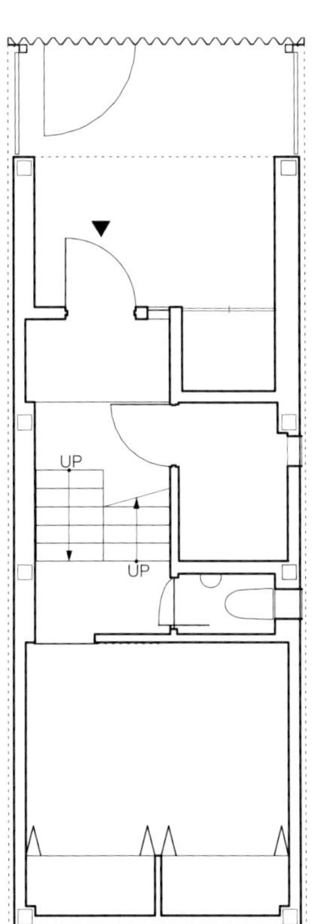

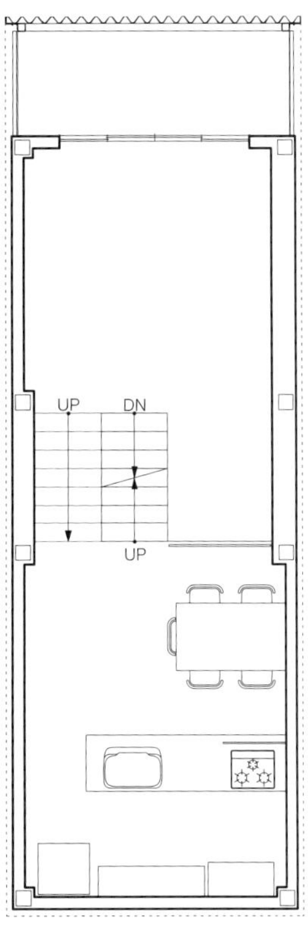

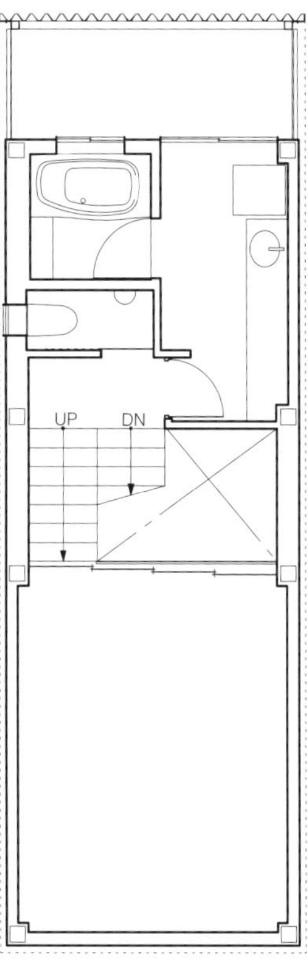

Andrew Maynard Architects

↑ | **Terraced house in context**
→ | **New extension**

Moor Street

Fitzroy

This aging house was home to a family for eight years, but as the family grew and the children began to grow up, it became apparent that the house had to undergo some changes. A small light well in the original house contained a maple tree and was a central aspect of the house. This light well has been expanded, improving the connection between the various levels of the house. The separate boxes on the upper levels contain the master bedroom. This is surrounded by the canopy of the maple tree to the south, and the branches of a large gum tree to the north, making the bedroom feel almost like a treehouse. The new extension also makes the most of views of the surroundings.

PROJECT FACTS

Address: Moor Street, Fitzroy 3065, Australia. **Client:** confidential. **Completion:** 2012. **Gross floor area:** 150 m². **Number of rooms:** 6. **Main materials:** wood, glass. **Situation:** part of existing development in suburban context.

←←| **Corridor,** high ceiling and modern timber floors
← | **Light-filled interior**
↓ | **Ground and first floor plans**

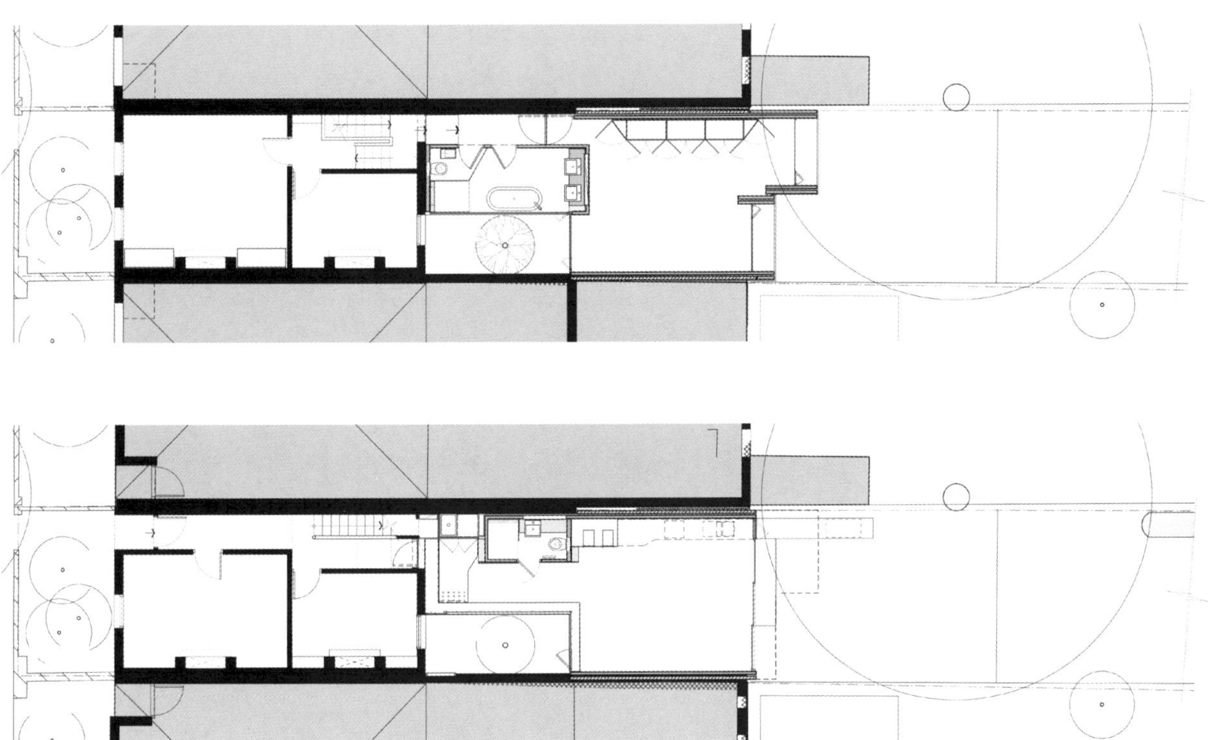

Johanne Nalbach

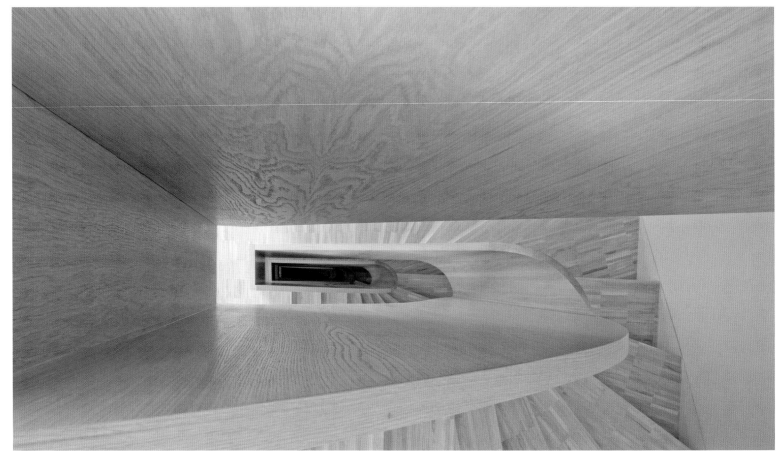

↑ | **Stairwell from above**
↓ | **Details,** interior, façade and garden

→ | **Façade,** view from street

Townhouse P15

Berlin

The openings in the brick façade tell of the rooms that lie behind them. The choice of materials and the craftsmanship give the building a rather modest yet expressive appearance. The raw material itself and the firing process determine the varying shades and colors of the individual bricks. These variations create different color effects depending on the character of the light. The choice of brick as building material also serves to create a connection to Berlin's architectural history; the unmistakably modern character of the house juxtaposes this intention. The depth of the house creates a tension between the interior and exterior, public and private, light and dark areas.

Address: Caroline-Von-Humboldt-Weg 32, 10117 Berlin, Germany. **Client:** confidential. **Completion:** 2008. **Gross floor area:** 1,000 m². **Number of rooms:** 8. **Main materials:** brick, concrete. **Situation:** part of new development in city center.

← | **Entire view**

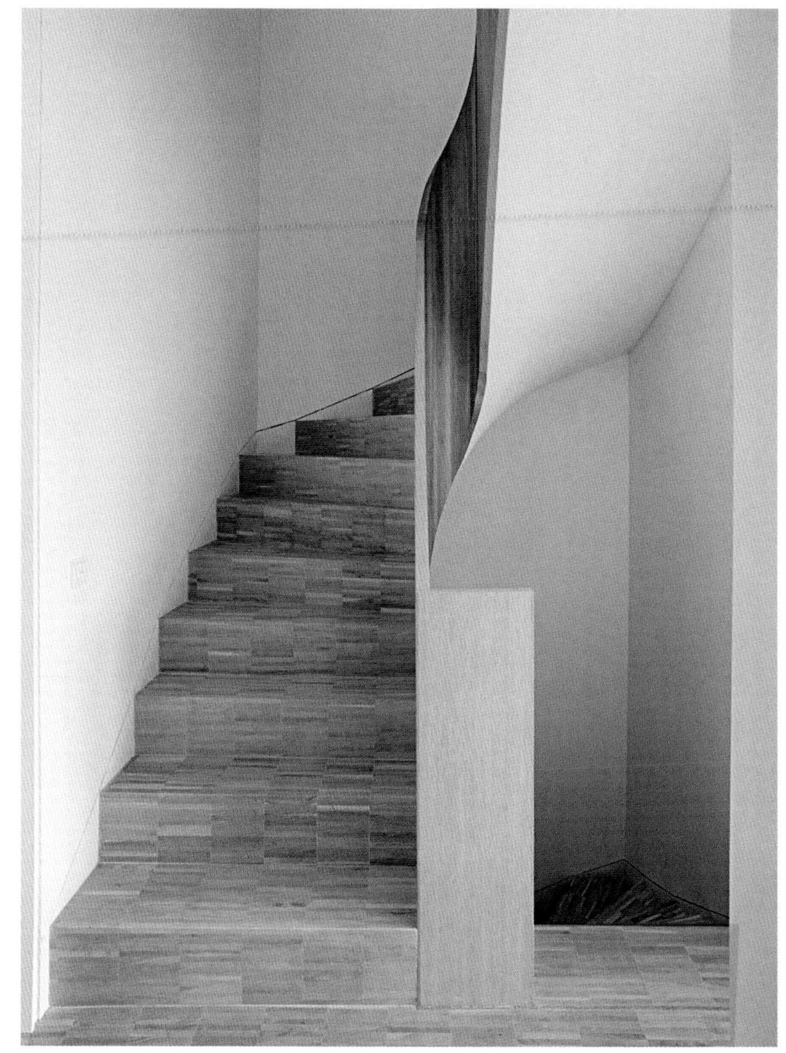

← | Staircase

↓ | Ground to fifth floor plans

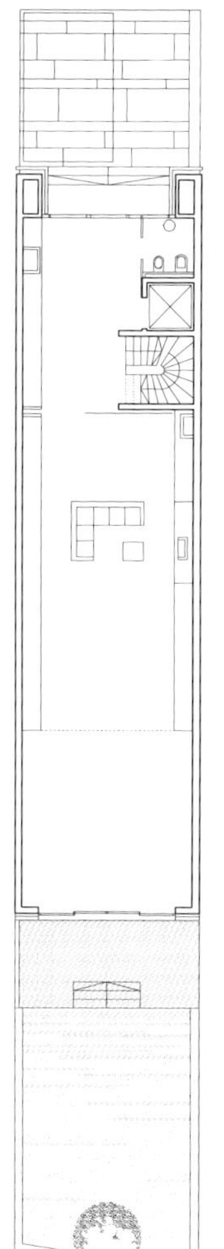

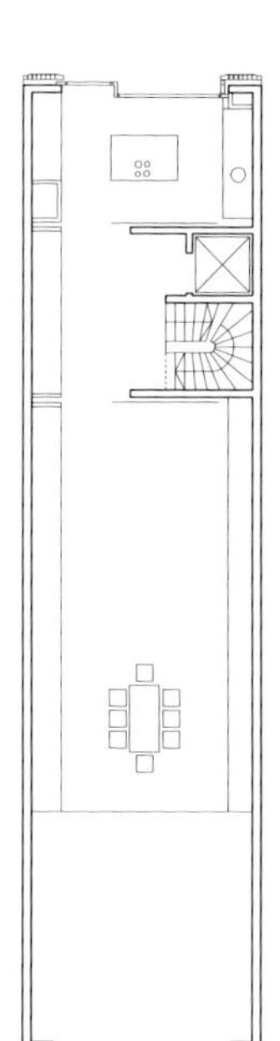

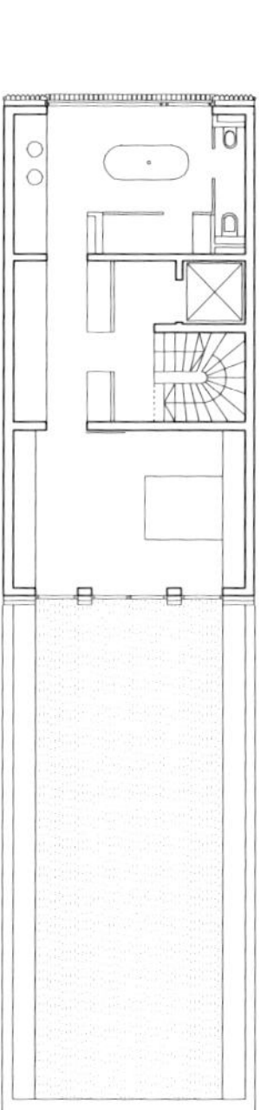

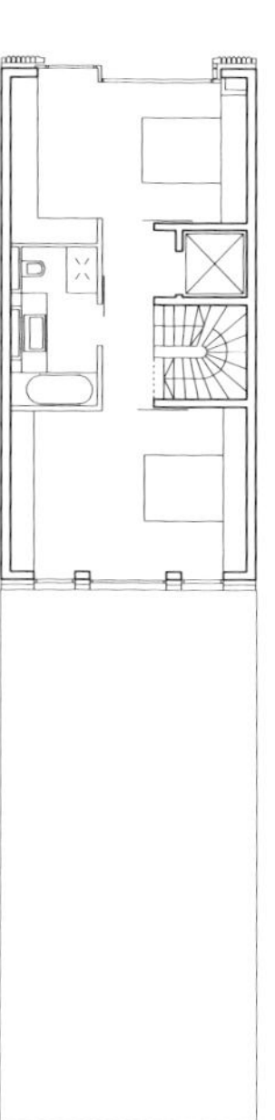

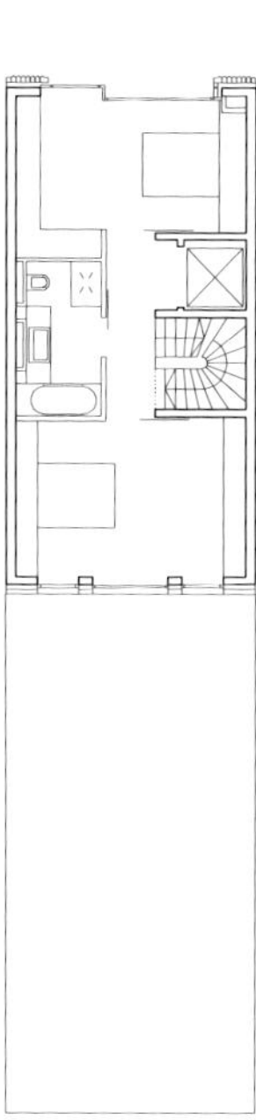

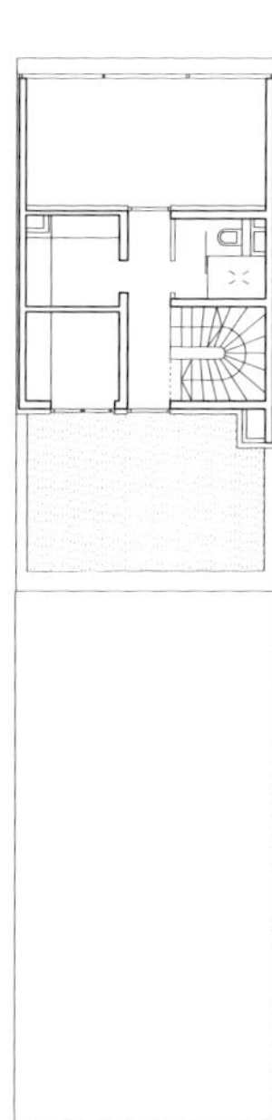

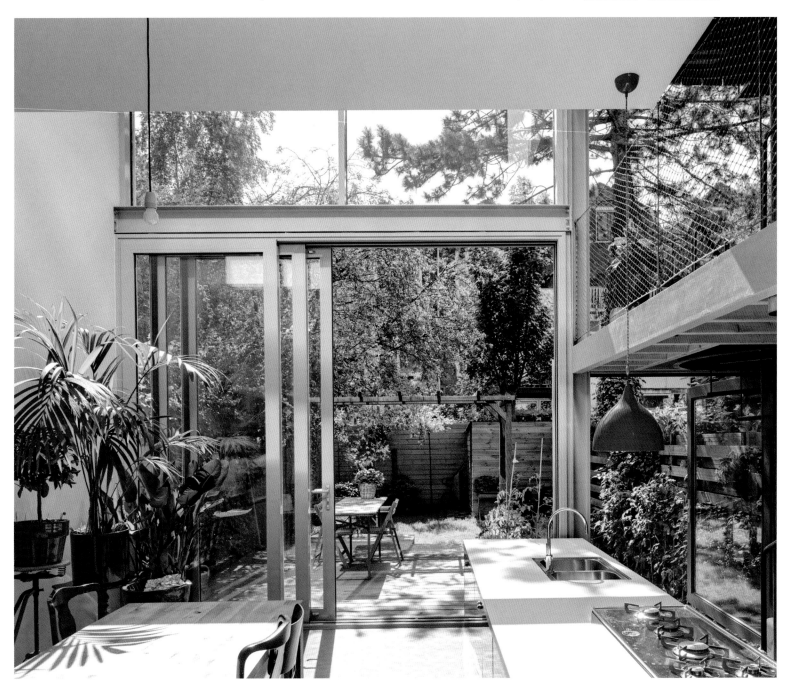

↑ | **Interior,** view of backyard

Joyce & Jeroen House

Den Haag

The huge potential of the structure and the original characteristics of the original early-20th-century house were, according to the clients, decisive for the purchase of the strong prolapsed and dilapidated building. The poor condition made a thorough restoration of the foundation and the main structure necessary. This, together with the high level of ambition of the client, lead to a rigorous redesign in which the architects used the spacious floor height to create new floors, voids and split levels at the backside of the house. The combination of the restored front of the house with its original detailing and the new extension at the back creates an interesting tension between classical and contemporary.

PROJECT FACTS

Address: Van Merlenstraat, 2518 TD Den Haag, the Netherlands. **Client:** Joyce Wierda, Jeroen Bogers. **Completion:** 2009. **Gross floor area:** 225 m². **Number of rooms:** 9. **Main materials:** Douglas fir, plywood, steel, aluminum, glass. **Situation:** part of existing development in city center.

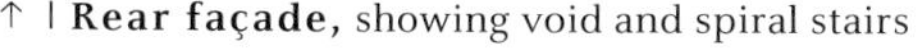

↑ | **Rear façade,** showing void and spiral stairs

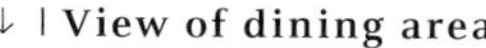

↓ | **View of dining area**

↑ | **Street façade**

↓ | **Ground and first floor plans**

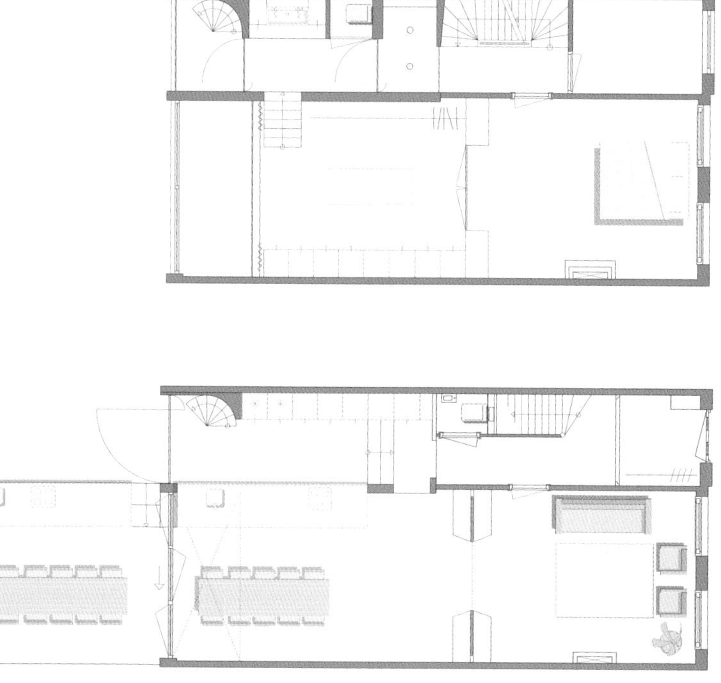

Barker Freeman Design Office (BFDO)

↑ | Front entrance
→ | Rear exterior at dusk

Brooklyn House

New York City

This wide wood frame house is located on a lot with a driveway and a two-story hayloft in the rear yard. The building was rebuilt and expanded to create a modern, light-filled family home. An entry porch is carved from the south-east corner to allow views of the nearby park. A secondary porch at the north-west corner allows access to the house from the rear yard and patio. Inside, the open plan living-dining-kitchen space includes a mix of minimal modern detailing and rich textured materials and reclaimed elements. The four-bedroom second floor is divided into children's and parent's wings separated by a pocket door.

PROJECT FACTS

Address: Reeve Place, 11218 New York City, NY, USA. **Client:** confidential. **Completion:** 2013. **Gross floor area:** 350 m². **Number of rooms:** 8. **Main materials:** cedar siding, walnut floors. **Situation:** part of existing development in urban context.

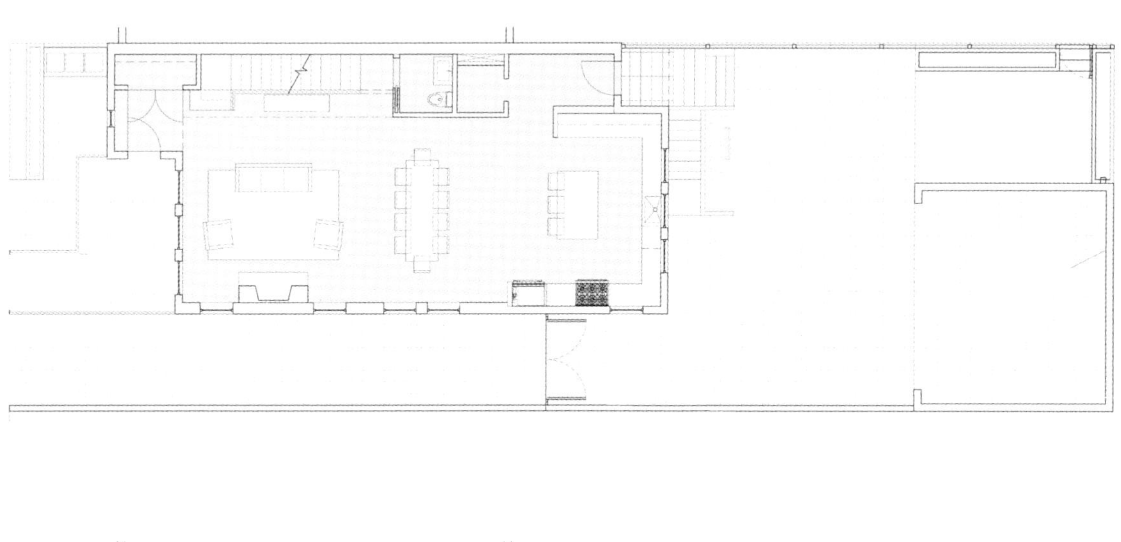

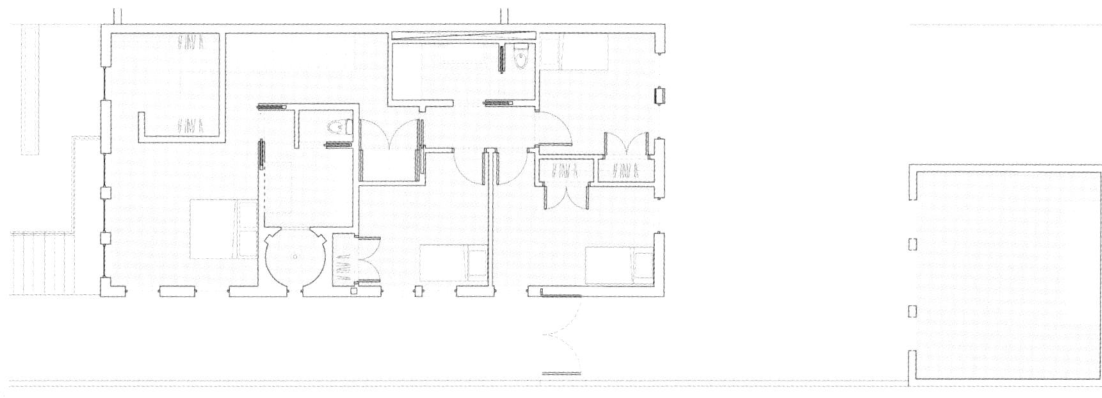

↑ | **Ground and first floor plans**
← | **Interior,** kitchen

← | Master bedroom
↓ | Living room

Ryo Matsui Architects

↑ | **Interior,** 5th floor
→ | **Inner courtyard,** 5th floor

Grass Building

Tokyo

This five-story townhouse comprises a residential unit, office, and retail businesses. Located near the city center, the design responds to the surrounding architecture and is an esthetic addition to the streetscape. The rooms facing the street have large windows and glass doors, which draw an abundance of light inside and allow easy access to the balcony. The modern design is complemented by the interior, which is bright and open. A tree incorporated into the large terraced area integrates nature into the design, creating a small green oasis in the heart of the city.

Address: 3-32-13 Shiba, Mínato-ku, Tokyo 105-0014, Japan. **Client:** confidential. **Completion:** 2010. **Gross floor area:** 305 m². **Number of apartments:** 4. **Number of rooms:** 8. **Additional use:** café, office. **Main materials:** concrete. **Situation:** part of existing development in urban context.

← | **Entire building**, night view

← | **Inner courtyard at dusk**
↙ | **General view,** city side
↓ | **Section**

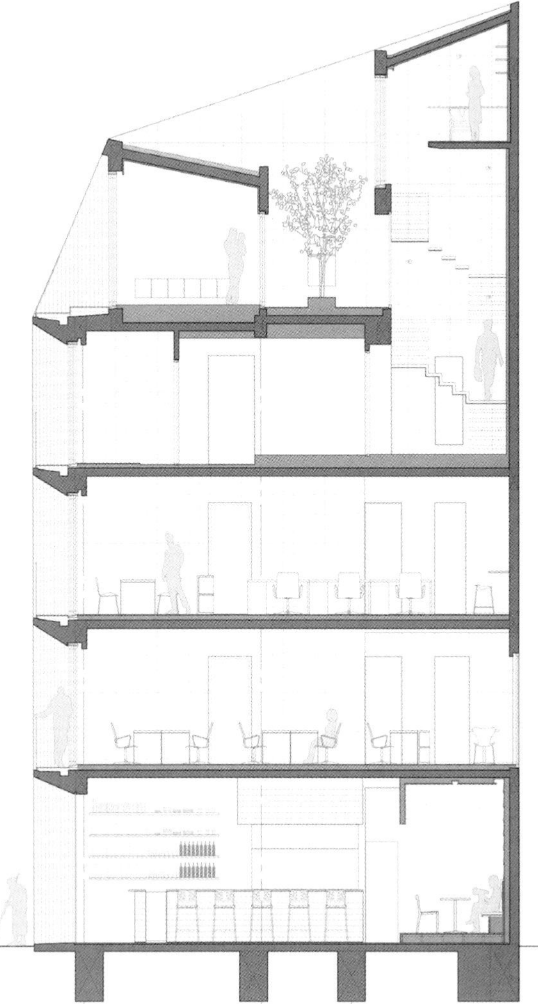

Level Architects

↑ | **Interior,** second floor
→ | **Stairwell,** living area

House in Fukasawa

Tokyo

Situated on a typical long and narrow urban plot in Tokyo, the length of the site was a key focus of the design. A wall design was incorporated on the north and south sides of the home to create a sense of privacy, but by making intentional cuts, light is either filtered in or shielded on the south side, and reflected into the home on the north side. The open second floor plan utilizes a variation of ceiling heights to differentiate space, as well as a set of steps around the living room to create a built-in sofa where cushions can be placed, amplifying a sense of openness. The center of the house hosts a stair and light well, allowing for light to filter through the home. The sectional design highlights the length of the house, allowing a creative use of line-of-sight and height differentiations, which make the house appear larger than it is.

PROJECT FACTS

Address: Fukusawa, Setagaya Ward, Tokyo, Japan. **Client:** confidential. **Completion:** 2013. **Gross floor area:** 116 m². **Number of rooms:** 5. **Main materials:** wood frame construction. **Situation:** part of existing development in urban context.

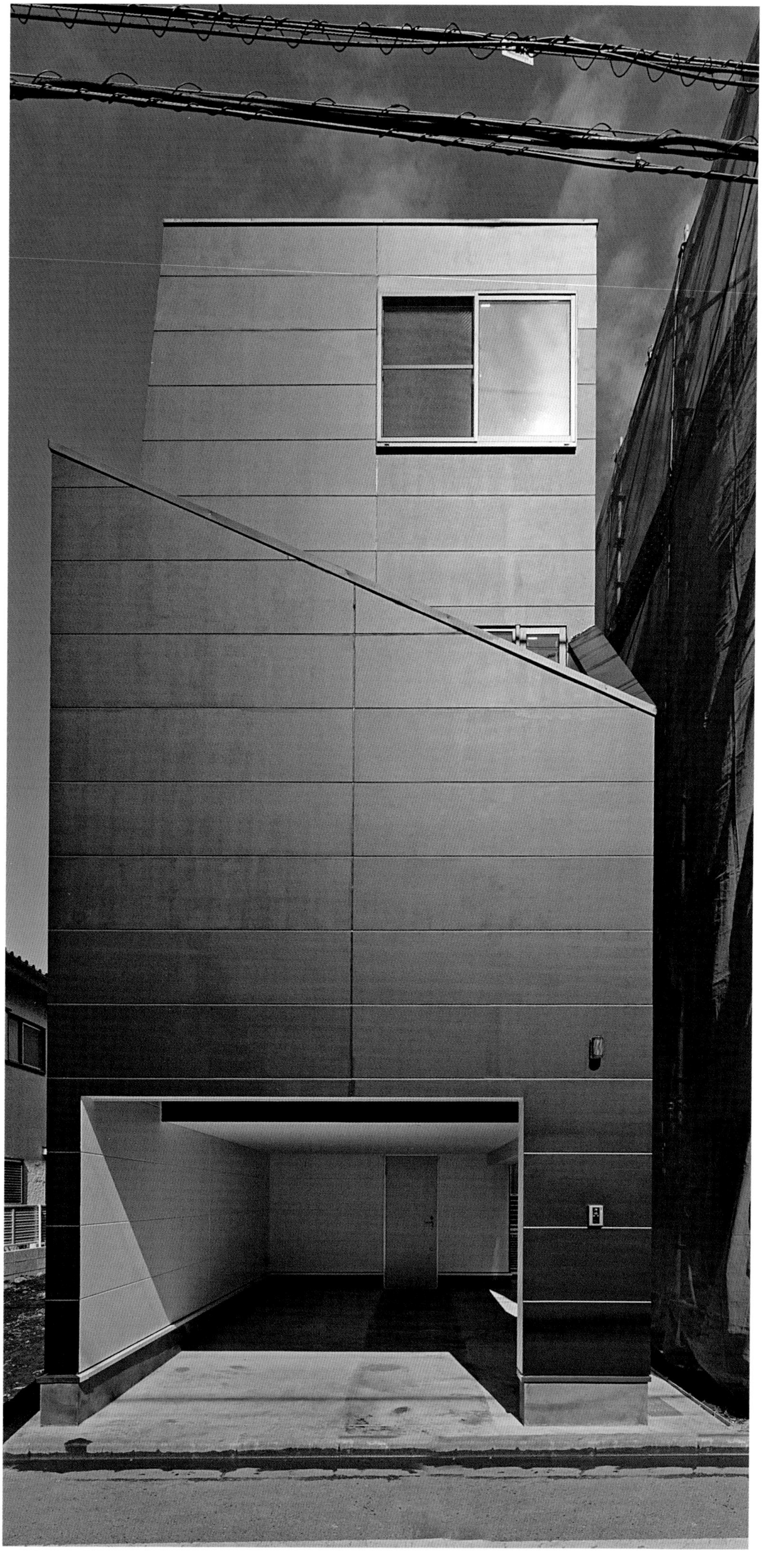

← | **Exterior,** façade
↓ | **Elevation**

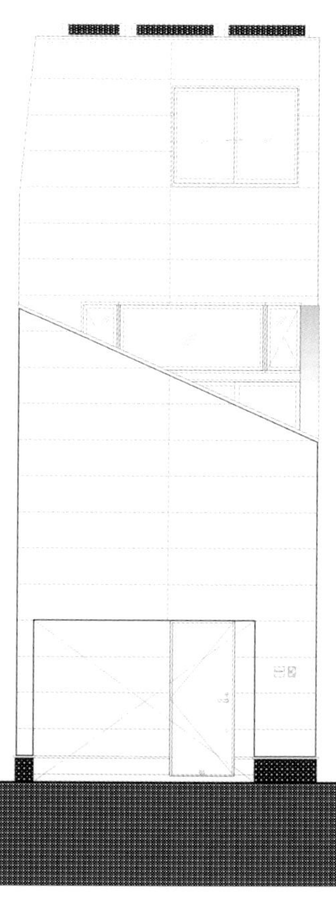

← | Interior from living room
↓ | Second, third and loft floor plans

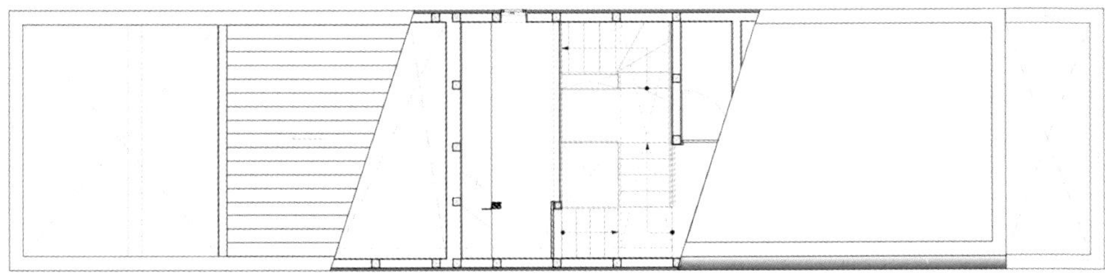

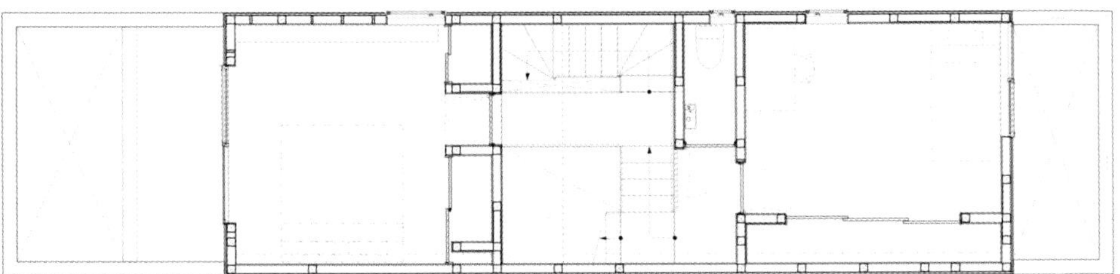

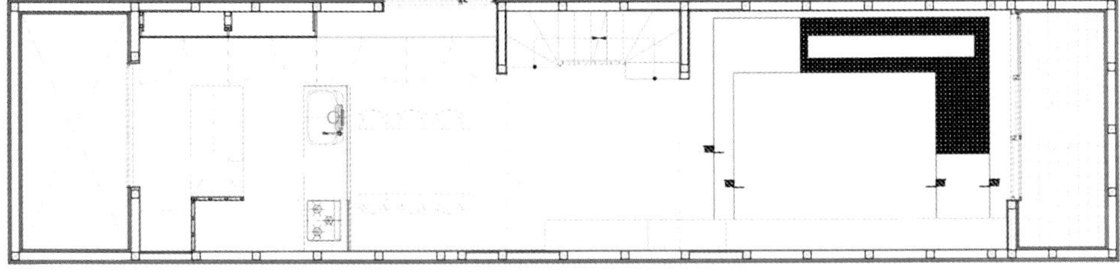

Alain Hinant + Jean Glibert

↑ | Staircase, dining room and garden

Transforming a Laundry Building

Uccle

This annex, attached to the rear of a group of three identical houses in the center of the commune of Uccle in the Brussels region once housed a laundry. The renovation has given the three-story house a visual unity, improved natural illumination and opened up views over the garden. A large open space was created at the center of the annex. A staircase unfurls in the middle of this, lit by skylights in the roof overhead. From the street, the view extends through a large bay window at the far end of the annex into the garden. By painting sections of the walls, floors and ceilings, the artist Jean Gilbert has created a mass of color that transcends the various levels and engages with the building through reflections in the glossy black paintwork.

PROJECT FACTS

Address: 36, rue du Doyenné, 1180 Uccle, Belgium. **Client:** confidential. **Completion:** 2011. **Gross floor area:** 120 m². **Artist:** Jean Glibert. **Number of rooms:** 4. **Main materials:** wood, steel. **Situation:** part of existing development in city center.

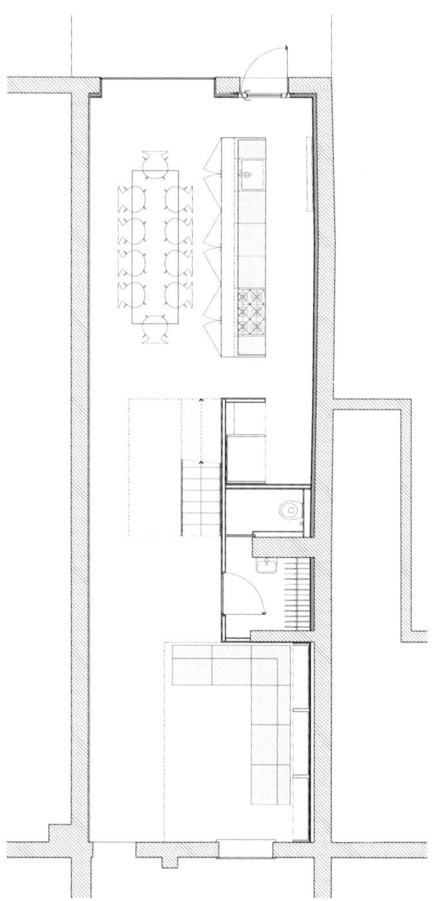

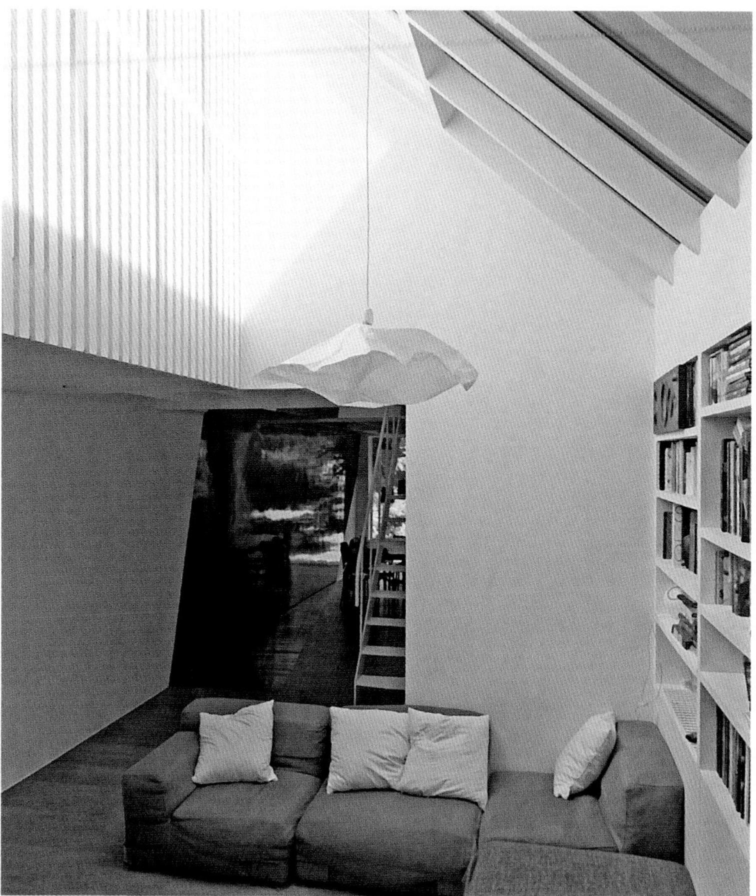

↑ | **Ground floor plan**
↓ | **Bedroom and office**

↑ | **Living room,** illuminated by windows above
↓ | **Stairwell,** striking blue paintwork

mm architekten Martin A. Müller Architekt

↑ | **Street view,** building in context
→ | **Staircase,** seating place, integrated closet

Closing the Gap

Lübeck

A clever exploitation of building regulations allows this building to occupy a narrow gap in the street fabric. The design deliberately develops a dialogue between the new building and its existing neighbors. The materials, height and proportions of the house match those of its neighbors, successfully integrating it into the streetscape. Lines of sight through the house help to make the garden and nature part of the design. The children's rooms are located on the first floor and can be either joined together or separated from each other by large sliding doors. The stairwell connects the various living areas on all three levels. The attic story houses a library and two roof terraces. Two large skylights help to draw daylight deep inside the house.

PROJECT FACTS

Address: Kronsforder Allee 39a, 23560 Lübeck, Germany. **Client:** Majbritt Paul, Lars Olaf Brüning. **Completion:** 2010. **Gross floor area:** 199 m². **Lighting design:** Fahlke & Dettmer. **Number of rooms:** 6. **Main materials:** reinforced concrete, wood, fair faced concrete, brick. **Situation:** detached building in urban context.

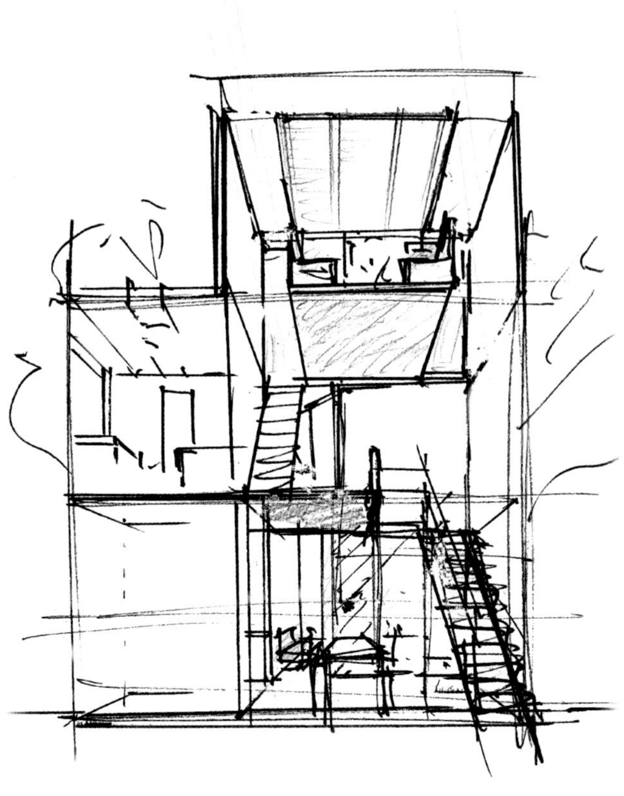

↖ | **Computer diagram**
↑ | **Sketch**
← | **Front view,** large windows open out the façade

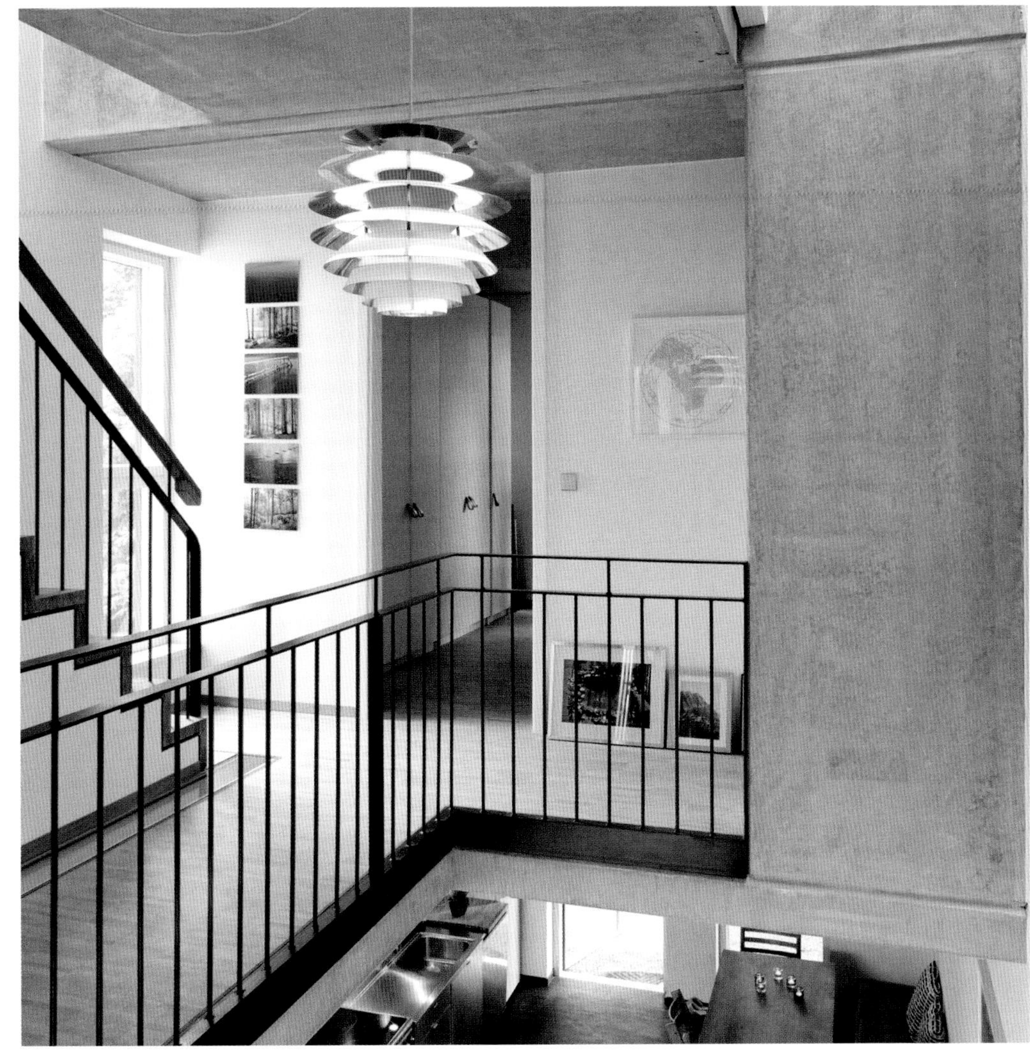

← | **Interior,** view of two levels
↓ | **Site and ground floor plans**

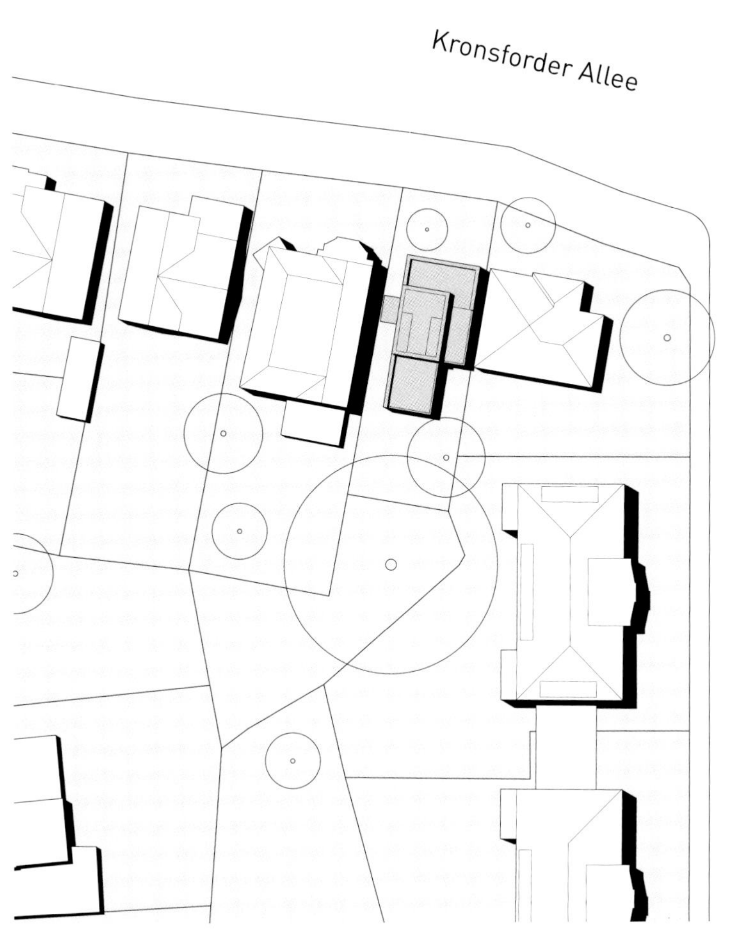

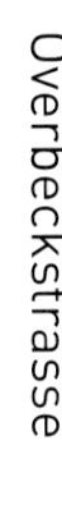

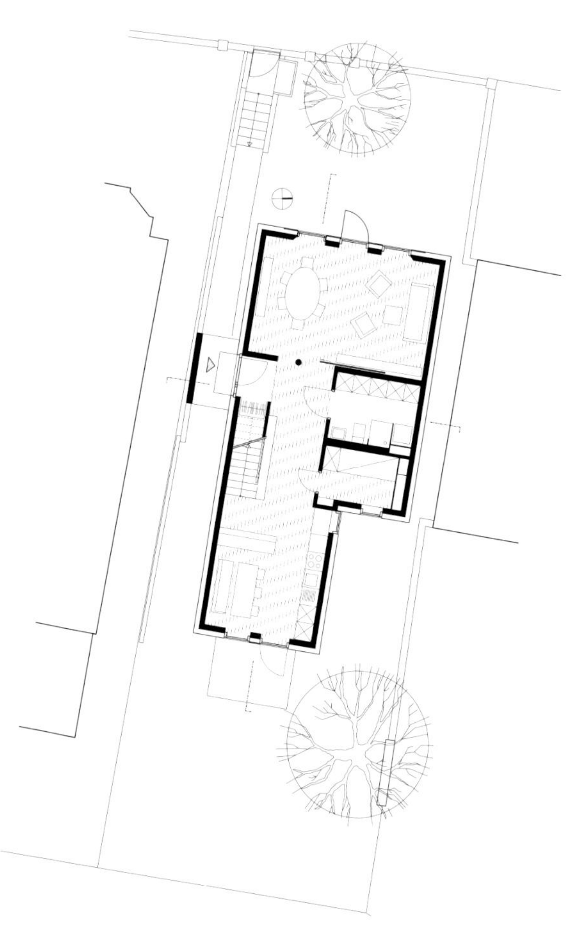

pier7 architekten

↑ | **Living area,** kitchen
→ | **Night view,** from street

House Re-Used

Düsseldorf

This project involved the complete renovation of a house from the 1950s, located directly adjacent to a park. The removal of some of the dividing walls has created large open-plan living areas that allow residents to experience both the park on one side and the courtyard on the other, almost as an extension of the living space. Atria have been cut into the existing building, creating a range of varied spatial relationships. A purist design reduces the space to just the essentials. The original underground car park no longer met modern requirements and has been converted into a useable space. The technical infrastructure has also been completely renewed. Sound insulation has been improved, which also presented an opportunity to add underfloor heating. Optimized insulation helps to raise the technical standard above current requirements.

Address: Faunastraße 41, 40239 Düsseldorf, Germany. **Client:** confidential. **Completion:** 2009. **Gross floor area:** 635 m². **Number of apartments:** 4. **Number of rooms:** 11. **Additional use:** office. **Main materials:** steel, concrete, wood, aluminum. **Situation:** part of existing development in urban context.

← | **Stairs**, detail
↓ | **Office**, ground floor

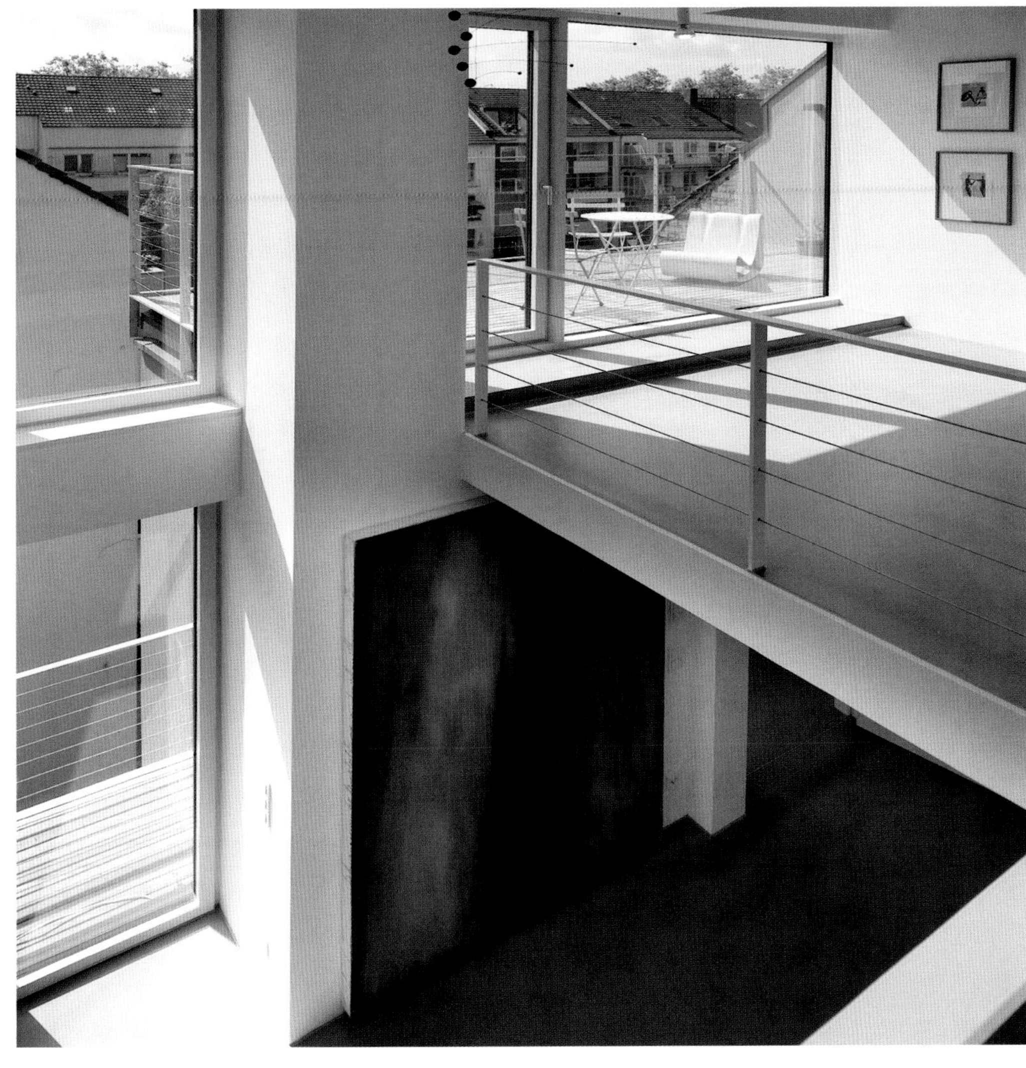

← | **Maisonette,** roof terrace in background
↓ | **Ground floor plan**

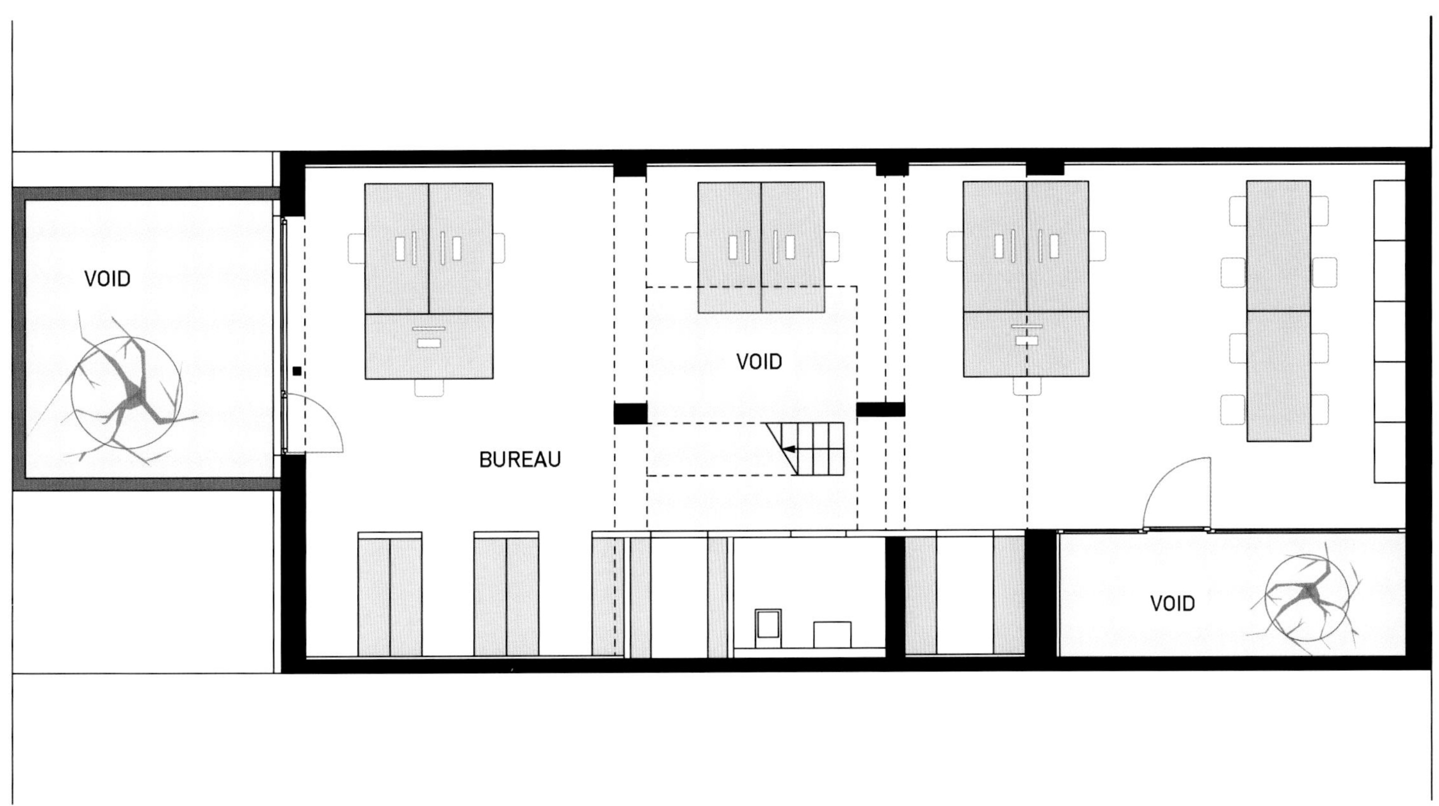

Eingartner Khorrami Architekten

↑ | **Roofscape,** new building in center

↓ | **Elevation**
→ | **Street façade,** worm's-eye view

House in the Old Town

Bad Mergentheim

Located in the densely developed Holzapfelgasse, this new four-story building incorporates two maisonettes and was built in place of a rather dilapidated house that formerly occupied the site. The upper two floors serve as a residence for the client himself. The house is oriented with the gable end facing the street, and the appearance and façade design have been carefully integrated into the streetscape. The façade of plaster, stone and wooden window frames is inspired by the region's historical and local traditions. The sculptural street façade and the slight staggering of the upper stories cites the typical division of the surrounding timber framed houses. The well-chosen details and expert implementation reflect traditions associated with city bourgeois architecture and reflect a commitment to high-quality urban development in the inner city.

Address: Holzapfelgasse 18, 97980 Bad Mergentheim, Germany. **Client:** confidential. **Completion:** 2011. **Gross floor area:** 529 m². **Color scheme:** Friederike Tebbe. **Number of apartments:** 2. **Number of rooms:** 6. **Additional use:** garage. **Main materials:** concrete, shell limestone, brick, bronze, oak. **Situation:** part of existing development in city center.

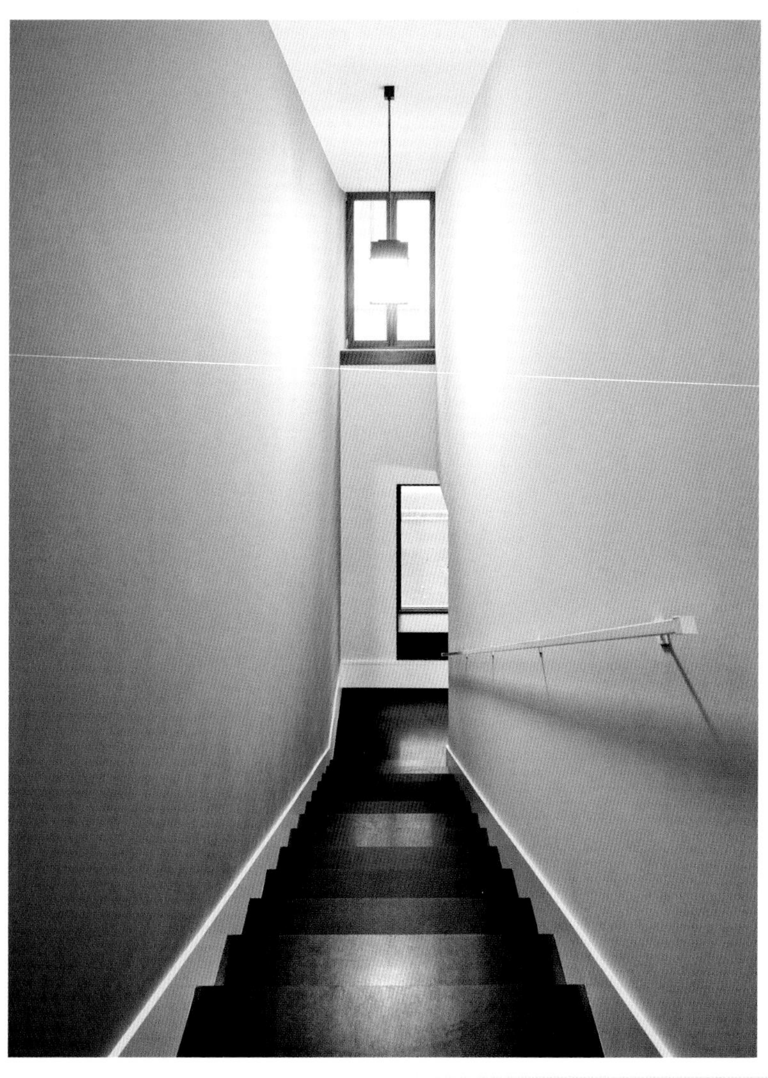

← | **Staircase**
↓ | **Interior,** second floor

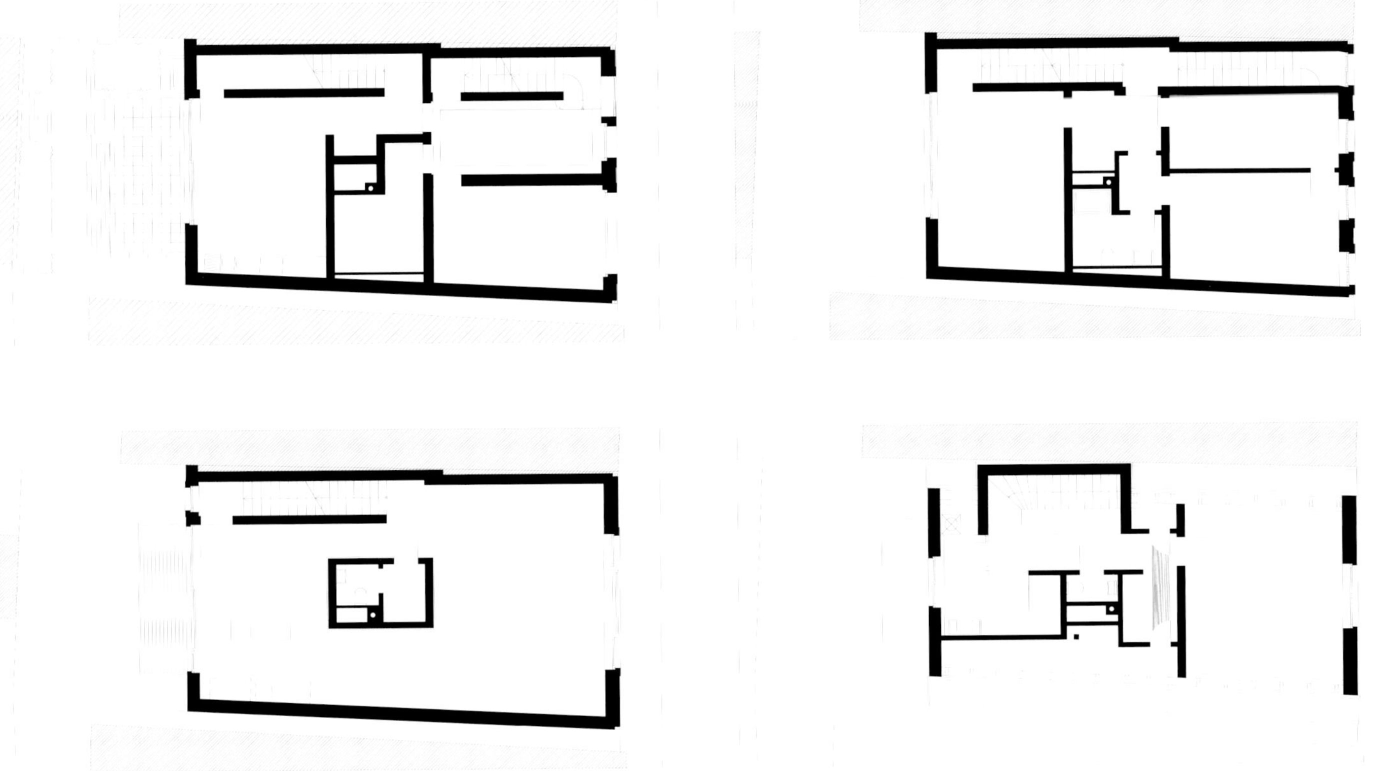

↑ | **Ground, first, second and third floor plans**
← | **Living area,** kitchen in background

Pablo Pita Architects

↑ | **Skylight**

Maternidade House

Porto

The Maternidade project involved the refurbishment of a 19th-century house to create a modern single-family home. The intervention was controlled by the context but respects the scale and dimensions of the original house. A key focal point of the design is light; a new skylight has been added that drawls light deep into the house. The large windows also draw an abundance of light inside and present a transparent and welcoming face to the street.

PROJECT FACTS

Address: Rua da Maternidade 39, 4050-369 Porto, Portugal. **Client:** Gonçalo Cruz, Lia Moreira. **Completion:** 2013. **Gross floor area:** 270 m². **Number of rooms:** 5. **Main materials:** eucalyptus flooring, plasterboard drywalls, aluminum. **Situation:** part of existing development in city center.

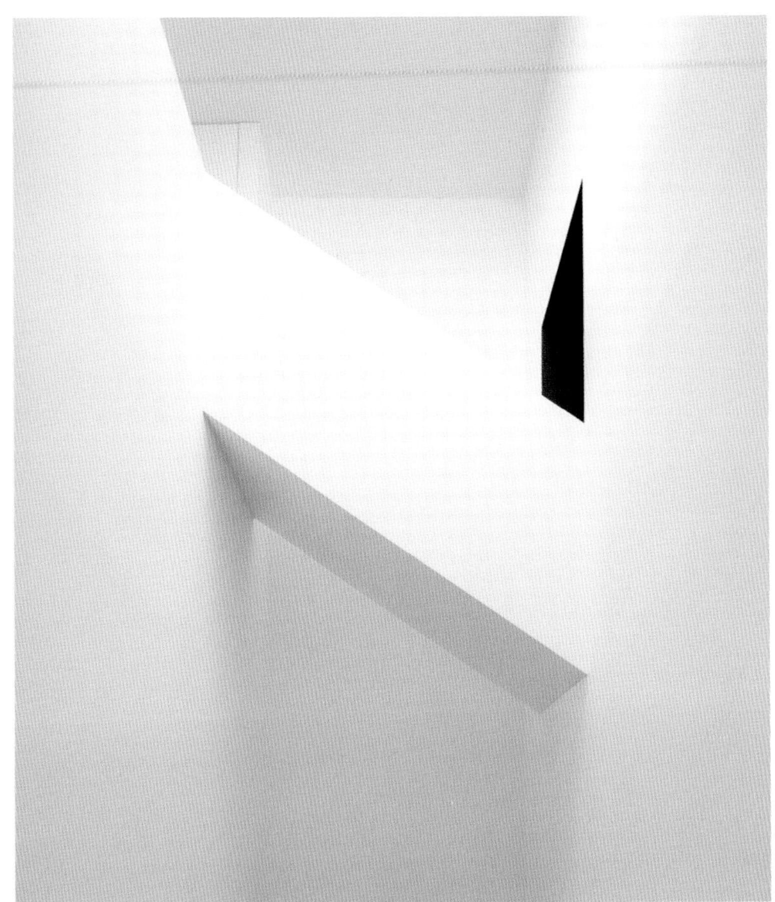

↑ | **Stairs**, with natural lighting from above

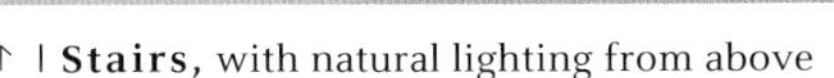

↓ | **Ground, first and second floor plans**

↑ | **Façade**, view from garden

↓ | **Interior**, bedroom

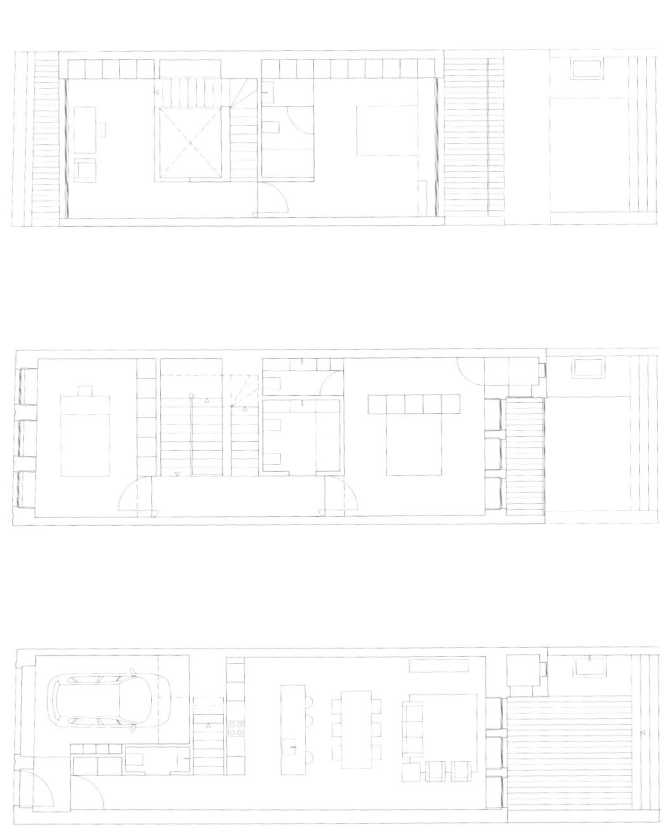

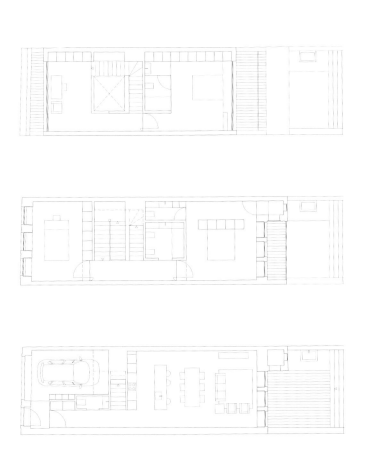

P8 Architecten

↑ | **Living area**
→ | **Windows,** swimming pool in background

House LKS

Lier

This house was designed for a young couple living in the center of Lier, Belgium. They were already living in the house next door and bought this property in order to extend their house. The existing house was demolished creating an area of 56 square meters. The clients wanted an extra living space, a patio, a lounge and a master bedroom. On the outside, the new house creates a strong contrast to the existing house. The white painted façade deliberately breaks with the classical proportions of the other houses in the street. A swimming pool is located on the ground floor of the new house positioned between two folding windows. In the winter it can be used as an interior swimming pool, while in the summer the two windows can be opened and it becomes an outdoor swimming pool.

PROJECT FACTS

Address: Lookstraat, 2500 Lier, Belgium. **Client:** Peter Claes, Sophie D'Hulst. **Completion:** 2012. **Gross floor area:** 250 m². **Planning partners:** David D'Hulst, Kalle Block. **Number of rooms:** 8. **Main materials:** masonry, concrete, wood. **Situation:** part of existing development in urban context.

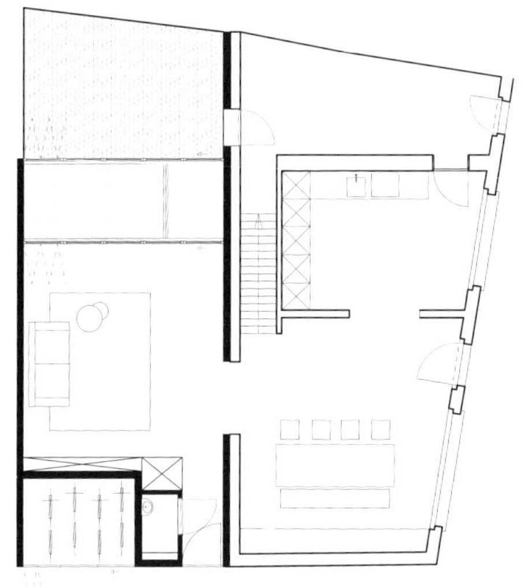

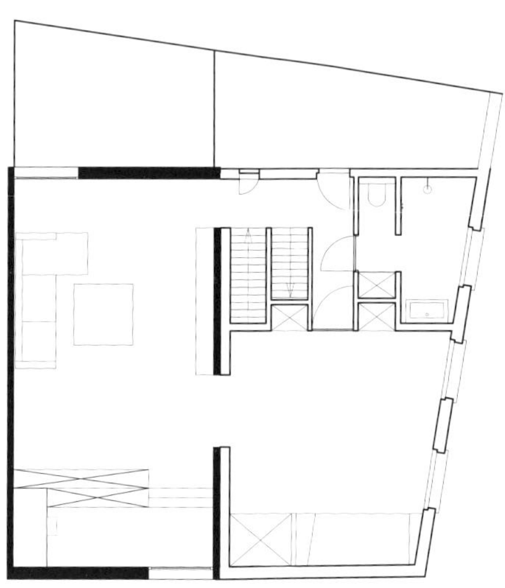

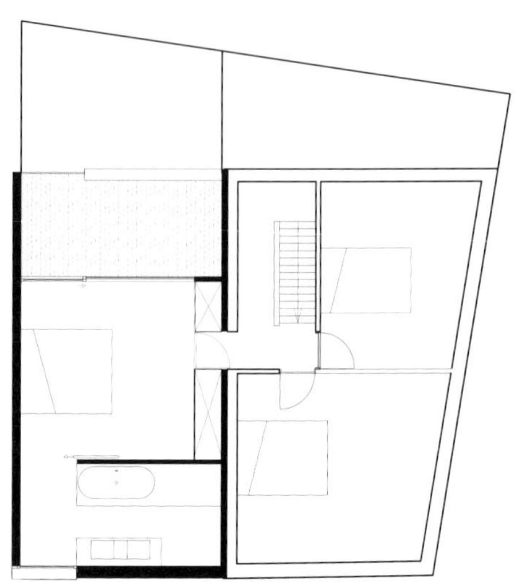

↑ | **Ground, first and second floor plans**
← | **Exterior,** street view

← | **Front view,** façade
↓ | **Connection between living area and children's room**

ANA Architects

↑ | **Exterior,** garden side

House SE

Amsterdam

House SE is built on the edge of the new suburban housing area IJburg, near Amsterdam. The house has a small garden on the waterside of the IJlake. In House SE all living areas are connected by a number of voids permeating the volume like an airy sponge. Routing, voids and visibility define different spatial relationships between communal and private spaces. The large kitchen is positioned on the ground floor and is connected to the garden on the waterfront. On the first floor a flexible room can be used for different purposes: working, playing or for accommodating guests. The living room offers a wide view over the wide lake. The three bedrooms are positioned on the third floor. The master bedroom has an ensuite bathroom.

Address: James Bradleystraat 30, 1086 ZM Amsterdam, the Netherlands. **Client:** confidential. **Completion:** 2009. **Gross floor area:** 238 m². **Number of rooms:** 6. **Main materials:** concrete, stone. **Situation:** part of existing development in suburban context.

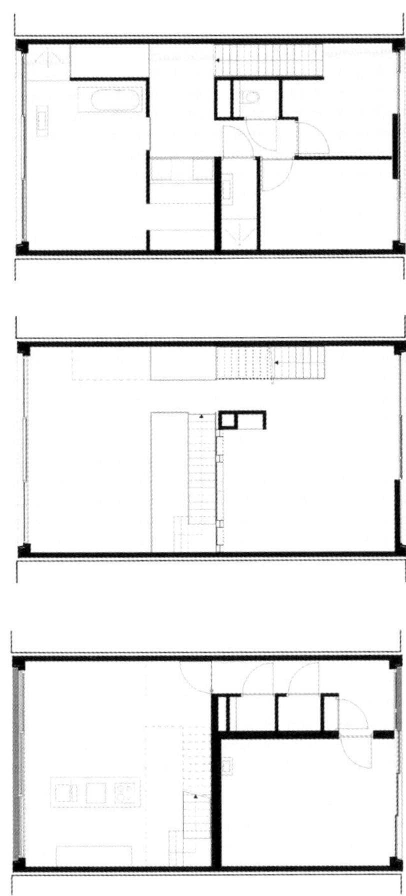

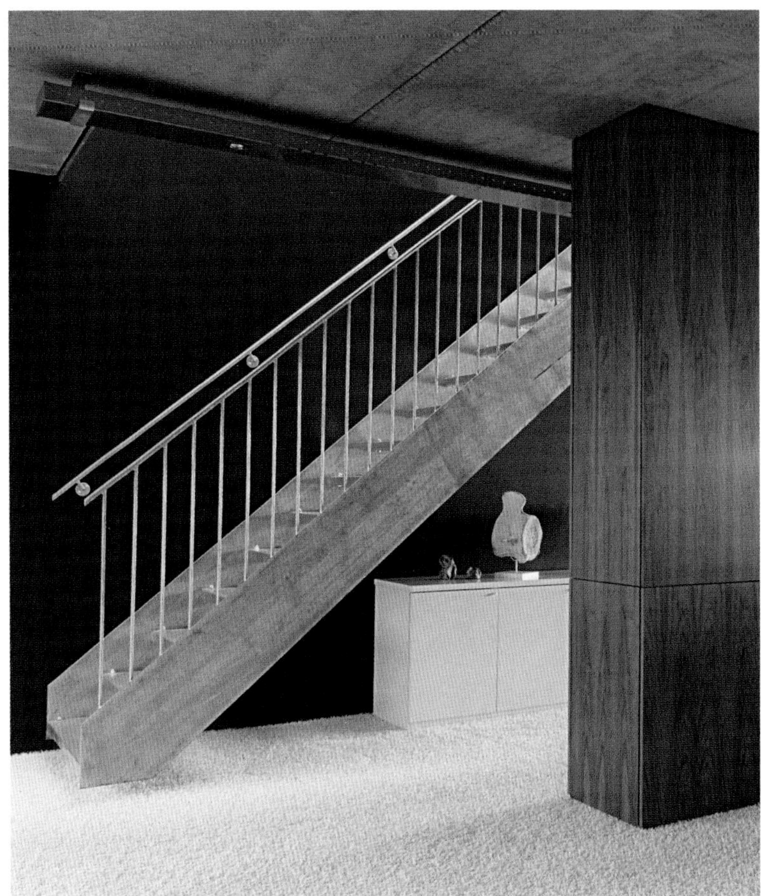

↑ | **Ground, first and second floor plans**
↓ | **Stairs**, illuminated from above

↑ | **Floating stairs**
↓ | **Interior**

Level Architects

↑ | **Living room,** in the evening
→ | **Interior,** second floor

House in Oimachi

Tokyo

Situated in a crowded neighborhood in Tokyo where light and ventilation are hard to maintain, the design uses an inner garden to create a sense of openness, light, and privacy. Due to the narrow site, this garden is suspended from the living room ceiling, giving the house a distinctive character. This central space becomes a core around which all the auxiliary rooms are pieced together, each receiving their own natural light and ventilation. The surrounding neighborhood may change over time, but the tranquil light filtering through the garden will always be constant.

PROJECT FACTS

Address: Oimachi, Shinagawa Ward, Tokyo, Japan. **Client:** confidential. **Completion:** 2010. **Gross floor area:** 100 m^2. **Number of rooms:** 5. **Main materials:** wood frame construction. **Situation:** part of existing development in urban context.

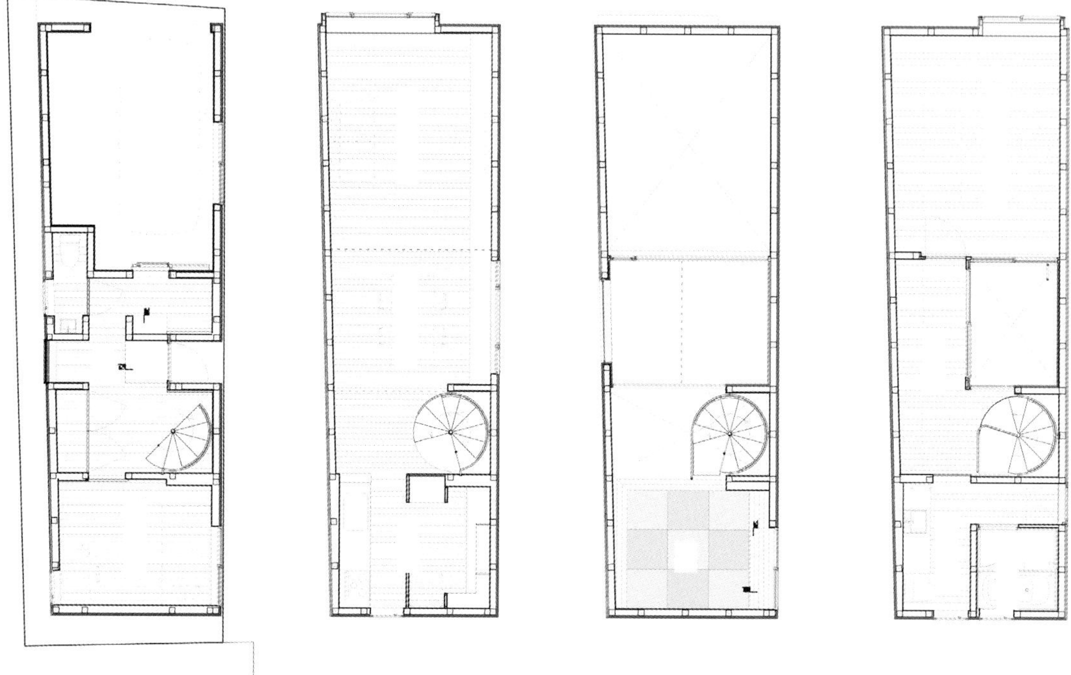

↑ | **First, second, mezzanine and third floor plans**
← | **Interior**, courtyard

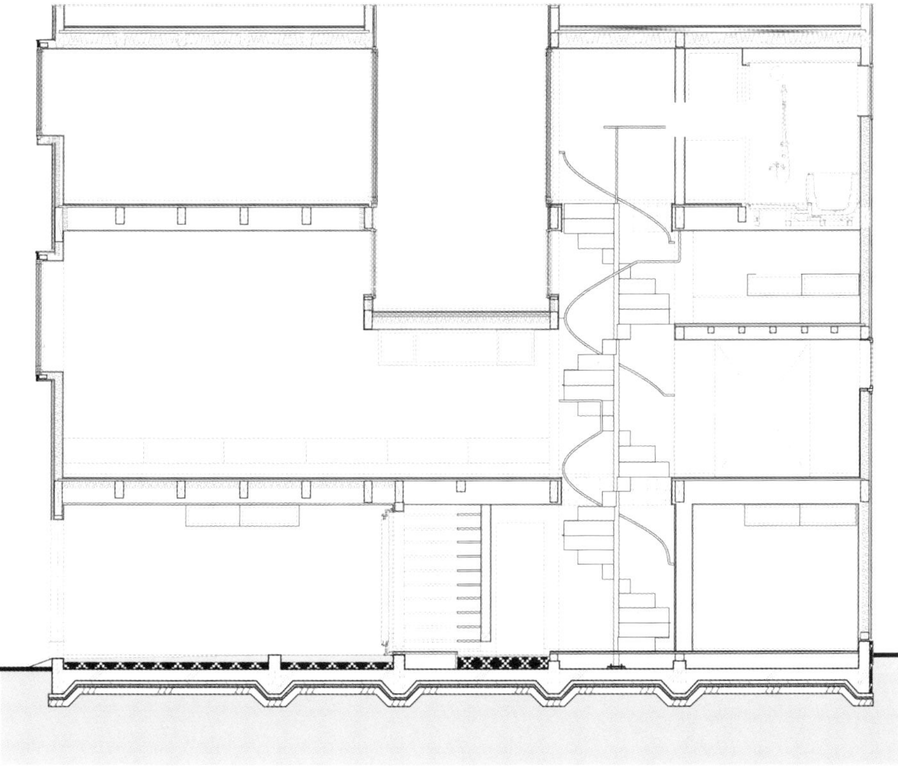

↖ | **Section**
↓ | **Exterior,** façade at night

Johanne Nalbach

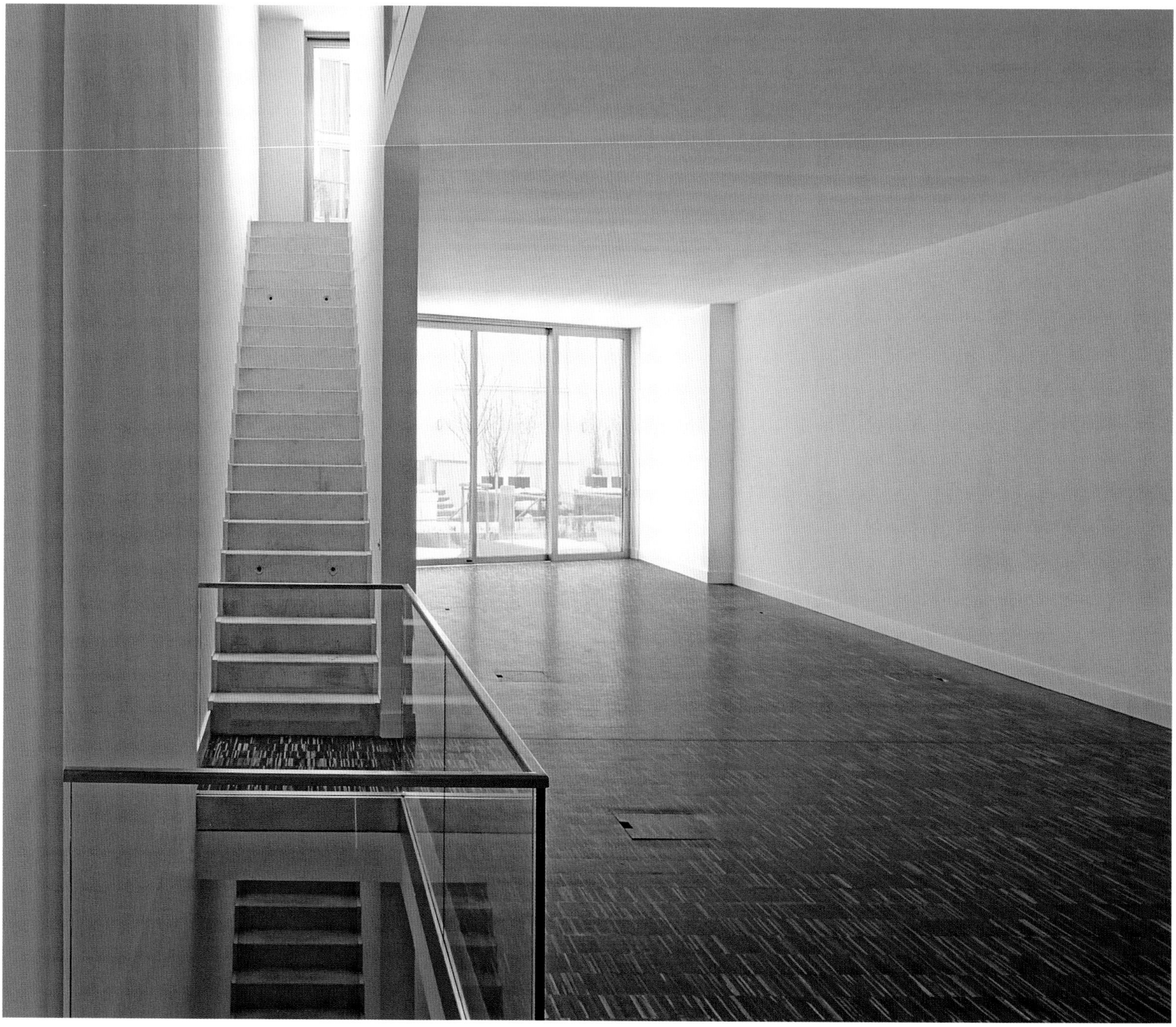

↑ | **Stairs,** illuminated from above
→ | **Entrance from street**

Townhouse 015

Berlin

The distribution of this five-story townhouse, located in an industrial and residential area, is clearly demonstrated by the arrangement of the façade. A narrow horizontal strip separates the different functions from each other. Despite this, the volume can still be understood as a dynamic unified whole. The building is characterized by a triad of white concrete, glazed balustrade elements and textile sun blinds that are presented as an 'urban curtain' in front of the apartments. The sloping walls allow light deep into the interior throughout the day and emphasize the sculptural effect of the building. Inside, a stair connects the individual levels and helps to underline the depth and slim character of the building.

PROJECT FACTS

Address: Oberwallstraße 10, 10117 Berlin, Germany. **Client:** confidential. **Completion:** 2009. **Gross floor area:** 900 m². **Number of rooms:** 6. **Additional use:** office. **Main materials:** plaster, concrete. **Situation:** part of new development in city center.

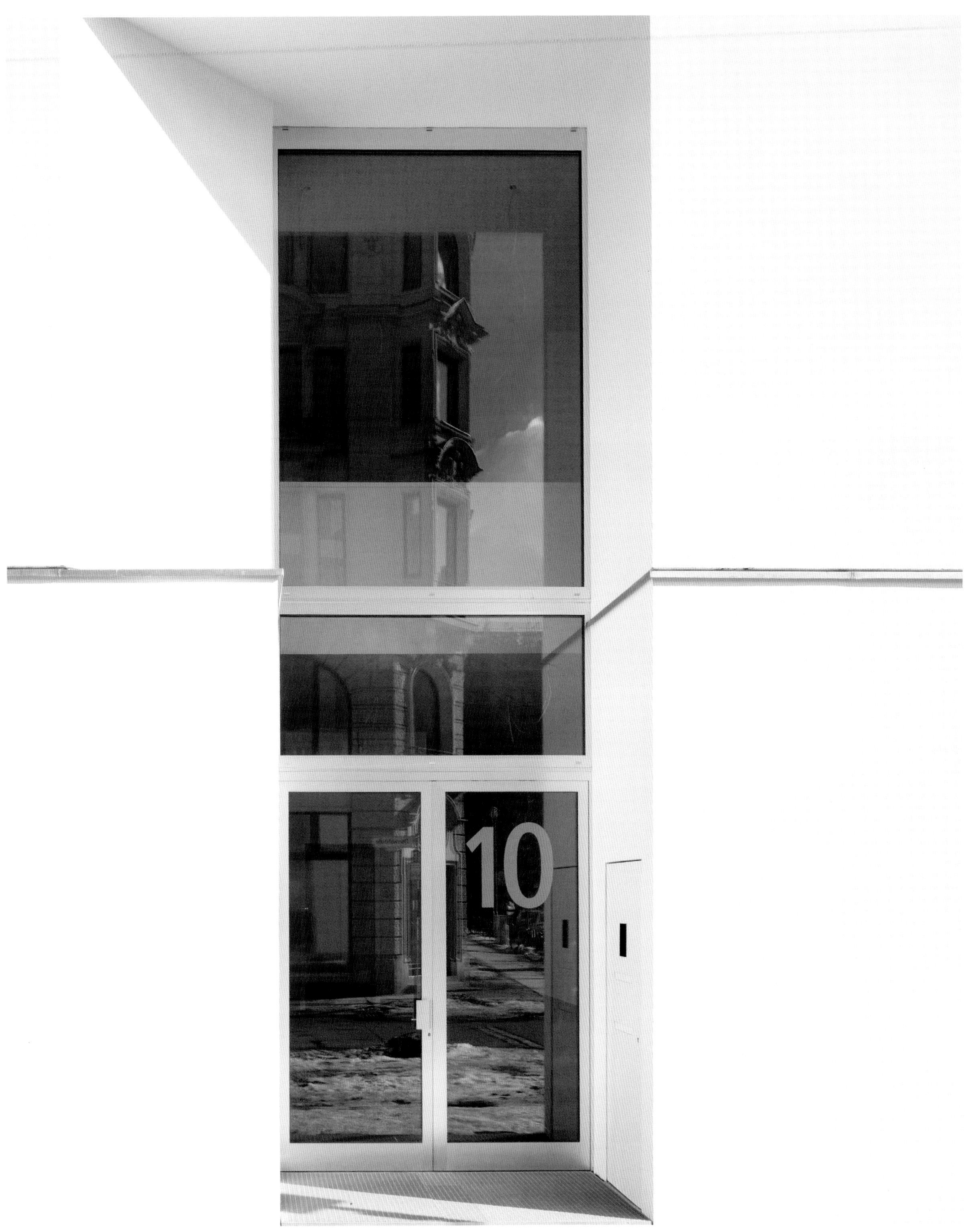

← | **Façade,** front view

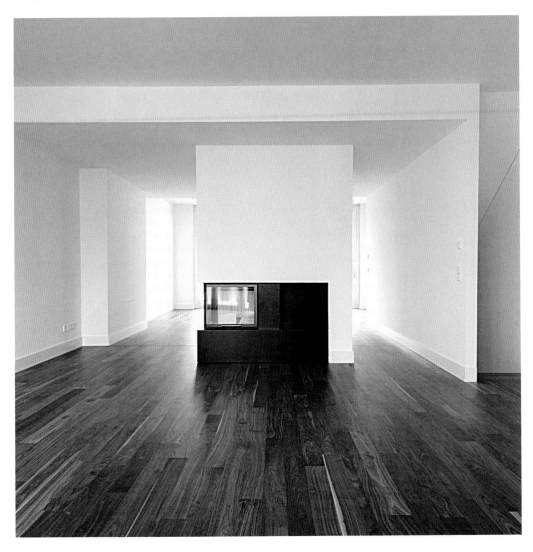

← | Fireplace

↓ | Ground to fifth floor plans

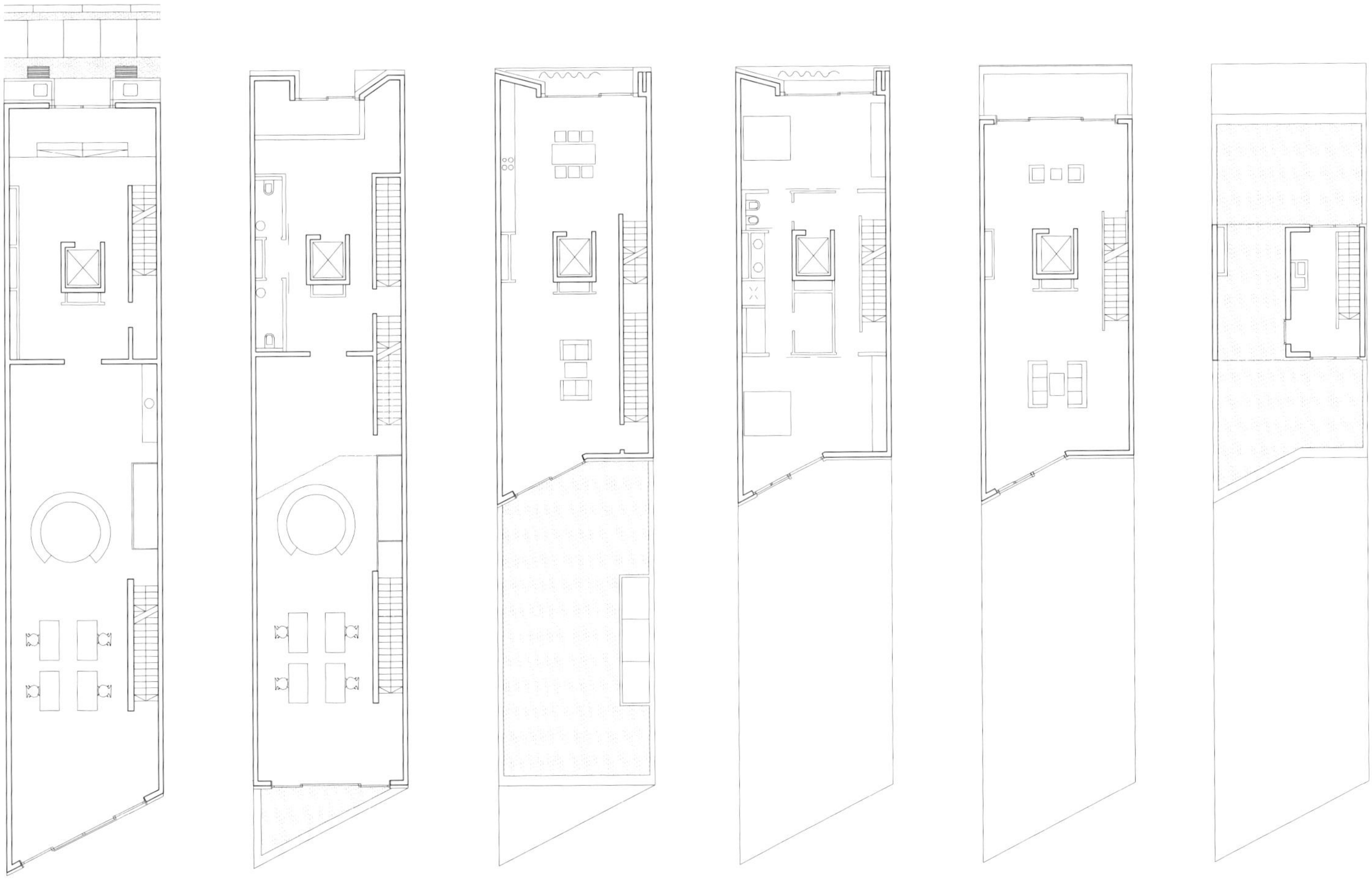

Areal Architecten

↑ | **Interior,** stairs leading to upper level
→ | **Street view,** front façade

Townhouse EM

Mechelen

This house in the Belgian city of Mechelen has an open-plan arrangement that allows natural light to flow throughout the space. The staircase also creates a vertical void through the center of the house, forming a light-shaft, illuminated by the skylights above. The use of simple materials and raw finishes gives the house a natural feel, emphasized by easy access to the terrace and garden. The light natural colors, combined with the open-plan arrangement also have to added advantage of making the house feel larger than it actually is.

PROJECT FACTS

Address: Vrijgeweidestraat 42, 2800 Mechelen, Belgium. **Client:** Chris Eeraerts, Barbara Morisse. **Completion:** 2013. **Gross floor area:** 340 m². **Co-designer:** Barbara Morisse. **Number of rooms:** 7. **Additional use:** office. **Main materials:** concrete, pre-painted brick, marble, wood. **Situation:** part of existing development in urban context.

←← | **Interior,** living room
← | **Open ceiling allows natural lighting**
↓ | **Ground, first and second floor plans**

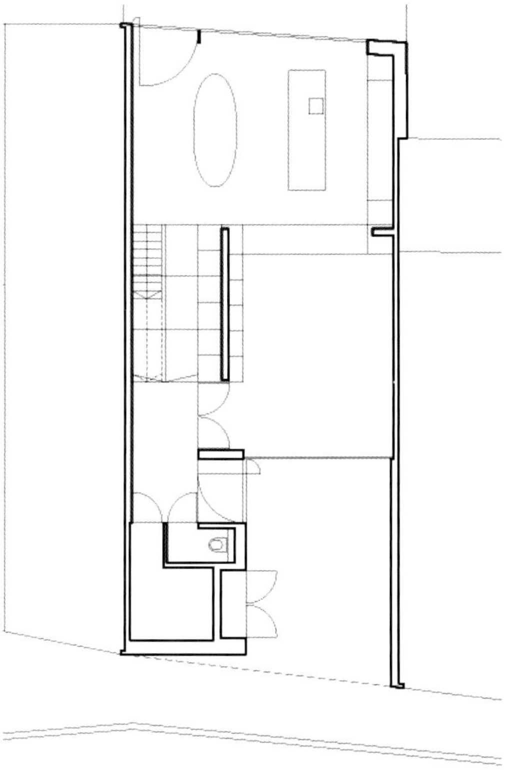

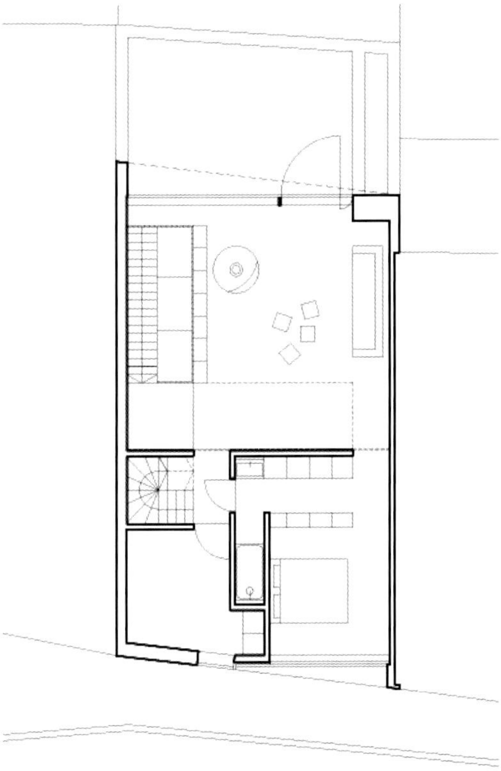

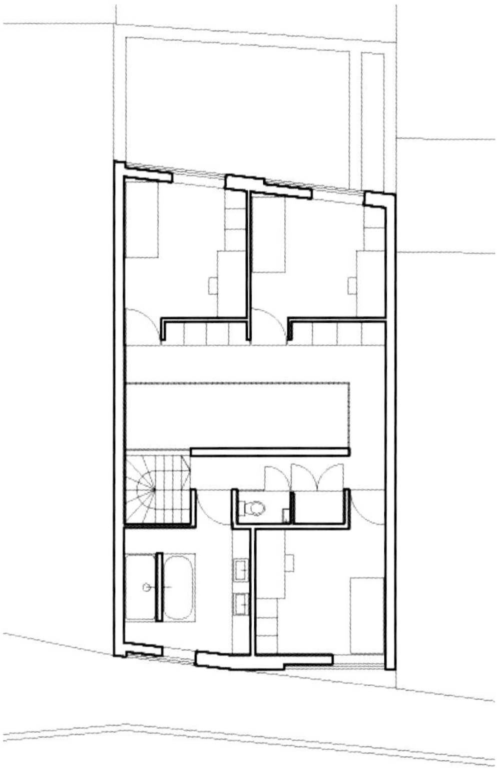

Ryo Matsui Architects

↑ | **Terrace,** city view
→ | **Balcony,** second floor

Balcony House

Tokyo

This four-story house is located in an area characterized by apartment buildings with small balconies. It is common practice in Tokyo to build a property right up to the site boundaries, so that all the available space is used and nothing is wasted. The balconies act as a buffer between the property and the road. Small trees and greenery have been added to the balconies, which not only offer privacy from prying eyes, but also bring a touch of nature to this urban environment. The large windows and balconies make the building appear larger than it actually is, creating a modern light-filled space where one can escape from the bustle of the city.

Address: Tokyo, Japan. **Client:** confidential. **Completion:** 2013. **Gross floor area:** 202 m². **Number of apartments:** 2. **Number of rooms:** 5. **Main materials:** concrete. **Situation:** part of existing development in urban context.

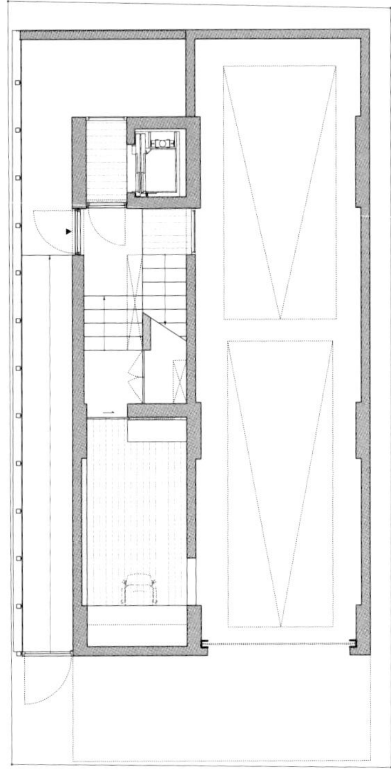

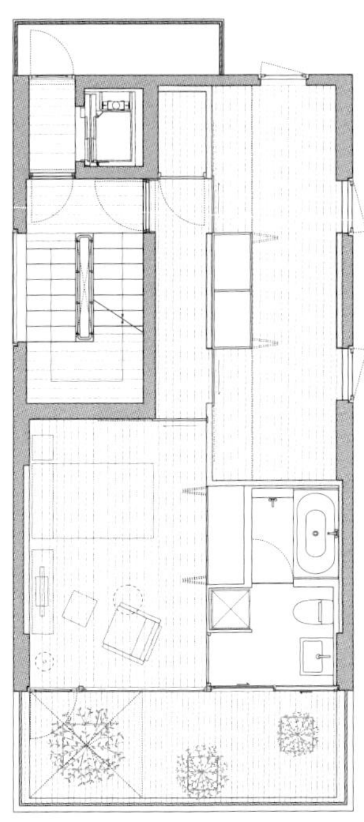

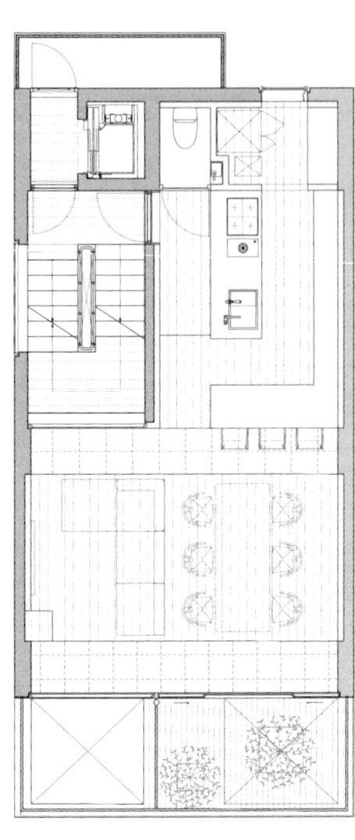

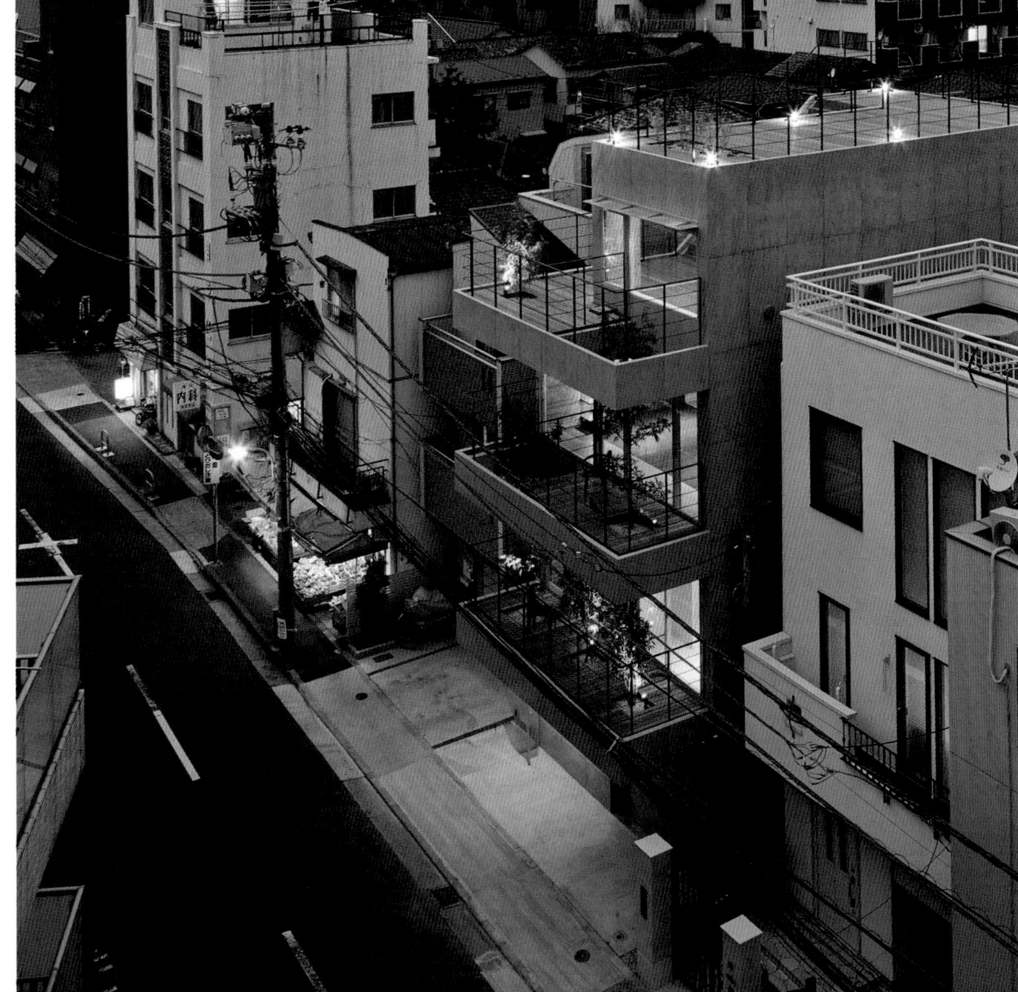

↑ | **Ground, first and second floor plans**
← | **Entire building,** night view

← | **Interior,** second floor

↓ | **Stairs and kitchen,** wood cladding

Barker Freeman Design Office (BFDO)

↑ | **Place to study,** upstairs
→ | **Rear exterior in the evening**

Rowhouse

New York City

This renovation of a Brooklyn townhouse for a family of four developed as a series of transformative insertions into the existing building volume. All interior partitions were removed and a large opening was inserted into the rear façade, creating one large room that would allow light to penetrate deep into the interior. The first floor was subdivided into four main spaces. The kitchen, pantry and powder room are contained within a volume that divides the front half of the house from the rear. Upstairs, three bedrooms and two baths were carved out of the existing apartment. A sky-lit, book-lined study separates the children's rooms from the master suite.

Address: Windsor Place, 11215 New York City, NY, USA. **Client:** confidential. **Completion:** 2012. **Gross floor area:** 242 m². **Number of rooms:** 8. **Main materials:** oak, aluminum storefront, marble. **Situation:** part of existing development in urban context.

105

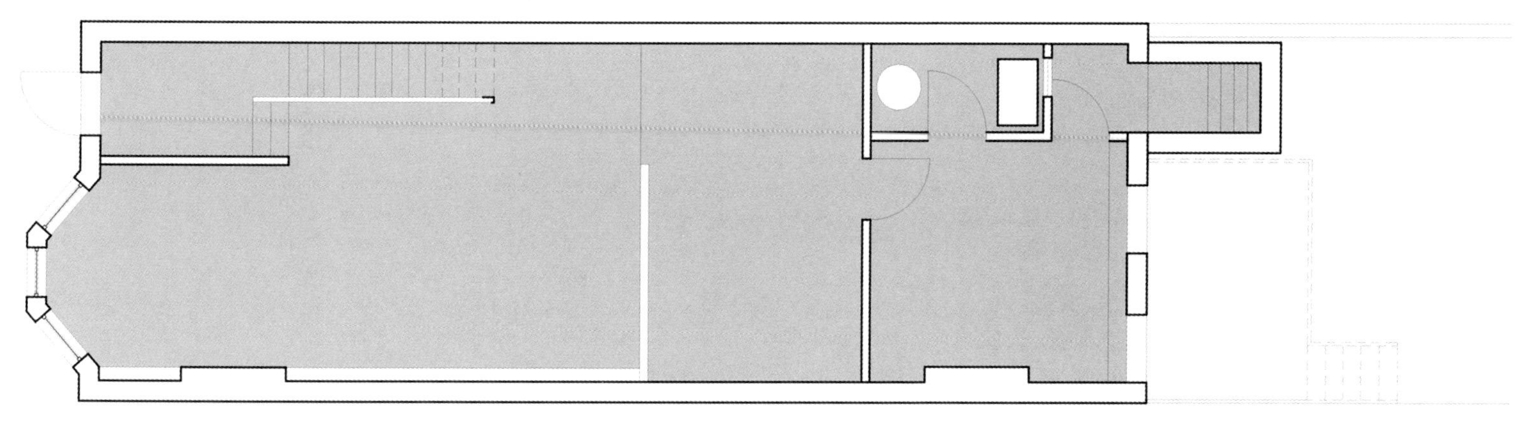

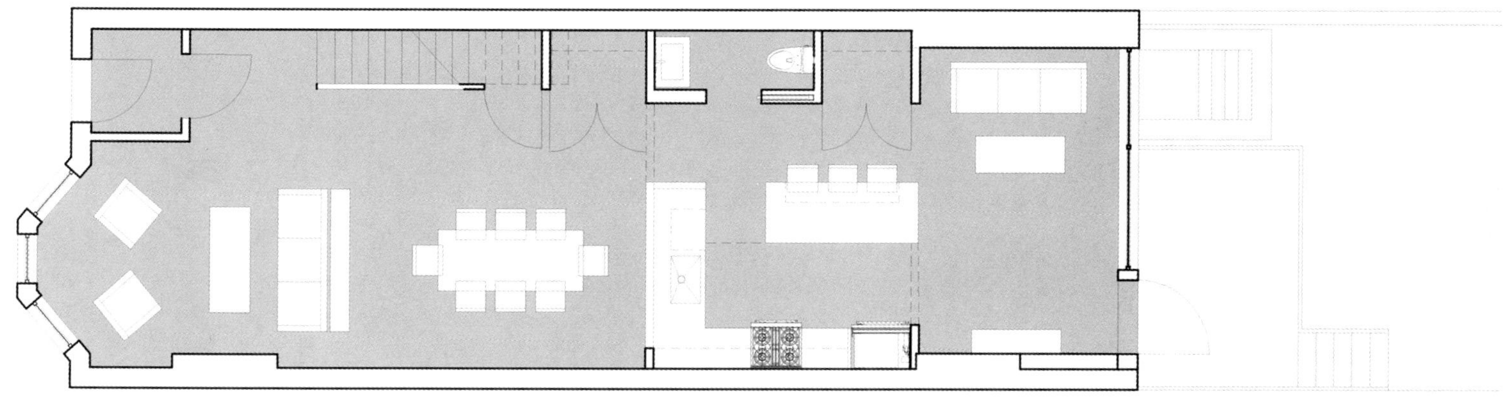

←←| **Exterior,** front façade
↑ | **Ground and first floor plans**
← | **Interior,** view of garden

LK Architekten

↑ | **Stairs,** open central area
→ | **Façade,** view from yard

Townhouse Schwalbengasse 32

Cologne

This townhouse has been built on a site just 4.6 meters wide. The entire area is 96 square meters and the house is built over 12 split-levels, this provides space for two separate units with different uses. The lower six levels provide space for work while the upper six contain the living areas. The open area in the center of the house allows for a light filled, continuous space, reaching from the cellar to the roof with views to many of the levels. Within the urban area, the house has a simple and unspectacular appearance, a clearly articulated house executed with simple and precise detail.

PROJECT FACTS

Address: Schwalbengasse 32, 50667 Cologne, Germany. **Client:** Regina Leipertz, Martin Kostulski. **Completion:** 2007. **Gross floor area:** 347 m^2. **Number of apartments:** 2. **Number of rooms:** 11. **Additional use:** office. **Main materials:** natural stone façade, aluminum, bamboo flooring. **Situation:** part of new development in city center.

↑ | **Roof terrace at dawn**

← | **Office unit,** view through open central space

← | Townhouse in context

↓ | Basement to fourth floor plans

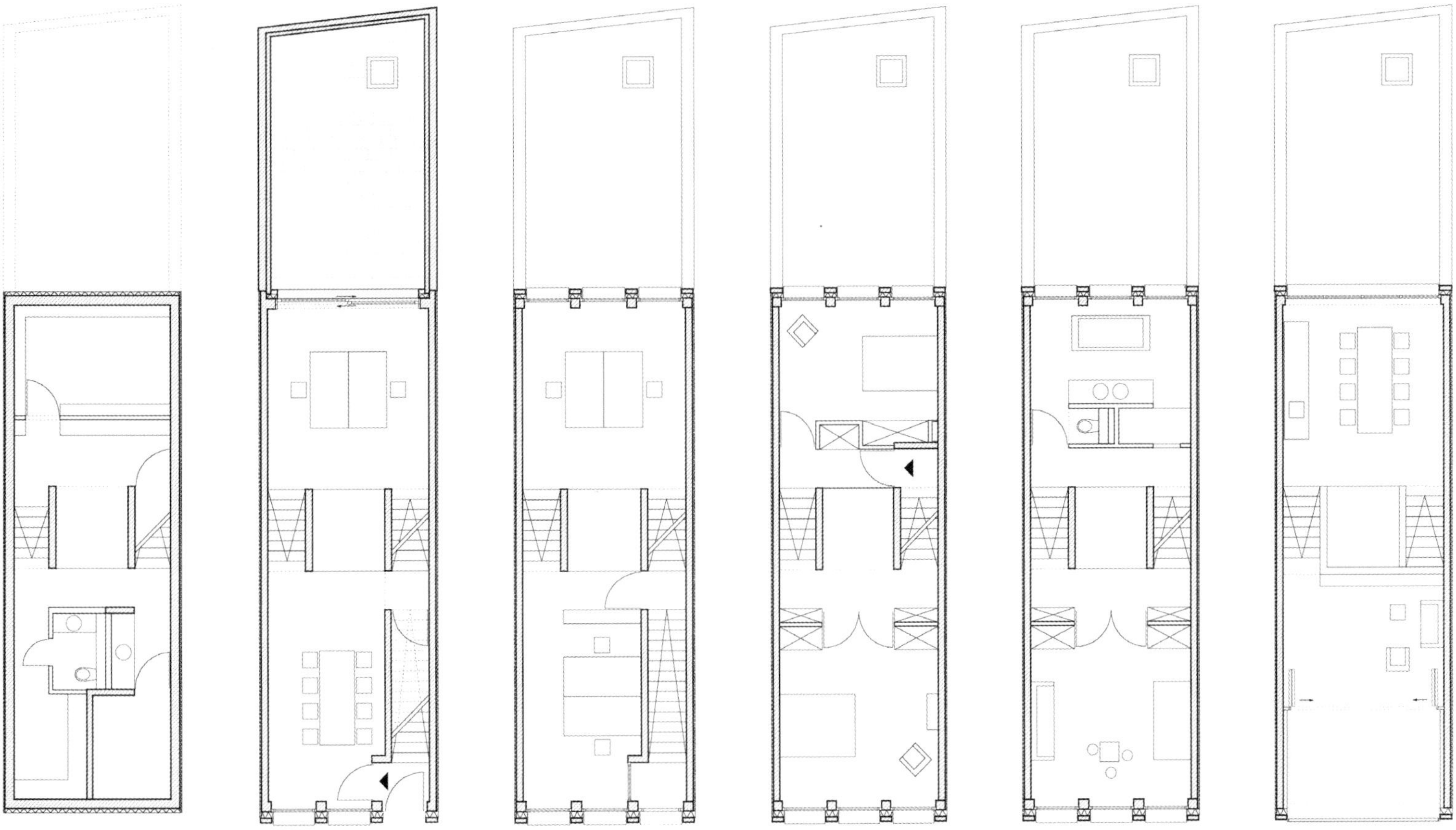

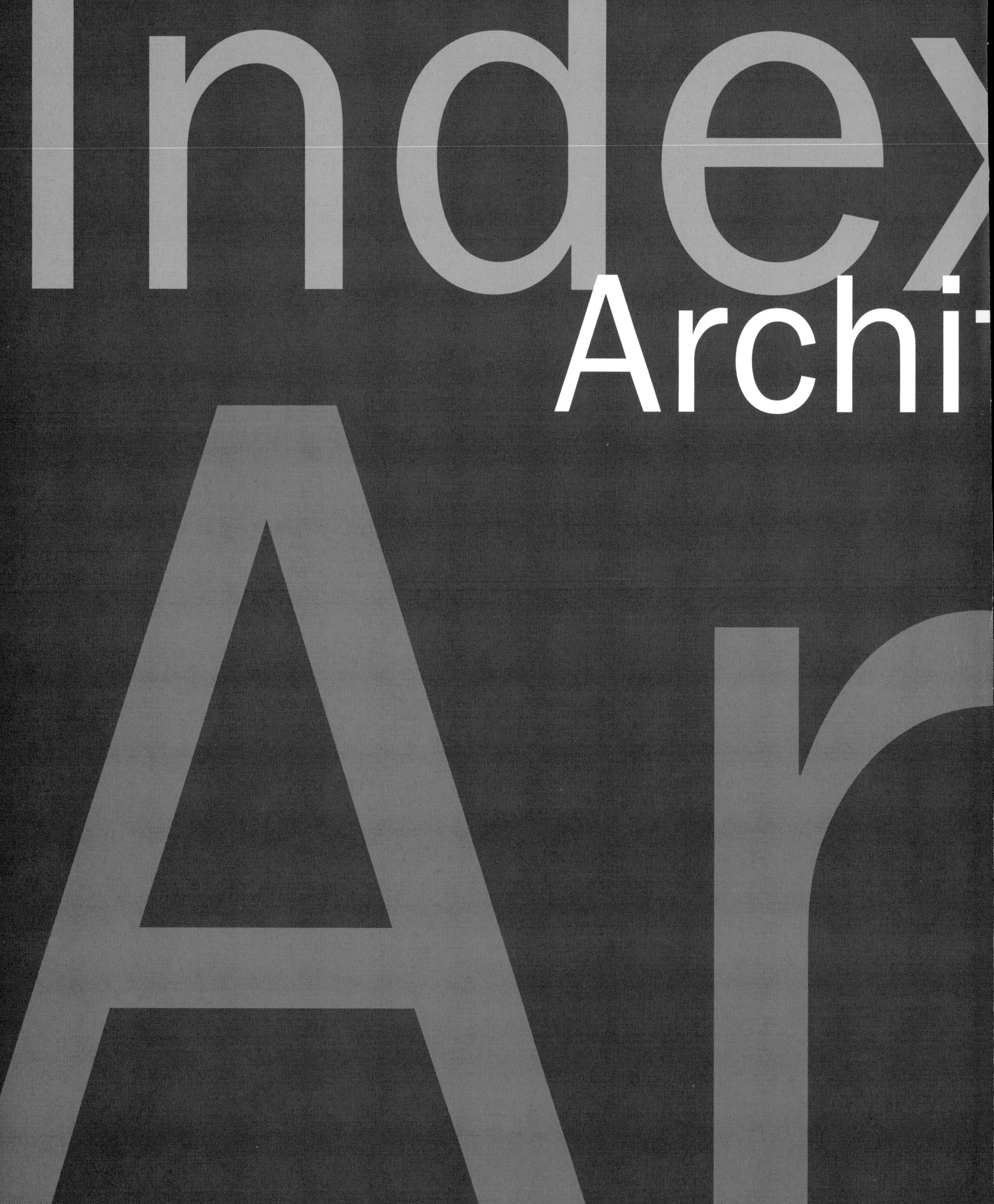
Index
Archi
Ar